Raspberry Pi Networking Cookbook
Second Edition

Connect your Raspberry Pi to the world with this essential collection of recipes for basic administration and common network services

Rick Golden

[PACKT] open source *
PUBLISHING
community experience distilled

BIRMINGHAM - MUMBAI

Raspberry Pi Networking Cookbook
Second Edition

First published: March 2013

Second edition: January 2016

Production reference: 1241215

Published by Packt Publishing Ltd.
Livery Place
35 Livery Street
Birmingham B3 2PB, UK.

ISBN 978-1-78528-021-4

www.packtpub.com

Credits

Author
Rick Golden

Reviewers
Stefan Pietzonke

Werner Ziegelwanger

Acquisition Editor
Vivek Anantharaman

Content Development Editor
Arshiya Ayaz Umer

Technical Editors
Mohit Hassija

Edwin Moses

Copy Editors
Vedangi Narvekar

Jonathan Todd

Project Coordinator
Shipra Chawhan

Proofreader
Safis Editing

Indexer
Priya Sane

Production Coordinator
Shantanu N. Zagade

Cover Work
Shantanu N. Zagade

About the Author

Rick Golden, in the summer of 1972, sat in the computer lab at SUNY Fredonia and completed his first CAI tutorial on programming in APL. He was 9 years old then.

He has been programming computers for over 40 years. He has designed and developed a multitude of projects, from low-level graphics and database drivers to large-volume e-commerce platforms.

At work, Rick is currently focused on developing software to improve healthcare by mining petabytes of healthcare claims to find opportunities to improve healthcare coordination. After work, Rick teaches 10-14 year olds how to program using Raspberry Pi computers.

I would like to thank my dad for giving me the opportunity to learn programming at such a young age, which was unheard of in the 1970s. His wisdom, patience, and faith in my programming abilities has encouraged me to become the man that I am today.

I would also like to thank my wife and family for supporting me during the many hours that I spent working on this book. Without their support, this book would not have been written.

Finally, I would like to thank Packt Publishing for giving me the opportunity to update this book and my editor, Arshiya Umer, for keeping me focused on my deadlines. Without her help and encouragement, this book would not have been published.

About the Reviewers

Stefan Pietzonke grew up in a village and wrote his first computer program at the age of 14. His first computer was an Amiga 500. He learned to program in Amiga BASIC. Now, he mostly writes programs in the C/C++ language.

He developed his own virtual machine called "Nano". The bytecode for the Nano VM can be created by using his assembler or compiler.

He also likes to conduct hardware projects. He built a robot from a computer mouse case. This robot is autonomous, drives around, and seeks light.

He has a blog (`http://midnight-koder.net/wordpress/`) about his software and hardware projects.

I want to thank my family for supporting me.

Werner Ziegelwanger studied game engineering and simulation and got his master's degree in 2011. His master's thesis was published with *Terrain Rendering with Geometry Clipmaps for Games* as the title. The publisher was Diplomica Verlag. His hobbies are programming, games, and all kinds of technical gadgets.

He worked as a self-employed programmer for some years and mainly did web projects. At that time, he started his own blog (`http://developer-blog.net`), which is about the Raspberry Pi, Linux, and open source.

Since 2013, Werner has worked as a Magento developer and the head of programming at mStage GmbH, an e-commerce company that is focused on Magento.

www.PacktPub.com

Support files, eBooks, discount offers, and more

For support files and downloads related to your book, please visit www.PacktPub.com.

Did you know that Packt offers eBook versions of every book published, with PDF and ePub files available? You can upgrade to the eBook version at www.PacktPub.com and as a print book customer, you are entitled to a discount on the eBook copy. Get in touch with us at service@packtpub.com for more details.

At www.PacktPub.com, you can also read a collection of free technical articles, sign up for a range of free newsletters and receive exclusive discounts and offers on Packt books and eBooks.

![PACKTLIB logo]

https://www2.packtpub.com/books/subscription/packtlib

Do you need instant solutions to your IT questions? PacktLib is Packt's online digital book library. Here, you can search, access, and read Packt's entire library of books.

Why Subscribe?

- ▸ Fully searchable across every book published by Packt
- ▸ Copy and paste, print, and bookmark content
- ▸ On demand and accessible via a web browser

Free Access for Packt account holders

If you have an account with Packt at www.PacktPub.com, you can use this to access PacktLib today and view 9 entirely free books. Simply use your login credentials for immediate access.

Table of Contents

Preface

A Raspberry Pi 2, with its 900MHz quad-core processor, has more processing power than a network server from the late-1990s. Created as an educational tool to inspire the next generation of programmers, the Raspberry Pi is also an excellent network server. It can be used to share files, host websites, create Internet access points, and analyze network traffic. Multiple Raspberry Pis can be clustered to create a single, highly available, and fault-tolerant super computer. This book shows you how.

The Raspberry Pi Foundation recognized that *computers had become so expensive and arcane that programming experimentation on them had to be forbidden by parents*. The parental restrictions on using computers had created a *year-on-year decline in the numbers and skills levels of the A Level students applying to read Computer Science*. So, the Foundation set out to create a computer that was "affordable, and powerful enough to provide excellent multimedia, a feature we felt would make the board desirable to kids who wouldn't initially be interested in a purely programming-oriented device".

2 million Raspberry Pis were sold in the first two years of its release, which was not limited to educators and school children. Hobbyists were also excited to use the inexpensive Linux-based computer in their projects. In February 2015, the quad-core Raspberry Pi 2 was released with significantly more power and memory than the original, which was more than enough memory and power for many typical server applications.

In this cookbook, you'll find a collection of server-side recipes for the Raspberry Pi, including recipes to set up file servers and web servers, create secure wireless access points, and analyze network traffic. There is even a recipe to create a highly available fault-tolerant supercomputer.

What this book covers

Chapter 1, *Installation and Setup*, has a number of beginner recipes to set up the Raspberry Pi as a network server, which include instructions on how to download and install new operating system images, boot for the first time, and the proper way to shut down the system.

Chapter 2, *Administration*, has more beginner recipes to configure the Raspberry Pi as a network server, which includes instructions on how to execute privileged commands, configure remote access, and manage user accounts.

Chapter 3, *Maintenance*, has intermediate and advanced recipes to maintain the Raspberry Pi server. You'll learn how to update software, read the built-in documentation, and upgrade the system.

Chapter 4, *File Sharing*, has a number of different intermediate recipes to share files.

Chapter 5, *Advanced Networking*, has a collection of advanced recipes to set up and monitor network applications, including a firewall, web server, wireless access point, and network protocol analyzer.

Chapter 6, *IoT - The Internet of Things*, has several intermediate recipes to connect your Raspberry Pi to the Internet of Things.

Chapter 7, *Clustering*, has advanced recipes to create a highly available fault-tolerant supercomputer from a cluster of Raspberry Pis.

What you need for this book

For most of the recipes in this book, you will need a little more than a basic Raspberry Pi setup (Raspberry Pi and a power supply) that is connected to a local area network.

You may choose to use a display, keyboard, and a mouse with the Raspberry Pi. However, most recipes have been written to remotely access the Raspberry Pi as a server.

Internet access is required to download software and connect to the Internet of Things.

Who this book is for

This book is for students, educators, hobbyists, and computer professionals who would like to use the Raspberry Pi as a network server.

Previous experience with the Raspberry Pi is not required. After completing the beginner and intermediate recipes in this book, you will gain the knowledge and experience that you will need to complete even the advanced recipes.

Sections

In this book, you will find several headings that appear frequently (Getting ready, How to do it, How it works, There's more, and See also).

To give clear instructions on how to complete a recipe, we use these sections as follows:

Getting ready

This section tells you what to expect in the recipe, and describes how to set up any software or any preliminary settings required for the recipe.

How to do it...

This section contains the steps required to follow the recipe.

How it works...

This section usually consists of a detailed explanation of what happened in the previous section.

There's more...

This section consists of additional information about the recipe in order to make the reader more knowledgeable about the recipe.

See also

This section provides helpful links to other useful information for the recipe.

Conventions

In this book, you will find a number of text styles that distinguish between different kinds of information. Here are some examples of these styles and an explanation of their meaning.

Code words in text, database table names, folder names, filenames, file extensions, pathnames, dummy URLs, user input, and Twitter handles are shown as follows: "Use the `chown` command to give the user `pi` ownership of the directory (`.`) and all of the files in it (`*`)."

Any command-line input or output is written as follows:

```
pi@web1 /var/www/html $ sudo chown pi:www-data . *
```

New terms and **important words** are shown in bold. Words that you see on the screen, for example, in menus or dialog boxes, appear in the text like this: "Press the *Tab* key to select **Finish** and then press the *Enter* key:"

> Warnings or important notes appear in a box like this.

> Tips and tricks appear like this.

Reader feedback

Feedback from our readers is always welcome. Let us know what you think about this book—what you liked or disliked. Reader feedback is important for us as it helps us develop titles that you will really get the most out of.

To send us general feedback, simply e-mail feedback@packtpub.com, and mention the book's title in the subject of your message.

If there is a topic that you have expertise in and you are interested in either writing or contributing to a book, see our author guide at www.packtpub.com/authors.

Customer support

Now that you are the proud owner of a Packt book, we have a number of things to help you to get the most from your purchase.

Downloading the color images of this book

We also provide you with a PDF file that has color images of the screenshots/diagrams used in this book. The color images will help you better understand the changes in the output. You can download this file from http://www.packtpub.com/sites/default/files/downloads/Raspberry_Pi_Networking_Cookbook_ColorImages.pdf.

Errata

Although we have taken every care to ensure the accuracy of our content, mistakes do happen. If you find a mistake in one of our books—maybe a mistake in the text or the code—we would be grateful if you could report this to us. By doing so, you can save other readers from frustration and help us improve subsequent versions of this book. If you find any errata, please report them by visiting `http://www.packtpub.com/submit-errata`, selecting your book, clicking on the **Errata Submission Form** link, and entering the details of your errata. Once your errata are verified, your submission will be accepted and the errata will be uploaded to our website or added to any list of existing errata under the Errata section of that title.

To view the previously submitted errata, go to `https://www.packtpub.com/books/content/support` and enter the name of the book in the search field. The required information will appear under the **Errata** section.

Piracy

Piracy of copyrighted material on the Internet is an ongoing problem across all media. At Packt, we take the protection of our copyright and licenses very seriously. If you come across any illegal copies of our works in any form on the Internet, please provide us with the location address or website name immediately so that we can pursue a remedy.

Please contact us at `copyright@packtpub.com` with a link to the suspected pirated material.

We appreciate your help in protecting our authors and our ability to bring you valuable content.

Questions

If you have a problem with any aspect of this book, you can contact us at `questions@packtpub.com`, and we will do our best to address the problem.

Installation and Setup

1

In this chapter, we will cover the following topics:

- ▶ Preparing for the initial boot
- ▶ Downloading new SD cards
- ▶ Booting with NOOBS
- ▶ Mac OS X disk utilities – diskutil and dd
- ▶ Image Writer for Windows – Win32DiskImager.exe
- ▶ Convert and copy for Linux – dd
- ▶ Booting Raspbian Linux for the first time
- ▶ Shutting down the Raspberry Pi

Introduction

This chapter introduces the Raspberry Pi. It begins by listing the components that you will need, such as a power supply, in addition to the Raspberry Pi.

The core recipes of this chapter describe how to download, install, and configure a number of common Raspberry Pi operating systems.

The last two recipes describe the initial boot of the official Raspbian Linux distribution and how to safely power off the Raspberry Pi.

Once you've completed this chapter, you will have downloaded, installed, and configured an operating system for your Raspberry Pi and booted your Raspberry Pi for the first time.

Preparing for the initial boot

This recipe explains which components are needed for the initial boot, in addition to the Raspberry Pi, before it can be powered on for the first time.

The Raspberry Pi Foundation has released a number of versions of the Raspberry Pi since it was first released in June 2012, which include Raspberry Pi B (April 2012), Raspberry Pi A (February 2013), Raspberry Pi Compute Module (April 2014), Raspberry Pi Model B+ (July 2014), and the Raspberry Pi 2 Model B (February 2015).

The original Raspberry Pi Model B has a memory of only 512 MB, a single-core processor, and two USB ports. The current model, the Raspberry Pi 2 Model B, has a memory of 1 GB, a quad-core processor, and four USB ports.

> The examples in this book feature the Raspberry Pi 2 Model B.

The Raspberry Pi is shipped without a case and power supply. There is no keyboard or monitor. Depending on how you intend to use the Raspberry Pi, you will need additional components. For the majority of the recipes in this book, you will only need a power supply, an SD card, and a network cable.

You may wish to attach additional peripherals, depending on how you intend to use the Raspberry Pi. An HDMI cable, a USB keyboard, and a USB mouse are needed if you'd like to use the Raspberry Pi as you would use a desktop computer. This recipe lists a number of different Raspberry Pi projects and the peripherals needed to complete them.

After completing this recipe, you will be ready for the initial boot of your Raspberry Pi.

Getting ready

To get started with this recipe, there are a few prerequisites that you must be familiar with.

The basic components

These are some of the basic components:

- The Raspberry Pi
- An SD card
- A 5V Micro USB Power Supply

The Raspberry Pi draws its power from a 5V micro USB power supply and needs an SD card for its operating system. While no further components are required to boot the Raspberry Pi, many of the networking solutions in this book will require additional components.

A single 4 GB SD Class 10 card has more than enough room and speed to host the base operating system as well as many useful applications. Because the SD card is where the Raspberry Pi stores its operating system, the speed of the operating system is dependent on the speed of the SD card. Class 10 cards will have better performance than Class 4 or Class 6 cards. The Embedded Linux Wiki maintains an SD Card compatibility table, which can be viewed by visiting `http://elinux.org/RPi_SD_cards`.

In addition to an SD Card, the Raspberry Pi will need additional components for many applications. For most of the recipes in this book, you will need only a network connection. For some, you may also need a display as well as a keyboard and mouse.

The following are a few examples of networking applications and the components that they will need.

Basic networking

By basic networking, we mean having a network connection. For the simplest networking solutions, the only additional component that the Raspberry Pi needs is a network connection—either a direct TCP cable connection, or a wireless network USB dongle. Once the network is configured and remote logins to the Raspberry Pi are possible, the Raspberry Pi can be remotely accessed, updated, and administered.

Media centers

As part of media centers, we will require an HDMI television or monitor.

For the simplest network media solutions, in addition to the basic networking components, the only additional component that the Raspberry Pi needs is an HDMI connection. Both audio and video can be streamed through the Raspberry Pi's HDMI connection. Furthermore, there is enough room on an SD card to store a small collection of music and video files in addition to the operating system.

Desktop computers

If you are using desktop computers, these will be required:

- An HMDI television or monitor
- A USB keyboard
- A USB mouse

The Raspberry Pi 2 has four USB ports, with enough power to support low-power devices, such as a USB keyboard or a USB mouse. With its quad-core processor, it is powerful enough to browse the Web, send e-mails, and edit documents or images. Because it runs the Linux operating system, the Raspberry Pi can also run hundreds of educational, scientific, and business programs. In short, the Raspberry Pi can run many useful open source desktop applications.

Network hubs

For network hubs, we will require these:

- A powered USB hub
- A USB LAN adapter
- A USB WLAN adapter (a Wi-Fi dongle)
- A USB hard drive
- A USB printer

When using the Raspberry Pi as a firewall or wireless access point, an additional LAN or WLAN network adapter is required. If the network adapter is powered from the USB connection, an additional powered USB connector will be required for the adapter to operate reliably.

Game consoles

- A powered USB hub
- USB game controllers

The Raspberry Pi is an excellent gaming platform if you wish to create games, or play single-player console games or multi-player network games. Many of the older text-based games can be played on the Raspberry Pi with just a keyboard or via a remote login. However, USB game controllers can also be connected to the Raspberry Pi to further enrich the gameplay of multimedia action games.

The initial setup

- The Raspberry Pi
- An SD card
- A 5V Micro USB power supply
- A network connection
- An HDMI TV or monitor
- A USB keyboard
- A USB mouse

A power supply, preformatted SD card, monitor, keyboard, and mouse are the bare minimum components that are needed for an initial setup. When connected with an HDMI to a television, the television will output audio as well as video.

How to do it...

Perform the following steps to boot the Raspberry Pi:

1. Download the latest disk image.
2. Write the disk image to an SD card.
3. Insert the formatted SD card into the Raspberry Pi.
4. Attach a display to the HDMI connector.
5. Attach a USB board and a USB mouse to the USB ports.
6. Attach a 5V micro USB power supply to the Raspberry Pi, and it boots.
7. Finally, shut down the Raspberry Pi.

How it works...

Before you can boot the Raspberry Pi, you'll need an SD card with a bootable disk image on it. The official Raspbian Linux image for the Raspberry Pi can be downloaded from `http://www.raspberrypi.org/downloads`.

Once the disk image has been downloaded, it needs to be written to an SD card (refer to the *Setting up new SD cards* recipe).

After the SD card has been prepared and inserted into the Raspberry Pi, the display, keyboard, and mouse can be connected to the Raspberry Pi. Then it is ready to be booted (refer to the *Booting Raspbian Linux* recipe).

Connect the power supply in the end! There is no on-off switch for the Raspberry Pi. When the power supply is connected, the Raspberry Pi immediately boots. Therefore, it is important to have all the cables connected and the SD card inserted before connecting the power supply.

When it is time to turn off the Raspberry Pi, the operating system must first be shut down, which is the opposite of booting (refer to the *Shutting down the Raspberry Pi* recipe).

There's more...

The Raspberry Pi 2 is a low-cost single-board computer (it costs only $35). It is sold bare bones and requires a power supply, a preformatted SD card to hold its operating system, a keyboard, and a display before it can do anything useful. However, it does have a number of standard I/O interfaces and on-board components that will enable it to connect to a large variety of devices.

Interfaces

The standard connectors and interfaces for the Raspberry Pi are as follows:

▸ **Power** (5V at 800 mA (4.0 W)): The Raspberry Pi has a Micro USB power connector that should be connected directly to a power supply that is neither the USB port on a computer, nor a USB hub.

▸ **SD card**: The Raspberry Pi is designed to be booted from a preformatted SD card (4 GB or greater is recommended; Class 10 SD cards deliver the best performance).

▸ **GPIO**: This is used in analog and digital I/O connection for expansion and experimentation.

▸ **Audio output** (3.5 mm jack—stereo): The Raspberry Pi does not have an audio input connector. However, a USB microphone or sound card can be added. Audio output includes the I2S protocol to connect to digital audio devices.

▸ **LEDs**: These are disk, power, and network traffic indicators. When these LEDs are flashing, the Raspberry Pi is actively processing. After shutting down, wait until the LEDs stop flashing before unplugging the Raspberry Pi.

▸ **USB 2.0** (four ports): There is limited power available on these ports. The devices connected to the Raspberry Pi via USB should either have their own power supply, or should be connected via a powered USB hub.

▸ **Network** (10/100 wired Ethernet RJ45): Be aware that the onboard networking competes for bandwidth with attached USB devices.

▸ **HDMI** (rev 1.3 and 1.4): This may be used for both video and audio output. Resolutions from 640x350 to 1920x1200, including the PAL and NTSC standards, are supported.

On-board components

The central on-board components for the Raspberry Pi are as follows:

▸ **SoC**: This stands for System on Chip. The one we require is Broadcom BCM2836 media processor. Here are its features:

  ❏ **CPU**: quad-core ARM Cortex-A7 at 900MHz

  ❏ **GPU**: 24 GFLOPS of compute power

  ❏ **Memory**: 1GB SDRAM

▸ **LAN9512**

  ❏ 10/100 MB Ethernet (Auto-MDIX)

  ❏ 4x USB 2.0

Recommended accessories

In addition to a power supply, the following accessories are recommended:

- ▸ **A Case**: This is a protective enclosure for the Raspberry Pi.
- ▸ **A powered USB hub**: This has its own power supply that is separate from that of the Raspberry Pi. This has enough power to support attached devices.

Power supply problems

It is difficult to say how much power is actually needed by the Raspberry Pi because the power needed varies depending on how busy the Raspberry Pi is and which peripherals are connected. However, problems related to an inadequate supply of power have been reported. These problems are reduced or eliminated when the power supply for the Raspberry Pi produces at least 800mA at 5V and the USB devices are connected indirectly through a powered USB Hub.

Symptoms

Here are some of the symptoms:

- ▸ A rainbow square glows in the upper-right corner of the display
- ▸ The network connection is unreliable
- ▸ The keyboard does not work after the Desktop GUI is started
- ▸ Intermittent SD card errors occur

Causes

Here are the causes:

- ▸ The power supply is rated less than 800mA
- ▸ A complex keyboard or a keyboard with a built-in USB hub, such as Apple Macintosh keyboards
- ▸ A USB hard disk or an extra large thumb drive is attached directly to the Raspberry Pi instead of indirectly through a powered USB hub

Solutions

Here are the solutions:

- ▸ Use a regulated power supply of at least 700mA at 5V
- ▸ Only connect simple USB devices directly to the Raspberry Pi
- ▸ Connect USB devices to a powered USB hub and only connect the hub directly to the Raspberry Pi

See also

▶ **Wikipedia—the Raspberry Pi** (`http://en.wikipedia.org/wiki/Raspberry_Pi`): This Wikipedia article about the Raspberry Pi includes a comparison of all the Raspberry Pi models, detailed information about each Raspberry Pi component, and an extended history of the Raspberry Pi.

▶ **The MagPi** (`http://www.raspberrypi.org/magpi`): The MagPi is the official Raspberry Pi magazine. Monthly issues are available online.

▶ **The Raspberry Pi website** (`http://www.raspberrypi.org`): The official Raspberry Pi website contains history, news, and documentation for the Raspberry Pi as well as a quick start guide, a forum, a wiki, and a download area.

▶ **R-Pi Hub— eLinux.org** (`http://elinux.org/R-Pi_Hub`): The R-Pi Hub is an Embedded Linux community's wiki page for Raspberry Pi users. This wiki page has a buying guide, a beginner's guide, a list of verified peripherals, and a list of Raspberry Pi distributions that is larger than what's found on the official website. It has a wealth of well-organized, up-to-date information.

▶ **The hardware history of the Raspberry Pi** (`http://elinux.org/RPi_HardwareHistory`): The Embedded Linux community has chronicled the history of the Raspberry Pi, including detailed specs and images for each version.

Downloading new SD cards

The following recipes explain how to create bootable SD cards from downloaded disk images using `Win32DiskImager.exe`, `dd`, and `diskutil`.

The Raspberry Pi does not come with an operating system. Before the Raspberry Pi can boot, it needs an SD card with the operating system installed. Preinstalled SD cards are available for purchase. However, downloading and installing an operating system image is not difficult.

Once you've completed this recipe, you will know how to download a Raspberry Pi operating system. The following recipes will show you how to write it to an SD card.

How to do it...

Perform the following steps to write an image to the SD card:

1. Download a Raspberry Pi image.
2. Write the image to an SD card.

How it works...

The easiest way to get started with the Raspberry Pi is to download the **NOOBS** (**New Out Of Box Software**) distribution from the Raspberry Pi Foundation website, which can be viewed by visiting `http://www.raspberrypi.org/downloads`. The files from this distribution can be copied directly to a formatted SD card. No additional disk utilities are required to create a bootable image (refer to the *Booting with NOOBS* recipe).

Included with NOOBS is the Raspberry Pi Foundation's recommended operating system distribution, Raspbian Linux. On the downloads page, you will also find a link to the Raspbian Linux disk image. There are links to a number of other third-party operating systems too. For more images for the Raspberry Pi, visit the Embedded Linux community's wiki page (`http://elinux.org/RPi_Distributions`).

Unlike NOOBS, once one of these individual operating system images is downloaded, you'll need to write it to an SD card using a special disk utility.

If you are using the Mac OS operating system, use `diskutil` and `dd` to write the operating system image to an SD card (refer to the Mac OS Disk Utilities recipe). If you are writing the SD card from a Windows computer, use `Win32DiskImager.exe` (refer to the *Image Writer for Windows* recipe). If you are using the Linux operating system to write the image to the SD card, use the `dd` command-line utility (refer to the *Convert and Copy for Linux* recipe).

See also

▶ The Raspberry Pi website—downloads (`http://www.raspberrypi.org/downloads`): The Raspberry Pi website's download page is where you can find links to the recommended versions of Raspberry Pi to optimize operating system distributions. Currently, the Raspberry Pi Foundation has links to the following operating system distributions:

- ❑ NOOBS and NOOBS Lite
- ❑ Raspbian (Jessie and Wheezy)
- ❑ Ubuntu Mate (a Linux desktop)
- ❑ Snappy Ubuntu Core (a developer distribution)
- ❑ Windows 10 IoT Core (a developer distribution)
- ❑ Open Source Media Center (OSMC)
- ❑ Open Embedded Linux Entertainment Center (OpenELEC)
- ❑ PINET (a classroom distribution)
- ❑ RISC OS (a non-Linux distribution)

The Raspbian Linux distribution is recommended by the Raspberry Pi Foundation. It also is the operating system distribution that is used throughout this book.

▶ **The Embedded Linux for the Raspberry Pi distributions** (http://elinux.org/ RPi_Distributions): The Embedded Linux community maintains an excellent wiki page on Raspberry Pi operating system distributions. The wiki page has a comparison table and links to downloadable image files. Many of these distributions are specialized for a specific use, such as penetration testing; use as a home theater, firewall, or an inexpensive desktop PC; or the development of software.

▶ **Windows 10IoT—Downloads** (https://ms-iot.github.io/content/ Downloads.htm): Windows for IoT and the other tools that you will need to develop for Windows IoT devices such as the Raspberry Pi are available at this website.

As of this revision, the Window 10 IoT distribution does not have a user interface. It is labeled as **Windows 10 IoT Core Insider Preview**. The tools needed to interact with the IoT Core are available from the downloads page of Windows 10 IoT.

Booting with NOOBS

This recipe explains how to use the Raspberry Pi Foundation's NOOBS to install a Raspberry Pi operating system.

NOOBS is not an operating system distribution. It is a tool that is used to install operating systems. By using NOOBS, you can select an operating system for your Raspberry Pi.

This is the easiest way to get started with the Raspberry Pi. No special disk utilities are required. Therefore, this recipe works from any computer that has an SD card writer.

Once you've completed this recipe, you will be able to use NOOBS to select an operating system for your Raspberry Pi.

Getting ready

Ingredients:

▶ A computer with an SD card writer

▶ An initial setup for the Raspberry Pi (refer to the *Preparing for the initial boot* recipe)

▶ A formatted SD card—4 GB or greater (class 10 has the best speed)

▶ The NOOBS ZIP file

The installation of NOOBS on an SD card is not operating system-specific.

Download the NOOBS ZIP file (NOOBS_v1_4_2.zip) from the Raspberry Pi website (https://www.raspberrypi.org/downloads/noobs/).

How to do it...

The following steps are required to copy NOOBS to an SD card:

1. Insert the formatted SD card into the computer.
2. Decompress the NOOBS ZIP file onto the SD card.
3. Eject the SD card.
4. Insert the SD card into the Raspberry Pi and power on the Raspberry Pi.
5. Select and install an operating system.

How it works...

The NOOBS installation process is not operating system-specific. The files in the NOOBS ZIP file simply need to be expanded onto a newly formatted SD card.

Once the files have been expanded onto the SD card, the SD card can be safely ejected from the computer and inserted into the Raspberry Pi.

After the SD card is firmly inserted into the Raspberry Pi and all of its other components are connected (the HDMI monitor, network connection, USB keyboard, and USB mouse), you can connect the power supply and boot the Raspberry Pi. Ensure that the power supply is connected in the end. Otherwise, your Raspberry Pi will not boot properly.

When the Raspberry Pi is finished booting NOOBS, you will be presented with a choice of operating systems. Select **Raspbian [RECOMMENDED]** from the top of the list by pressing the Spacebar or clicking on it with the mouse. Click on **Install (i)** or press the *I* key to install the Raspbian Linux operating system.

> Raspbian Linux is the operating system that is used throughout this book.

NOOBS will then extract the Raspbian Linux operating system and reboot the Raspberry Pi. As NOOBS is extracting the operating system, you will be presented with a few tips on how to use the Raspberry Pi, including the default username and password (the default username is `pi` and the default password is `raspberry`).

After the Raspberry Pi is rebooted, you will be ready to use the `raspi-config` command to complete the installation (refer to the *Booting Raspbian Linux for the first time* recipe).

There's more...

NOOBS is the easiest way to get started with the Raspberry Pi. It is an installation tool and not a complete operating system.

In this recipe, you used NOOBS to install the Raspbian Linux operating system. NOOBS can also be used to install a number of other operating systems, including Arch, OpenELEC, Pidora, and RaspBMC.

By using NOOBS, Raspbian Linux can be configured so that it boots directly into an easy-to-use programming environment called **Scratch**. NOOBS also has a built-in configuration editor that can be used by experts to apply additional tweaks to the boot configuration.

See also

> ▸ NOOBS (the New Out of Box Software) at `https://github.com/raspberrypi/noobs`

NOOBS is designed to make it easier to select and install operating systems for the Raspberry Pi without having to worry about manually imaging an SD card.

Mac OS X disk utilities – diskutil and dd

This recipe explains how to use the `diskutil` and `dd` disk utilities that are found on a Mac OS X computer to install a Raspberry Pi operating system image on an SD card.

You should have already downloaded a Raspberry Pi disk image and you should be ready to write the disk image onto an SD card.

Once you've completed this recipe, you will be able to write an SD card from a Mac OS X computer.

Getting ready

Ingredients:

> ▸ A computer running Mac OS X with an SD card writer
> ▸ An SD card of 4 GB or greater (class 10 has the best performance)
> ▸ A Raspberry Pi operating system image file

Both the `diskutil` and `dd` disk utility commands are installed by default with the Mac OS X operating system. The `diskutil` command is used to administer disk devices, and the `dd` command is used to copy data to and from a disk device.

The dd command requires administrative privileges. Use the sudo command to temporarily give the user administrative privileges.

How to do it...

The following steps need to be performed to write a disk image to an SD card on a Linux computer:

1. Open a Terminal.
2. Determine the name of the SD drive by using the following command:
   ```
   diskutil list
   ```
3. Unmount the mounted SD card by using the following command:
   ```
   diskutil unmountdisk /dev/disk2
   ```
4. Use dd to copy the disk image to the SD card (this requires sudo), as follows:
   ```
   sudo dd bs=1M if=raspbian.img of=/dev/rdisk2
   ```

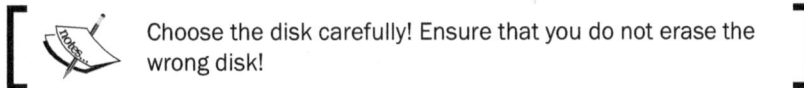

> Choose the disk carefully! Ensure that you do not erase the wrong disk!

Here is an example of a Terminal session that shows the diskutil and dd commands being used to discover the name of the SD card's disk drive, unmount the SD card, and write a Raspberry Pi disk image to the SD card:

```
macosx:~ $ diskutil list

/dev/disk0
    #:                     TYPE NAME              SIZEIDENTIFIER
    0:   GUID_partition_scheme*500.3 GB    disk0
    1:                 EFI EFI209.7 MB    disk0s1
    2:      Apple_CoreStorage499.4 GB    disk0s2
    3:           Apple_Boot Recovery HD        650.0 MB    disk0s3
/dev/disk1
    #:                     TYPE NAME              SIZE          IDENTIFIER
    0:           Apple_HFS Macintosh HD      *499.1 GB    disk1
/dev/disk2
    #:                     TYPE NAME              SIZE          IDENTIFIER
    0: FDisk_partition_scheme NO_NAME *4.0 GB    disk2
```

1:	DOS_FAT_32 NO_NAME	4.0 GB	disk2s1

```
macosx:~ $ diskutilumountdisk /dev/disk2

macosx:~ $ cd Downloads

macosx:Downloads $ dd bs=1M if=raspbian.img of=/dev/rdisk2
```

How it works...

The `diskutil` command is used to find the name of the SD card and unmount the disk.

The command is first used with the `list` subcommand to show information about each mounted disk drive.

After the SD card is inserted, the SD card appears in this list as `/dev/disk2`.

Now that we know that the SD card disk device is `/dev/disk2`, the SD card is unmounted by using the `unmountdisk` subcommand.

Finally, the `dd` command is used to write the Raspberry Pi disk image to the SD card:

- Each written disk block is 1 MB (`bs=1M`)
- The input file (`if`) is `raspbian.img`
- The output file (`of`) is the SD card disk device (`/dev/rdisk2`)

Note that the output file is named `/dev/rdisk2` and not `/dev/disk2`. The extra `r` asks Mac OS X to use the raw mode when writing to the disk. The raw mode is much faster, if you want to write, than the default mode.

There's more...

The `diskutil` command utility is a feature-rich tool that is used to modify, verify, and repair disks on Mac OS X. More information about the `diskutil` command can be found by using the built-in man pages (`man diskutil`).

Before the image is copied to the SD card in the preceding example, the disk partition is unmounted (`diskutil unmountdisk`). It is important to unmount the disk before formatting or overwriting it.

When the image is copied with the dd command,

- ▸ if= specifies the input file (raspbian.img)
- ▸ of= specifies the output file (/dev/rdisk2)
- ▸ bs= specifies the size of the blocks written to the disk

The dd utility can also be used as a backup tool. Just exchange the input file (if=) and output file (of=).

Use the following command to create a backup using the disk from the preceding example:

```
dd bs=1M if=/dev/rdisk2 of=backup-2015-06-20.img
```

Pressing *Ctrl + T* while the dd command is running will cause the command to report its progress.

More information about the dd command can be found in its man pages (man dd).

See also

- ▸ **Disk Utility** (http://en.wikipedia.org/wiki/Disk_Utility): The diskutil command can be used to unmount disks from a system. This Wikipedia article explains in detail all the features of the diskutil command.

- ▸ **diskutil – modify, verify, and repair local disks** (https://developer.apple.com/library/mac/documentation/Darwin/Reference/ManPages/man8/diskutil.8.html): The diskutil command is part of the Mac OS X operating system. The Apple man page for diskutil describes the command and its options.

- ▸ **dd – convert and copy a file** (https://developer.apple.com/library/mac/documentation/Darwin/Reference/ManPages/man1/dd.1.html): The dd command can be used to copy images to and from disks. The Apple man page for dd gives details about the command and its options.

Image Writer for Windows – Win32DiskImager.exe

This recipe shows how to install a Raspberry Pi operating system image on an SD card using the open source Image Writer for Windows, Win32DiskImager.exe.

You should have already downloaded a Raspberry Pi disk image, and you should be ready to write the disk image onto an SD card using a Windows PC.

To complete this recipe, you will also need an Internet connection to download Image Writer for Windows.

Once you've completed this recipe, you will be able to write Raspberry Pi images to SD cards from a Windows computer.

Getting ready

Here are the ingredients:

- A computer running Windows with an SD card writer
- An SD card of 4 GB or greater (class 10 has the best performance)
- A Raspberry Pi operating system image file
- A precompiled `Win32DiskImager` binary

The precompiled binary of `Win32DiskImager` is distributed as a ZIP file and can be downloaded from `https://launchpad.net/win32-image-writer`.

How to do it...

The following steps are required to write a disk image to an SD card on a Windows computer:

1. Download the `Win32DiskImager` ZIP file from `https://launchpad.net/win32-image-writer`.
2. Expand the ZIP file to a folder on disk, such as `C:\Win32DiskImager`.
3. Run `Win32DiskImager.exe` from the install folder.
4. Select the downloaded Raspberry Pi disk image as the source image file and the location of your SD card writer as the target device.
5. Click on the **Write** button to copy the image to the SD card.

Writing an image to disk takes about 5 minutes for a 2 GB image file. Once the image is written to the SD card, the SD card can be ejected and used to boot the Raspberry Pi.

How it works...

First, you will need to download and install Image Writer for Windows (`Win32DiskImager`). The `Win32DiskImager` is a single standalone executable and can be installed to a folder that is located anywhere on your PC.

Double-click on the expanded `Win32DiskImager` executable to start the application.

Once the application has started, select the downloaded Raspberry Pi disk image as the source Image File and then select the location of the SD card writer as the target device. When you click on the **Write** button, the `Win32DiskImager` writes the Raspberry Pi disk image to the SD card.

There's more...

The `Win32DiskImager` is also an excellent backup tool! After booting and configuring the Raspberry Pi, a backup can be made to preserve the image in case the SD card is damaged or lost.

To create a backup, perform the following steps:

1. Run `Win32DiskImager.exe`.
2. Select SD card as the source and a new image file as the target.
3. Click on the **Read** button to read the SD card in a new image on the disk.

The steps needed to back up a Raspberry Pi disk image from an SD card are similar to those required to write the image. The only difference is that during a backup, the SD card is the source of the copy, and a new image on the disk is the target.

A new backup should be created after each update to the Raspberry Pi's operating system, application software, or configuration.

See also

▸ **Image Writer for Windows** (`https://launchpad.net/win32-image-writer`): This utility was originally written to read and write disk images for a specific Linux distribution. However, it has now been generalized and is now a popular tool for many development projects, such as the Raspberry Pi. The Image Writer for Windows homepage has details about this disk image utility.

Convert and copy for Linux – dd

This recipe explains how to install an operating system image on an SD card using the `dd` standard Linux utility.

You should have already downloaded a Raspberry Pi disk image, and you should now be ready to write the disk image onto an SD card using a Linux PC.

Most versions of Linux and Mac OS have the `dd` command installed. This powerful version of the copy command (`cp`) can be used to write blocks of data to devices such as an SD card.

Once you've completed this recipe, you will be able to write an SD card from a Linux computer.

Getting ready

Here are the ingredients:

- ▸ A computer running Linux with an SD card writer
- ▸ An SD card with a capacity of 4 GB or greater (class 10 has the best performance)
- ▸ A Raspberry Pi operating system image file

The dd utility is normally installed by default with most Linux distributions. If it is not installed, use the appropriate Linux installation utility to install it.

All the commands in this example are executed as a privileged user (root).

How to do it...

Perform the following steps to write a disk image to an SD card on a Linux computer:

1. Determine the name of the SD drive by using the df command.

   df

2. Unmount the mounted disk partitions with umount, as follows:

   umount /dev/mmcblk0p1

3. Use dd to copy the disk image to the SD card, as follows:

   dd bs=1M if=rasbian.img of=/dev/mmcblk0

Here is an example of a Terminal session that shows the df command being used to discover the name of the SD card drive, the umount command being used to unmount the SD card, and the dd command being used to write a Raspberry Pi disk image to an SD card:

```
user@host ~ $ df -vh

Filesystem       Size  Used  Avail Use% Mounted on
/dev/sda1        9.1G  7.3G  1.4G  85% /
udev             992M     0  992M   0% /dev
/dev/sda3        9.1G  4.9G  3.8G  57% /sys1
/dev/sda4        9.1G  4.2G  4.4G  49% /sys2
/dev/mmcblk0p    3.8G  1.2G  2.6G  32% /media/A181-918F

user@host ~ $ umount /dev/mmcblk0p1

user@host ~ $ dd bs=1M if=raspbian.img of=/dev/mmcblk0
```

How it works...

The name of the SD drive is discovered using the `df` command.

The `df` command shows how much disk space is free on each mounted disk drive. After the SD card is inserted, the primary partition (`p1`) of the SD card appears in this list as `/dev/mmcblk0p1`. Therefore, the SD card disk device is `/dev/mmcblk0` (note that `p1` is missing).

Now that we know that the SD card disk device is `/dev/mmcblk0`, the SD card is unmounted using the `umount` command (note that there is no n in `umount`).

Finally, the `dd` command is used to write the Raspberry Pi disk image to the SD card:

- Each written disk block is 1 MB (`bs=1M`)
- The input file (`if`) is `raspbian.img`
- The output file (`of`) is the SD card disk device (`/dev/mmcblk0`)

Pressing *Ctrl + T* while the `dd` command is running will cause the command to report its progress.

There's more...

The `dd` utility is one of the core Gnu utilities found in most Linux distributions. It is a low-level utility that simply copies blocks of data from one file to another.

The preceding example shows how the `df` command can be used to determine the name of the SD card disk drive. The first partition of the SD disk, `/dev/mmcblk0p1`, is mounted at `/media/A1B1-918F`. Disk images cover a whole disk and not just one partition. Therefore, the correct name of the disk drive in the preceding example is `/dev/mmcblk0` (note the missing `p1`).

Before the image is copied to the SD card in the preceding example, the disk partition is unmounted. It is good practice to unmount all disk partitions before formatting or overwriting a disk.

When the image is copied with the `dd` command,

- `if=` specifies the input file (`raspbian.img`)
- `of=` specifies the output file (`/dev/mmcblk0`)
- `bs=` specifies the size of the blocks written to the disk

The `dd` utility can also be used as a backup tool. Just exchange the input file (`if=`) and output file (`of=`).

Use the following command to create a backup using the disk from the preceding example:

```
dd bs=1M if=/dev/mmcblk0 of=backup-2015-06-20.img
```

See also

▶ **dd (Unix)** (http://en.wikipedia.org/wiki/Dd_(Unix)): This Wikipedia article explains the original application of the dd command.

▶ **dd – convert and copy a file** (http://manpages.debian.net/cgi-bin/man.cgi?query=dd): The Debian man page for dd describes the command and its options.

▶ **dd (gnu - coreutils)** (http://www.gnu.org/software/coreutils/manual/html_node/dd-invocation.html): The GNU Operating System manual reference for dd has a detailed description.

Booting Raspbian Linux for the first time

This recipe explains how to boot the official Raspbian Jessie Linux distribution and use the raspi-config command to complete the installation of the Raspberry Pi remotely.

When the Raspberry Pi boots for the first time, it automatically boots into the **graphical user interface** (**GUI**) mode—the Raspberry Pi Desktop. The Raspberry Pi also starts a secure shell server on the initial boot. Therefore, the installation can be completed without a display attached to the Raspberry Pi.

In this recipe, the raspi-config command is run from a remote shell (SSH or PuTTY) to complete the installation of the Raspberry Pi. Details of the use of raspi-config can be found in *Chapter 2, Administration*.

> The installation of the Raspberry Pi can also be completed from the GUI using the **Raspberry Pi Configuration** tool, which is found in the **Preferences** menu.

Once this recipe is complete, you will have booted the Raspberry Pi for the first time.

Getting ready

Here are the ingredients:

▶ A basic networking setup for the Raspberry Pi (refer to the *Preparing for the initial boot* recipe)

▶ An SD card formatted with a Raspbian Linux image

▶ A network connection

For this recipe, the SD card should already be formatted with a Raspbian Jessie disk image, or the Raspbian operating system should have been selected using NOOBS and the Raspberry Pi should be connected to the local network, where another computer is being used to connect to the Raspberry Pi remotely.

How to do it...

Perform the following steps to boot the Raspberry Pi for the first time:

1. Insert the SD card into the Raspberry Pi and plug in the power supply. The Raspberry Pi should start booting.

2. After a short initial boot, the Raspberry Pi will announce itself on the local network using the `raspberrypi.local` hostname.

3. Log in to the Raspberry Pi using a secure shell. The default password for the user with a username of `pi` is raspberry (*Chapter 2, Administration*, has two remote access recipes).

   ```
   golden-macbook:~ rick$ ssh pi@raspberrypi.local
   ```

   ```
   The authenticity of host 'raspberrypi.local (fe80::ba27:ebff:fe57:796d%
   en5)' can't be established.
   RSA key fingerprint is da:2a:c1:d4:93:f8:02:2c:36:71:ae:6b:9e:83:a6:d4.

   Are you sure you want to continue connecting (yes/no)? yes

   pi@raspberrypi.local's password:

   The programs included with the Debian GNU/Linux system are free software;
   the exact distribution terms for each program are described in the
   individual files in /usr/share/doc/*/copyright.

   Debian GNU/Linux comes with ABSOLUTELY NO WARRANTY, to the extent
   permitted by applicable law.
   Last login: Thu Sep 24 15:33:00 2015

   pi@raspberrypi ~ $
   ```

4. Use the `raspi-config` command to update the operating system. This is a privileged command, and it requires the `sudo` prefix to run. More information on *Executing commands with privileges* can be found in *Chapter 2, Administration*.

   `pi@raspberrypi ~ $ sudo raspi-config`

5. Note that the `raspi-config` main menu has several options to update the Raspberry Pi operating system:

```
┌──────────┤ Raspberry Pi Software Configuration Tool (raspi-config) ├──────────┐
│                                                                               │
│    1 Expand Filesystem              Ensures that all of the SD card s          │
│    2 Change User Password           Change password for the default u         │
│    3 Boot Options                   Choose whether to boot into a des          │
│    4 Internationalisation Options   Set up language and regional sett          │
│    5 Enable Camera                  Enable this Pi to work with the R          │
│    6 Add to Rastrack                Add this Pi to the online Raspber          │
│    7 Overclock                      Configure overclocking for your P          │
│    8 Advanced Options               Configure advanced settings                │
│    9 About raspi-config             Information about this configurat          │
│                                                                               │
│                                                                               │
│                                                                               │
│                   <Select>                        <Finish>                    │
│                                                                               │
└───────────────────────────────────────────────────────────────────────────────┘
```

6. The following are the primary configuration options:

   - **Expand Filesystem**: This resizes the root partition to fill the SD card (not necessary if you used NOOBS)

   - **Change User Password**: This changes the default password (should be the first thing that you do).

   - **Boot Options**: Choose to boot the Raspberry Pi in the text mode or the desktop GUI (this book exclusively uses the text mode).

   - **Internationalisation Options**: This changes the display language and the default keyboard layout (the default language is British English and UK is the default keyboard layout)

   - **Enable Camera**: This enables the use of the Raspberry Pi camera

   - **Add to Rastrack**: This includes the Raspberry Pi in the Raspberry Pi Foundation's usage statistics

   - **Overclock**: This puts the Raspberry Pi into the Turbo mode (the newest model, Raspberry Pi 2, only has one speed to choose from)

- ❏ **Advanced Options**: This is for additional configuration options for advanced users (such as overscan, SSH, memory split, and audio)

- ❏ **About raspi-config**: This provides information about `raspi-config`

7. Select **1 Expand Filesystem** to expand the filesystem on the SD card to use all the available space on the SD Card. *Chapter 2, Administration*, has a recipe for *Expanding the size of the filesystem*.

8. Select **2 Change User Password** to change the default password.

9. Select **Finish** to complete the configuration and reboot the system.

How it works...

Upon booting, the Raspberry Pi registers its hostname (`raspberrypi.local`) with the local **Multicast Domain Name Server** (**mDNS**). Most home gateways and local area networks include an mDNS that provides domain name registration services for mobile devices and computers that dynamically connect to the network.

Once the Raspberry Pi has booted and registered its hostname, a secure shell client is used to connect to the Raspberry Pi using the `raspberrypi.local` hostname, the username as `pi` and the password as `raspberry`. *Chapter 2, Administration*, has two remote access recipes, one for Windows (PuTTY), and one for Mac OS X and Linux (SSH).

The Raspbian Linux operating system distribution includes the `raspi-config` utility. This configuration utility should be run once upon the first boot of the operating system to expand the filesystem and change the default password.

The `raspi-config` command is privileged and requires the `sudo` prefix to be run. More information on *Executing commands with privileges* can be found in *Chapter 2, Administration*.

When the `raspi-config` main menu appears, you can use the keyboard arrow keys, the *Tab* key, the Spacebar, or the *Return* key to navigate the menus.

Chapter 2, Administration, has a number of recipes that use the `raspi-config` command to configure the Raspberry Pi. For now, just use the **Expand Filesystem** and **Change User Password** menu items and the *Expand the size of the filesystem* and *Changing the login password* recipes.

> If you have used NOOBS, it is not necessary to expand the filesystem. NOOBS has already expanded the filesystem.

Selecting **Finish** from the main menu will cause the Raspberry Pi to reboot.

Once rebooted, the Raspberry Pi is ready for use!

See also

▶ **Multicast DNS** (https://en.wikipedia.org/wiki/Multicast_DNS): This Wikipedia article describes how mDNS is used to resolve host names to IP address with small local area networks.

Shutting down the Raspberry Pi

This recipe shows how the Raspberry Pi can be powered off safely.

Before powering off the Raspberry Pi, it is important to first shut down the operating system so that all of the applications and services on the Raspberry Pi have a chance to complete any disk writing that may be in progress and to prepare for the next boot.

External devices, such as hard disks, also need time to shut down and flush their buffers. The `shutdown` command also gives the devices attached to the Raspberry Pi an opportunity to clean up and prepare for the next boot.

After completing this recipe, you will be able to power off the Raspberry Pi safely.

Getting ready

Here are my ingredients:

▶ An Initial Setup for the Raspberry Pi (refer to the *Preparing for initiating the boot* recipe)

▶ An SD card formatted with the official Raspbian Linux image

The Raspberry Pi should already be powered on and booted before implementing this recipe.

How to do it...

Perform the following steps to shut down the Raspberry Pi:

1. If you have not already done so, log in to the Raspberry Pi as the user `pi` (the default password is `raspberry`):

```
Raspbian GNU/Linux 7raspberrypi tty1

Raspberrypi login: pi
Password:
```

```
Last Login: Sun Jun 21 19:45:35 UTC 2015 on tty1
Linux raspberrypi 3.18.11-v7+ #781SMP PREEEMPT Tue Apr 21 18:07:59 BST
2015armv7l


The programs included with the Debian GNU/Linux system are free
software;The exact distribution terms for each program are described in
the individual files in /user/share/doc/*/copyright.


Debian GNU/Linux comes with ABSOLUTELY NO WARRANTY, to the extent
permitted by applicable law.


pi@raspberrypi ~ $
```

2. Shut down and halt (-h) the operating system. This command is privileged. Use the `sudo` prefix to run the shutdown command as a privileged user, as follows:

    pi@raspberrypi ~ $ **sudo shutdown –h now**

    ```
    Broadcast message from root@raspberrypi (pts/0) (Sun Jun 21 19:53:03
    2015):
    The system is going down for system halt NOW!
    ```

3. After the `shutdown` command is executed, the Raspberry Pi will begin its shutdown process, displaying messages from applications, devices, and services, as they clean up and prepare for the next boot.

4. Once the operating system has shut down, the Raspberry Pi will halt, leaving only a single red LED lit on the Raspberry Pi (as long as the LEDs are flashing, the Raspberry Pi is still busy shutting down).

5. The power supply can now be unplugged from the Raspberry Pi.

How it works...

If you have not already logged into the Raspberry Pi, you will need to log in to the Raspberry Pi before shutting it down.

The default user is `pi`. You should have already changed the default user's password during the first boot (refer to the *Booting Raspbian Linux for the first time* recipe). In case you have not changed it, the default password is `raspberry`.

After logging in, the `shutdown` command is executed with the –h option, which tells the Raspberry Pi to halt after the operating system is shut down.

The `shutdown` command is privileged. Therefore, the `sudo` command is used as a prefix to temporarily grant privileges. More information on *Executing commands with privileges* can be found in *Chapter 2, Administration*.

There's more...

The shutdown command can also be used to reboot the system. Just use the -r reboot option instead of the -h halt option.

Rebooting the system when you're logged in as the user pi can be done with the help of the following command:

pi@raspberrypi ~ $ **sudo shutdown -r now**

Synonyms exist for the shutdown command, which include poweroff and reboot.

To power off the system instead of using shutdown -h, you can also use the following command:

pi@raspberrypi ~ $ **sudo poweroff**

Instead of shutdown -r, you can also use the following command:

pi@raspberrypi ~ $ **sudo reboot**

More information about these commands can be found in their man pages.

See also

> ▸ **halt, reboot, poweroff – stop the system** (http://manpages.debian.net/cgi-bin/man.cgi?query=halt): There are alternatives to the shutdown command. The Debian man page for halt, poweroff, and reboot describes these commands in detail.

> ▸ **shutdown – bring the system down** (http://manpages.debian.net/cgi-bin/man.cgi?query=shutdown): The shutdown command can be used to halt (-h) or reboot (-r) the system. The Debian man page for shutdown describes the command and all of its options in detail.

2

Administration

In this chapter, we will cover the following topics:

- ▶ Executing commands with privileges (`sudo`)
- ▶ Expanding the size of a filesystem (`raspi-config`)
- ▶ Configuring memory usage (`raspi-config`)
- ▶ Configuring remote access (`raspi-config`)
- ▶ Obtaining remote access by using SSH
- ▶ Obtaining remote access by using PuTTY
- ▶ Changing the login password (`passwd`)
- ▶ Adding a user (`adduser`)
- ▶ Giving a user sudo privileges (`id` and `usermod`)

Introduction

The recipes in this chapter are for the basic administration of the Raspberry Pi. This chapter starts with a recipe that shows how you can use the `sudo` command to execute other commands that require superuser privileges. The next three recipes use the `raspi-config` command-line tool to complete the following three initial configuration tasks:

- ▶ Expanding the filesystem to use all the space on an SD card
- ▶ Changing the memory allocation for better performance
- ▶ Enabling remote access to the Raspberry Pi

The following two recipes show how the Raspberry Pi can be accessed remotely:

- ▶ Using the `SSH` command-line client from Linux or Mac OS X computers
- ▶ Using the PuTTY client from Windows computers

The final three recipes in this chapter, which are as follows, are for user administration:

- ▶ How to change the password of the default user whose username is `pi`
- ▶ How to create a new user login
- ▶ How to add a user to the privileged `sudo` user group

Once you've completed this chapter, you will be able to administer the Raspberry Pi remotely via a network connection without a keyboard or display.

Executing commands with privileges (sudo)

This recipe shows how you can execute privileged commands using `sudo`.

The default Raspberry Pi user (`pi`) is an ordinary user and not a super-user. The `sudo` command is used to temporarily grant an ordinary user the privileges of a super-user.

After you've completed this recipe, you will be able to execute commands with super-user privileges by using `sudo` as a command prefix.

Getting ready

The following ingredients are required for this recipe:

- ▶ You need an initial setup or a basic networking setup for the Raspberry Pi that has been powered on. You also need to be logged in as the user whose username is `pi` (refer to the recipes in *Chapter 1, Installation and Setup,* for instructions on how to boot and log in and the recipes given later in this chapter for instructions on how to log in remotely).
- ▶ A network connection is an optional requirement.

If the Raspberry Pi has remote access enabled, this recipe can be completed remotely using SSH or PuTTY (refer to the *Remote access (SSH)* and *Remote access (PuTTY)* recipes that are given later in this chapter).

How to do it...

This recipe executes a privileged command, first without and then with privileges:

1. First, try executing a privileged command, such as reboot, as an ordinary user, as follows:

   pi@raspberrypi ~ $ **reboot**

   reboot: must be superuser.

   pi@raspberrypi ~ $

2. Then, try executing the command again with super-user privileges, as follows:

   pi@raspberrypi ~ $ **sudo reboot**

   Broadcast message from root@raspberrypi (pts/0) (Sat Jun 27 21:16:19 2015):

   The system is going down for reboot NOW!

How it works...

The sudo command is for nonprivileged users who wish to temporarily grant another command super-user privileges (as a super-user would do something).

In this recipe, the privileged command, reboot, was first executed without super-user privileges by the ordinary user pi. The reboot command then reported an error by stating that must be superuser. An ordinary user cannot execute the reboot command.

Finally, the sudo command was used like a super-user prefix to temporarily give the ordinary user, pi, super-user privileges. Then, the system was rebooted as requested.

There's more...

The following are a few more commands that can be used.

Switch user (sudo –u)

The sudo command is really a *switch user* and *do something* command.

By default, the sudo command temporarily switches to the root user, who's the superuser. When a command is run as the root user, the command has all the privileges that the root user enjoys.

When executed with the –u command-line argument, sudo can be used to impersonate any user on the system, temporarily giving one command all the privileges of another user.

For more information on creating additional users for the Raspberry Pi, refer to the *Adding a user* recipe at the end of this chapter.

Here is an example of using the sudo command to switch to another user that already exists on your Raspberry Pi, the user whose username is nobody. The user nobody has no privileges (that is its purpose – to have no privileges; it is a security feature), but we can use nobody to show how the sudo command works. This example creates and deletes two files – a file that belongs to the user pi and another that belongs to the user nobody:

```
pi@raspberrypi ~ $ ls -l /tmp

total 0

pi@raspberrypi ~ $ touch /tmp/i-belong-to-pi

pi@raspberrypi ~ $ ls -l /tmp

total 0
-rw-r--r-- 1 pi pi 0 Jun 27 21:54 i-belong-to-pi

pi@raspberrypi ~ $
```

Note that there is now one file in the temporary directory and this file is owned by the user pi (the third column of the ls -l command's output contains the file's owner):

```
pi@raspberrypi ~ $ sudo -u nobody touch /tmp/i-belong-to-nobody

pi@raspberrypi ~ $ ls -l /tmp

total 0
-rw-r--r-- 1 nobody nogroup 0 Jun 27 21:55 i-belong-to-nobody
-rw-r--r-- 1 pi     pi      0 Jun 27 21:54 i-belong-to-pi

pi@raspberrypi ~ $
```

There are now two files in the /tmp directory. One file, i-belong-to-pi, belongs to the user pi and the other file, i-belong-to-nobody, belongs to the user nobody.

Now, let's try to remove the two files that we created from the temporary directory, as follows:

```
pi@raspberrypi ~ $ rm /tmp/i-belong-to-pi

pi@raspberrypi ~ $ ls -l /tmp

total 0
-rw-r--r-- 1 nobody nogroup 0 Jun 27 21:55 i-belong-to-nobody

pi@raspberrypi ~ $
```

Removing the `i-belong-to-pi` file worked. There is only file left in the directory:

```
pi@raspberrypi ~ $ rm /tmp/i-belong-to-nobody

rm: remove write-protected regular empty file `/tmp/i-belong-to-nobody'? y
rm: cannot remove `/tmp/i-belong-to-nobody': Operation not permitted

pi@raspberrypi ~ $
```

Removing the `i-belong-to-nobody` file does not work because the file is owned by the user `nobody`.

If you want to delete the `i-belong-nobody` file, you will first have to switch to the user `nobody` using the `sudo` command, as follows:

```
pi@raspberrypi ~ $ sudo -u nobody rm /tmp/i-belong-to-nobody

pi@raspberrypi ~ $ ls -l /tmp

total 0

pi@raspberrypi ~ $
```

Using `sudo -u nobody` worked! There are no files left in the `/tmp` directory.

Password

The Raspbian Linux distribution's default configuration requires no password when using `sudo` for users in the `sudo` group.

If you are using another Linux distribution, you may be required to enter a password when using `sudo`. If you are required to enter a password, use the same password as the one that you used when logging in to the Raspberry Pi.

The sudo group

If you have added additional users to the Raspberry Pi, you will also need to add them to the sudo user group if you wish those users to use privileged commands, such as shutdown and reboot, or change files in the configuration directory (/etc). Users that are not in the sudo group will not be able to execute privileged commands or change privileged files.

The recipes at the end of this chapter have more information about user administration, including how to add users to the sudo user group.

See also

> ▸ **sudo, sudoedit – execute a command as another user** (http://manpages. debian.net/cgi-bin/man.cgi?query=sudo): The switch user command temporarily executes a command as another user. The Debian manual page for the sudo command describes all of its features and options.

> ▸ **touch – change file timestamps** (http://manpages.debian.net/cgi-bin/ man.cgi?query=touch): The touch command will create a file if it does not exist. The Debian man page for the touch command describes all of its features and options.

Expanding the size of a filesystem (raspi-config)

This recipe shows how you can use the raspi-config command to expand the Raspberry Pi's filesystem so that it uses all the available disk space on an SD card.

The operating system images for the Raspberry Pi are compacted and compressed to use as little disk space as possible. This reduction in the size of an operating system image helps improve the speed of downloading the image. When these reduced images are copied to an SD card, it is very likely that the SD card will still have space left over. Larger SD Cards (greater than 8 GB) will be mostly empty!

> If you used NOOBS to install the Raspberry Pi, you do not need to expand the filesystem. NOOBS has already expanded the filesystem for you.

This recipe uses the `raspi-config` command-line utility to expand the filesystem of the operating system image so that it includes all the available space on an SD card.

After you've completed this recipe, the filesystem that your Raspberry Pi uses for storage will be expanded to include all the available space on the SD card.

Getting ready

The following ingredients are required for this recipe:

► You need an initial setup or a basic networking setup for the Raspberry Pi that has been powered on. You also need to be logged in as the user `pi` (refer to the recipes in *Chapter 1, Installation and Setup*, for instructions on how to boot and log in and the recipes later in this chapter for instructions on how to log in remotely).

► A network connection is an optional requirement.

If the Raspberry Pi has remote access enabled, this recipe can be completed remotely using SSH or PuTTY (refer to the *Remote access (SSH)* and *Remote access (PuTTY)* recipes provided later in this chapter).

The SD card used in the examples for this recipe has a storage of 32 GB.

How to do it...

Use the following steps to expand the Raspberry Pi's filesystem:

1. Use the `df` command to see how much disk space is available, as follows:
   pi@raspberrypi ~ $ **df –h**

Filesystem	Size	Used	Avail	Use%	Mounted on
/dev/root	3.9G	3.1G	596M	84%	/
devtmpfs	459M	0	459M	0%	/dev
tmpfs	463M	0	463M	0%	/dev/shm
tmpfs	463M	13M	451M	3%	/run
tmpfs	5.0M	4.0K	5.0M	1%	/run/lock
tmpfs	463M	0	463M	0%	/sys/fs/cgroup
/dev/mmcblk0p1	56M	20M	37M	36%	/boot
tmpfs	93M	0	93M	0%	/run/user/1000

   pi@raspberrypi ~ $

2. Note that the **Size** (column 2) of the root filesystem (`/dev/root`) is only `3.9 G`, even though the actual disk size is much larger.

3. Execute the `raspi-config` command to expand the size of the root file system, as follows:

   pi@raspberrypi ~ $ **sudo raspi-config**

4. The `raspi-config` main menu is then displayed:

```
┌─────────┤ Raspberry Pi Software Configuration Tool (raspi-config) ├─────────┐
│                                                                             │
│    1 Expand Filesystem            Ensures that all of the SD card s         │
│    2 Change User Password         Change password for the default u        │
│    3 Boot Options                 Choose whether to boot into a des        │
│    4 Internationalisation Options Set up language and regional sett        │
│    5 Enable Camera                Enable this Pi to work with the R         │
│    6 Add to Rastrack              Add this Pi to the online Raspber         │
│    7 Overclock                    Configure overclocking for your P         │
│    8 Advanced Options             Configure advanced settings               │
│    9 About raspi-config           Information about this configurat         │
│                                                                             │
│                                                                             │
│                 <Select>                         <Finish>                   │
│                                                                             │
└─────────────────────────────────────────────────────────────────────────────┘
```

5. Press the *Enter* key to select the first menu item, `Expand Filesystem`. Use the up and down arrow keys to change the selection.

6. After a brief moment, the screen displays this:

```
┌─────────────────────────────────────────────────────────────────┐
│                                                                   │
│ Root partition has been resized.                                  │
│ The filesystem will be enlarged upon the next reboot              │
│                                                                   │
│                          <Ok>                                     │
│                                                                   │
└─────────────────────────────────────────────────────────────────┘
```

7. Press the *Enter* key; you will return to the main menu.

8. Press the *Tab* key to select **Finish** and then press the *Enter* key:

```
|                                                                    |
|                                                                    |
|  Would you like to reboot now?                                     |
|                                                                    |
|                                                                    |
|                  <Yes>                      <No>                   |
|                                                                    |
```

9. Press the *Enter* key to select **Yes**. The Raspberry Pi will reboot.

10. After logging back in, use the df -h command to check out the available disk space on the root filesystem (/), as follows:

pi@raspberrypi ~ $ **df -h /**

Filesystem   Size Used Avail Use% Mounted on
/dev/root   29G   3.1G   24G 12% /

pi@raspberrypi ~ $

How it works...

This recipe begins by displaying the amount of disk space that is available on the Raspberry Pi. The df command displays how much disk space is free (df is short for disk free). The -h command-line argument asks df to display the result in a human-readable format. The output of the command shows that the /dev/root filesystem has a total of 3.9 GB and 84% of the filesystem is in use, leaving only 596 MB available.

Then, the raspi-config command is run to expand the root filesystem. The first command in the raspi-config command's main menu, Expand Filesystem, is selected to resize the Raspberry Pi's root partition (/dev/root).

After resizing the root filesystem, the Raspberry Pi needs to be rebooted. Once rebooted, the size of the root filesystem is checked once again. The amount of available disk space is now 24 GB!

There's more...

The best time to expand the root filesystem is right after the installation – before you install new software or require additional disk space.

The `raspi-config` utility is used to configure many basic components of the Raspberry Pi. Examples of its use can be found in the recipes named *Configuring remote access* and *Configuring memory usage*.

See also

▶ Raspi-config

▶ (https://www.raspberrypi.org/documentation/configuration/raspi-config.md): A reference page for the `raspi-config` command can be found in the Raspberry Pi Foundations documentation.

▶ RPi raspi-config (http://elinux.org/RPi_raspi-config): This documentation at the Embedded Linux website shows how the `raspi-config` script helps you configure the Raspberry Pi.

Configuring memory usage (raspi-config)

This recipe shows how the `raspi-config` utility is used to change the Raspberry Pi's memory split to maximize the amount of memory available for the CPU.

This book features solutions that do not require a display. Many of these solutions will benefit from having the additional memory that the display is using.

However, if you are using the Raspberry Pi as a desktop computer, you may want to maximize the amount of video memory. Internet content displayed in web browsers, such as images and video, as well as computer games will benefit from a high video memory.

After you have completed this recipe, you can choose your own balance between memory dedicated for the video core and the memory available for the CPU.

Getting ready

The ingredients required for this recipe are an initial setup or a basic networking setup for the Raspberry Pi that has been powered on. You also need to be logged in as the user `pi` (refer to the recipes in *Chapter 1, Installation and Setup*, for instructions on how to boot and log in).

How to do it...

Use the following steps to configure the Raspberry Pi's memory usage:

1. Execute the `raspi-config` command, as follows:

   pi@raspberrypi ~ $ **sudo raspi-config**

2. The `raspi-config` main menu is then displayed:

   ```
   ┌──────────┤ Raspberry Pi Software Configuration Tool (raspi-config) ├──────────┐
   │                                                                              │
   │      1 Expand Filesystem            Ensures that all of the SD card s        │
   │      2 Change User Password         Change password for the default u       │
   │      3 Boot Options                 Choose whether to boot into a des        │
   │      4 Internationalisation Options Set up language and regional sett        │
   │      5 Enable Camera                Enable this Pi to work with the R         │
   │      6 Add to Rastrack              Add this Pi to the online Raspber        │
   │      7 Overclock                    Configure overclocking for your P        │
   │      8 Advanced Options             Configure advanced settings              │
   │      9 About raspi-config           Information about this configurat        │
   │                                                                              │
   │                 <Select>                      <Finish>                       │
   │                                                                              │
   └──────────────────────────────────────────────────────────────────────────────┘
   ```

3. Use the up and down arrow keys to change the selection. Then, press the *Enter* key to select **Advanced Options**.

4. The **Advanced Options** menu is displayed, as follows:

   ```
   ┌──────────┤ Raspberry Pi Software Configuration Tool (raspi-config) ├──────────┐
   │                                                                              │
   │      A1 Overscan          You may need to configure oversca                  │
   │      A2 Hostname          Set the visible name for this Pi                   │
   │      A3 Memory Split      Change the amount of memory made                   │
   │      A4 SSH               Enable/Disable remote command lin                  │
   │      A5 Device Tree       Enable/Disable the use of Device                   │
   │      A6 SPI               Enable/Disable automatic loading                   │
   │      A7 I2C               Enable/Disable automatic loading                   │
   │      A8 Serial            Enable/Disable shell and kernel m                  │
   │      A9 Audio             Force audio out through HDMI or 3                   │
   │      A0 Update            Update this tool to the latest ve                  │
   │                                                                              │
   │                 <Select>                      <Back>                         │
   │                                                                              │
   └──────────────────────────────────────────────────────────────────────────────┘
   ```

5. Select **Memory Split** from the menu to change the memory split.

6. You are prompted to enter an amount of memory for the GPU:

```
┌─────────────────────────────────────────────────────────────────┐
│ How much memory should the GPU have?  e.g.  16/32/64/128/256      │
│                                                                   │
│ 16_____ │
│                                                                   │
│              <Ok>                        <Cancel>                 │
│                                                                   │
└─────────────────────────────────────────────────────────────────┘
```

7. Enter `16` and press the *Enter* key to give the Raspberry Pi's GPU the minimum amount of memory.

8. You are returned to the main menu of `raspi-config`.

9. Select **Finish** from the main menu and reboot the Raspberry Pi.

How it works...

One of the selections available from the **Advanced Options** menu of the `raspi-config` configuration tool is to specify the memory split between the **Graphics Processing Unit** (**GPU**) used for video processing and the CPU used for general processing. In this recipe, you entered 16 MB, the minimum value for the GPU.

The Raspberry Pi shares 256 MB of its total memory (1 GB for the Raspberry Pi 2) between its CPU and GPU. The memory can be split in the following five different ways:

▶ 16 MB for the GPU and 1008 MB for the CPU

▶ 32 MB for the GPU and 992 MB for the CPU

▶ 64 MB for the GPU and 960 MB for the CPU

▶ 128 MB for the GPU and 896 MB for the CPU

▶ 256 MB for the GPU and 768 MB for the CPU

For many of the recipes in this book, the GPU only needs a minimum of 16 MB of memory. These recipes don't require a display and will benefit if the maximum amount of memory is assigned to the CPU (1008 MB). This will improve the CPU's overall performance.

For solutions that require a display, more memory should be allocated to the GPU. Multimedia solutions, such as OMXPlayer or XBMC distributions, will benefit from having a maximum of 256 MB of Video Core memory.

Even when the maximum amount of memory is assigned to the GPU, the Raspberry Pi 2 will still have 768 MB of memory left for use by the CPU. To experiment with the recipes in this book, 768 MB is more than enough memory. However, for higher performance or long-term use, the recipes that do not require a display will benefit from having the full 1008 MB available for the CPU.

There's more...

The `raspi-config` utility is used to configure many basic components of the Raspberry Pi. Examples of its use can be found in the recipes in this chapter that are named *Expanding the size of the filesystem* and *Configuring remote access*.

Configuring remote access (raspi-config)

This recipe shows how to use the `raspi-config` utility to configure remote access to the Raspberry Pi.

For most network applications, a graphical user interface (a GUI desktop) is not needed. The memory and processing power spent creating a GUI desktop can be invested in a better in the network application. The majority of the recipes in this book are written so that they can be used remotely without a graphical user interface.

> If you have installed a Raspbian Linux distribution (as recommended in *Chapter 1, Installation and Setup*), secure remote access via the SSH protocol is already enabled.
>
> Raspbian Linux has remote access via SSH enabled by default.

After you've completed this recipe, your Raspberry Pi will be securely accessible on your local network from another PC using the **Secure Shell** (**SSH**) protocol.

Getting ready

The following ingredients are needed for this recipe:

- An initial setup or a basic networking setup for the Raspberry Pi that has been powered on. You also need to be logged in as the user `pi` (refer to the recipes in *Chapter 1, Installation and Setup*, for instructions on how to boot and log in and the recipes later in this chapter for instructions on how to log in remotely).

- A network connection is an optional requirement.

If the Raspberry Pi has remote access enabled, this recipe can be completed remotely using SSH or PuTTY (refer to the *Remote access (SSH)* and *Remote access (PuTTY)* recipes that are given in the later parts of this chapter).

How to do it...

Use the following steps to configure remote access to the Raspberry Pi:

1. Execute the `raspi-config` command, as follows:

   `pi@raspberrypi ~ $ sudo raspi-config`

2. The `raspi-config` main menu is then displayed:

```
┌───────────┤ Raspberry Pi Software Configuration Tool (raspi-config) ├───────────┐
│                                                                                 │
│    1 Expand Filesystem             Ensures that all of the SD card s            │
│    2 Change User Password          Change password for the default u            │
│    3 Boot Options                  Choose whether to boot into a des            │
│    4 Internationalisation Options  Set up language and regional sett            │
│    5 Enable Camera                 Enable this Pi to work with the R             │
│    6 Add to Rastrack               Add this Pi to the online Raspber            │
│    7 Overclock                     Configure overclocking for your P             │
│    8 Advanced Options              Configure advanced settings                  │
│    9 About raspi-config            Information about this configurat            │
│                                                                                 │
│               <Select>                         <Finish>                         │
│                                                                                 │
└─────────────────────────────────────────────────────────────────────────────────┘
```

3. Use the up and down arrow keys to change the selection and then press the *Enter* key to select **Advanced Options**.

4. The **Advanced Options** menu is displayed:

```
┌──────────┤ Raspberry Pi Software Configuration Tool (raspi-config) ├──────────┐
│                                                                                │
│    A1 Overscan                   You may need to configure oversca             │
│    A2 Hostname                   Set the visible name for this Pi              │
│    A3 Memory Split               Change the amount of memory made              │
│    A4 SSH                        Enable/Disable remote command lin             │
│    A5 Device Tree                Enable/Disable the use of Device              │
│    A6 SPI                        Enable/Disable automatic loading              │
│    A7 I2C                        Enable/Disable automatic loading              │
│    A8 Serial                     Enable/Disable shell and kernel m             │
│    A9 Audio                      Force audio out through HDMI or 3             │
│    A0 Update                     Update this tool to the latest ve             │
│                                                                                │
│               <Select>                        <Back>                           │
│                                                                                │
└────────────────────────────────────────────────────────────────────────────┘
```

5. Select **SSH** from the **Advanced Options** menu to enable remote access.

6. The following screen appears:

```
┌──────────────────────────────────────────────────────────────┐
│                                                                │
│  Would you like the SSH server enabled or disabled?            │
│                                                                │
│               <Enable>                  <Disable>              │
│                                                                │
└──────────────────────────────────────────────────────────────┘
```

7. Use the *Tab* key to select the option and then press the *Enter* key or choose **Enable**.

8. After a brief moment, the SSH server is enabled:

```
|                                                        |
| SSH server enabled                                     |
|                                                        |
|                          <Ok>                          |
|                                                        |
```

9. Click on **Ok** to return to the main menu.

10. Click on **Finish** from the main menu and then click on **Yes** to reboot the Raspberry Pi and enable remote access.

How it works...

One of the selections available in the `raspi-config` main menu is to enable the Open SSH Secure Shell server. The Open SSH server enables secure access to the Raspberry Pi over a network connection. Once enabled, the SSH server will be started automatically each time the Raspberry Pi boots.

To disable remote access, disable the Open SSH server. The server can be disabled from the `raspi-config` utility using the same steps in this recipe, except that **Disable** should be selected when the utility asks, "Would you like the SSH server enabled or disabled?".

The Secure Shell server runs on the Raspberry Pi. A client program – such as SSH on Mac OS X or Linux, or PuTTY on Windows – can be used to connect to the Secure Shell server. The client program is a virtual terminal that, once connected, permits a user to interact remotely with the Raspberry Pi as though it is connected directly with a keyboard and display. The virtual terminal cannot run X Windows directly. Therefore, you will need another tool to view the Raspberry Pi's GUI desktop remotely.

There's more...

This `raspi-config` utility is used to configure many of the basic components of the Raspberry Pi. More examples of its use can be found in the recipes named *Expanding the size of the filesystem* and *Configuring memory usage*.

The *Remote access (SSH)* and *Remote access (PuTTY)* recipes in this chapter have instructions on how to connect remotely from Mac OS X, Linux, and Windows using an SSH client.

In *Chapter 5, Advanced Networking*, the *Connecting to the desktop remotely* recipe shows how to access the Raspberry Pi's GUI desktop remotely.

- ▸ See also
- ▸ **Secure Shell** (`http://en.wikipedia.org/wiki/Secure_Shell`): This Wikipedia article about the Secure Shell shows how it is a network protocol for secure data communication. The article highlights the history of the protocol, explains its architecture and vulnerabilities, and contains links to the current implementations.
- ▸ **OpenSSH** (`http://www.openssh.org/`): Open SSH was a SSH1 and SSH2 implementation that was originally designed as a part of the FreeBSD project. It is now a part of most Linux distributions, including Raspbian Linux.

Obtaining remote access by using SSH

This recipe shows how to access the Raspberry Pi remotely using the `ssh` command.

After the Raspberry Pi has been configured to automatically start the Secure Shell server when it boots (see the previous recipe named *Configuring remote access* in this chapter), it is possible to access the Raspberry Pi remotely using the Secure Shell client, `ssh`.

The `ssh` command is built into the current version of the Mac OS X operating systems and is also available for most Linux distributions. For Microsoft Windows operating systems, another utility will be required (refer to the recipe named *Remote Access (PuTTY)*.

This recipe starts by logging directly into the Raspberry Pi using an attached keyboard and display to discover the IP address of the Raspberry Pi. Once the IP address is known, the recipe shows how to log in to the Raspberry Pi from another computer using SSH.

After you've completed this recipe, you will no longer be required to log in directly to the Raspberry Pi with an attached keyboard. You will also not need a display. You will be able to remotely administer your Raspberry Pi from another PC on the same network.

Getting ready

The following ingredients are needed for this recipe:

- ▸ You need an initial setup for the Raspberry Pi that has been powered on. You also need to be logged in as the user `pi` (refer to the recipes in *Chapter 1, Installation and Setup*, for instructions on how to boot and log in).
- ▸ A network connection is required.
- ▸ A PC that runs on Mac OS X, Linux, or other Unix-based operating system is also required.

How to do it...

Perform the following steps to remotely access the Raspberry Pi using the `ssh` command:

1. On a Max OS X or Linux PC, use the `ssh` command to log in as the user `pi` on the host named `raspberrypi.local`, as follows:

    golden-macbook:~ rick$ **ssh pi@raspberrypi.local**

    The authenticity of host 'raspberrypi.local (192.168.2.10)' can't be established.
    RSA key fingerprint is f3:de:d3:58:eb:66:1e:23:2c:6e:cf:c9:12:0c:e3:e2.

2. Since this is the first time you have connected to your Raspberry Pi remotely using a secure shell, the Raspberry Pi shares its security fingerprint for future identification.

3. When prompted, answer `yes` to `Are you sure you want to continue connecting (yes/no)?`, as follows:

    Are you sure you want to continue connecting (yes/no)? yes

4. After entering `yes`, you are told that your Raspberry Pi's security fingerprint is being permanently added to the list of known hosts. Then, you are prompted for a password:

    Warning: Permanently added 'raspberrypi.local' (RSA) to the list of known hosts.

    pi@raspberrypi.local's password:

5. Enter the password for the user `pi` on the Raspberry Pi (if you have not yet changed it, the default password is `raspberry`). You will then be shown a logon message and a command prompt:

    The programs included with the Debian GNU/Linux system are free software;
    the exact distribution terms for each program are described in the
    individual files in /usr/share/doc/*/copyright.

    Debian GNU/Linux comes with ABSOLUTELY NO WARRANTY, to the extent
    permitted by applicable law.

    Last login: Mon Nov 23 00:43:40 2015 from fe80::12dd:b1ff:feee:dfc6%eth0

    pi@raspberrypi ~ $

6. Type `exit` to log out:

```
pi@raspberrypi ~ $ exit

logout
Connection to raspberrypi.local closed.

golden-macbook:~ rick$
```

How it works...

This recipe starts by using the `ssh` command to log in to the Raspberry Pi using its default username, `pi`, and its default hostname, `raspberrypi.local`. The default password is `raspberry`.

The format of the login parameter to the `ssh` command is `user@hostname`. The example shows `pi@raspberrypi.local` because we want to log in to the `raspberrypi` host on the local network as the user `pi`.

Since this is the first time that we are logging in to the Raspberry Pi from the golden-macbook computer, the golden-macbook computer says that it cannot establish the authenticity of the Raspberry Pi. So, the Raspberry Pi shares its secure digital fingerprint (`f3:de:d3:58:eb:66:1e:23:2c:6e:cf:c9:12:0c:e3:e2`). Once we agree to accepting a connection from this new computer, the golden-macbook computer says that it will store the fingerprint permanently.

Digital fingerprints

Secure digital fingerprints are one part of the SSH protocol. Each computer has its own digital fingerprints that are as unique to the computer as human fingerprints are to humans. The golden-macbook computer stores the Raspberry Pi's fingerprints for reference to prevent *spoofing* that can be done by another computer. The other computer should not have the same digital fingerprints as those in the Raspberry Pi.

After the Raspberry Pi's fingerprint has been accepted and stored, we are prompted for the password of the user `pi` at the `raspberrypi.local` host. After entering the password, we are presented with the Raspberry Pi's login message, the date of the last login, and a command prompt.

For this recipe, there is nothing more left to do. So, we will enter `exit` at the command prompt, and the remote connection to the Raspberry Pi is closed.

Hostname

It is not always possible to log in using the default hostname, which is `raspberrypi.local`. Sometimes, you will need to discover the IP address of the Raspberry Pi before you can log in.

If you have connected the Raspberry Pi to a keyboard and display, you can use the `hostname` command to discover the IP address of the Raspberry Pi. The `-I` option asks the command to display all the IP addresses for the Raspberry Pi:

```
pi@raspberrypi ~ $ hostname -I

192.168.2.12

pi@raspberrypi ~ $
```

After the IP address is discovered (192.168.2.12), it can be used to log in remotely to the Raspberry Pi, as follows:

```
golden-macbook:~ rick$ ssh pi@192.168.2.12

pi@192.168.2.12's password:
```

There's more...

Let's have a look at some other requirements for a remote login.

Finding out the IP address of the Raspberry Pi

Before the remote login is possible, the network address of the Raspberry Pi must be known. The `hostname` command can be used to directly discover the IP address from the Raspberry Pi via an attached keyboard and display. It is also possible to discover the IP address from the configuration interface of the local network gateway or DSL router. The following screenshot shows how the IP Address of a device named `raspberrypi` is displayed in a DSL router's configuration interface:

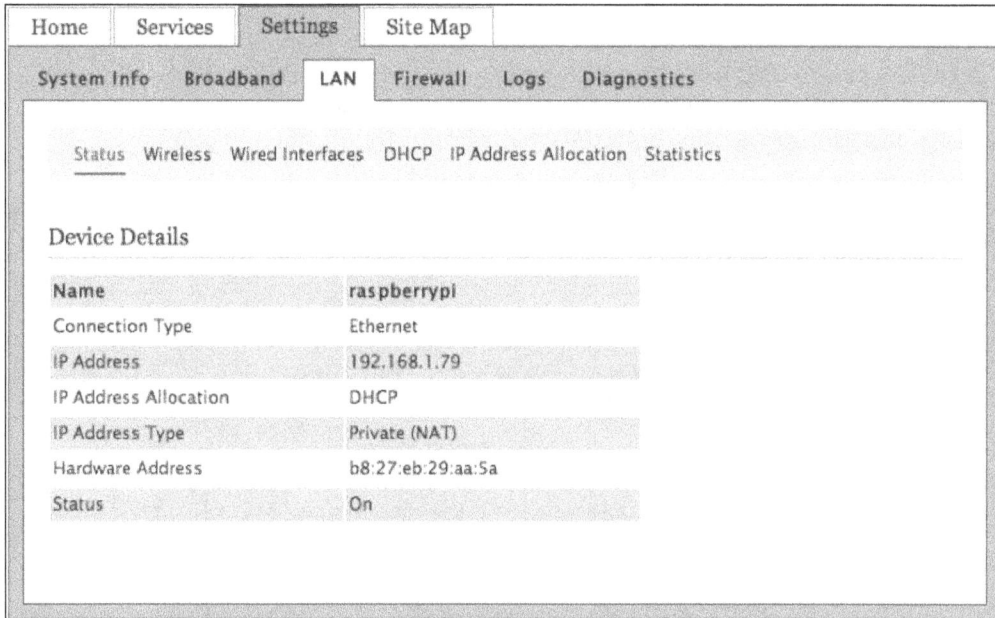

Home	Services	Settings	Site Map

System Info   Broadband   LAN   Firewall   Logs   Diagnostics

Status   Wireless   Wired Interfaces   DHCP   IP Address Allocation   Statistics

Device Details

Name	raspberrypi
Connection Type	Ethernet
IP Address	192.168.1.79
IP Address Allocation	DHCP
IP Address Type	Private (NAT)
Hardware Address	b8:27:eb:29:aa:5a
Status	On

The IP address of a device, such as the Raspberry Pi, is a mapping between the permanent hardware address of the device's network interface (`b8:27:eb:29:aa:5a`) and its current address in the topology of the local network (192.168.1.79). In the previous example, the network ID that was assigned is `79` for the device named `raspberrypi` in the 192.168.1 subnet of the local network.

Most home and small office networks attempt to assign network IDs semi-permanently to the same device (the hardware address). So, once discovered, it is not likely that the Raspberry Pi's IP address will change.

Spoofing the secure fingerprint

SSH, the Secure Shell utility, uses encryption to ensure that communication between the Raspberry Pi and other computers on the network remains secure. On the first launch, the Secure Shell server creates a unique security key that, like a fingerprint, can be used to uniquely identify that particular Secure Shell server. The first time a Secure Shell client connects to a Secure Shell server at a specific IP address, the client prompts the user to verify that the server has the correct fingerprint. Then, it stores the key to identify the server during the next connection.

The Secure Shell client will prevent logins to a machine with the same IP address but a different security key. This helps prevent a hacker from spoofing a device by stealing its IP address. The following example shows what happens when SSH suspects a hacker. In this case, it is only a new installation of the Raspberry Pi:

```
golden-macbook:~ rick$ ssh pi@192.168.2.10


@@@@@@@@@@@@@@@@@@@@@@@@@@@@@@@@@@@@@@@@@@@@@@@@@@@@@@@@@@@@@@@@@@@@
@    WARNING: REMOTE HOST IDENTIFICATION HAS CHANGED!     @
@@@@@@@@@@@@@@@@@@@@@@@@@@@@@@@@@@@@@@@@@@@@@@@@@@@@@@@@@@@@@@@@@@@@
IT IS POSSIBLE THAT SOMEONE IS DOING SOMETHING NASTY!
Someone could be eavesdropping on you right now (man-in-the-middle
attack)!
It is also possible that a host key has just been changed.
The fingerprint for the RSA key sent by the remote host is
f3:de:d3:58:eb:66:1e:23:2c:6e:cf:c9:12:0c:e3:e2.
Please contact your system administrator.
Add correct host key in /Users/A601012/.ssh/known_hosts to get rid of this
message.
Offending RSA key in /Users/A601012/.ssh/known_hosts:58
RSA host key for 192.168.2.10 has changed and you have requested strict
checking.
Host key verification failed.


golden-macbook:~ rick$
```

Each new install creates new digital fingerprints

Each new installation of a computer generates new digital fingerprints. Therefore, the Raspberry Pi's digital fingerprints will change. The digital fingerprint that the golden-macbook just received no longer matches the one that it has stored. Hence, access to the Raspberry Pi is denied. The same safety check that prevents a hacker from completing a successful man-in-the-middle attack also prevents a login to a newly reinstalled Raspberry Pi.

The old, invalid digital fingerprint of the Raspberry Pi is still stored on the golden-macbook and can be removed using the –R option of the `ssh-keygen` command, as shown in the following piece of code:

```
golden-macbook:~ rick$ ssh-keygen -R 192.168.2.10

# Host 192.168.2.10 found: line 3 type RSA
/Users/golden/.ssh/known_hosts updated.
Original contents retained as /Users/golden/.ssh/known_hosts.old

golden-macbook:~ rick$
```

Once the old invalid digital fingerprint has been removed, `ssh` will no longer block access to that IP address. The next login using `ssh` works the same as the first time. The Raspberry Pi will share its new digital fingerprint, and it will be stored to prevent future *attacks*.

See also

- ▶ **hostname – show or set the system's host name** (`http://manpages.debian.net/cgi-bin/man.cgi?query=hostname`): The `hostname` command can be used to display the IP address of the Raspberry Pi. The Debian manual page for hostname describes all the command's options and also has notes on how to change the hostname of the system.

- ▶ **ssh – OpenSSH SSH client (remote login program)** (`http://manpages.debian.net/cgi-biń/man.cgi?query=ssh`): The Debian manual page for SSH gives details about the command and its options.

- ▶ **ssh-keygen – key generation, management and conversion** (`http://manpages.debian.net/cgi-bin/man.cgi?query=ssh-keygen`): By using the –R option, `ssh-keygen` can be used to remove old digital fingerprints from the `known_hosts` file. The Debian manual page for `ssh-keygen` has information about the command and how it supports the secure shell (SSH) protocol.

Obtaining remote access by using PuTTY

This recipe shows how to create a secure connection to the Raspberry Pi by using PuTTY, one of the most commonly used Windows Secure Shell clients.

PuTTY, the Windows Secure Shell client, is not built into the Windows operating system. However, it is a commonly used third-party utility for secure communication. Before you can begin this recipe, you will need to download PuTTY from the Internet and install it on the Windows PC (the download URL is in the next section).

> There are also versions of PuTTY that are available for Mac OS X and Linux.

Once you've completed this recipe, you will be able to remotely administer the Raspberry Pi from a Windows PC.

Getting ready

The following ingredients are used in this recipe:

- You will require an initial setup or a basic networking setup for the Raspberry Pi that has been powered on. You also need to be logged in as the user pi (refer to the recipes in *Chapter 1, Installation and Setup,* for instructions on how to boot and log in).
- A network connection is needed.
- You need to have a Windows PC with PuTTY installed.

You can find a download link for PuTTY with instructions for its installation at
`http://www.chiark.greenend.org.uk/~sgtatham/putty/`

How to do it...

Perform the following steps to access the Raspberry Pi remotely by using the PuTTY command:

1. Start PuTTY on the Windows PC by double-clicking on `PuTTY.exe`.

2. When PuTTY is started, the PuTTY Configuration screen is displayed, as shown in the following screenshot:

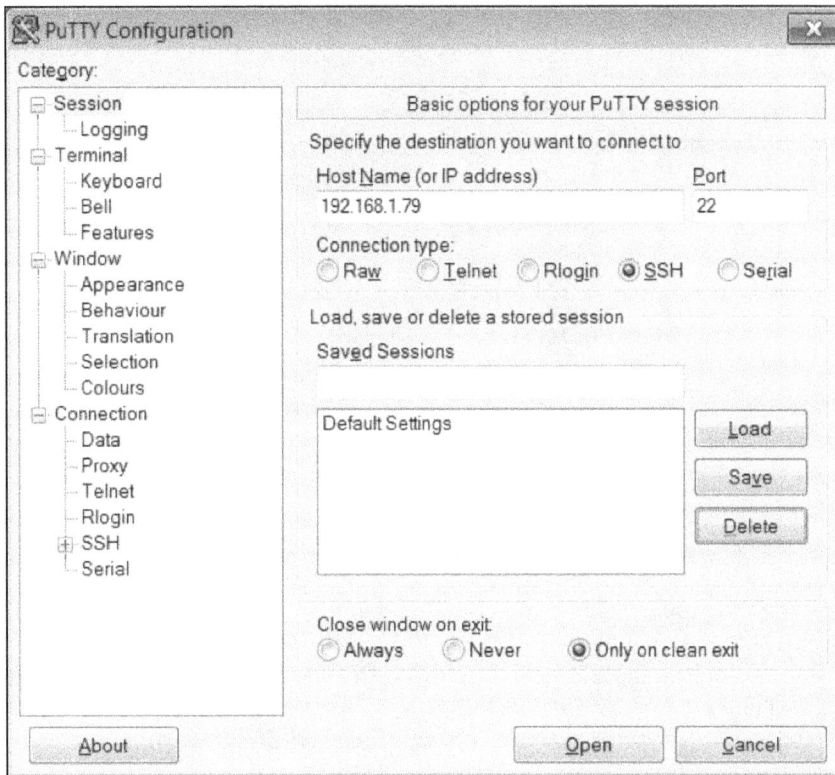

In the screenshot, the configuration window for PuTTY is being configured to connect to a Raspberry Pi whose IP address is 192.168.1.79.

3. Enter the Raspberry Pi's IP address in the **Host Name** field and click on **Open** to connect to the Raspberry Pi.

```
PuTTY Security Alert                                              [ x ]

  ⚠   The server's host key is not cached in the registry. You
       have no guarantee that the server is the computer you
       think it is.
       The server's rsa2 key fingerprint is:
       ssh-rsa 2048 39:49:70:f9:7e:92:38:bb:3a:4d:67:e0:0e:1a:dd:d5
       If you trust this host, hit Yes to add the key to
       PuTTY's cache and carry on connecting.
       If you want to carry on connecting just once, without
       adding the key to the cache, hit No.
       If you do not trust this host, hit Cancel to abandon the
       connection.

                        [ Yes ]      [ No ]       [ Cancel ]
```

4. The first time you connect remotely to the Raspberry Pi, PuTTY will display a warning message that says that the Raspberry Pi's digital fingerprint (or the host key) has not been registered with PuTTY because this is the first time that PuTTY has seen the digital fingerprint of the Raspberry Pi.

5. Click on the **Yes** button to accept the Raspberry Pi's digital fingerprint and continue.

6. After you've accepted the security warning, you will be asked for a username and password. Enter `pi` as the username and then enter the password that you configured during installation for the user whose username is `pi` (`raspberry` is the default password). The following screenshot shows a successful login using PuTTY:

```
pi@raspberrypi: ~
login as: pi
pi@192.168.1.79's password:
Linux raspberrypi 3.2.27+ #102 PREEMPT Sat Sep 1 01:00:50 BST 2012 armv6l

The programs included with the Debian GNU/Linux system are free software;
the exact distribution terms for each program are described in the
individual files in /usr/share/doc/*/copyright.

Debian GNU/Linux comes with ABSOLUTELY NO WARRANTY, to the extent
permitted by applicable law.

Type 'startx' to launch a graphical session

Last login: Sun Sep  9 23:11:52 2012
pi@raspberrypi ~ $
```

7. Type `exit` to log out.

How it works...

This recipe begins by starting the PuTTY client.

The IP address of the Raspberry Pi is entered into the **Host Name** field and the **Open** button is clicked to establish a secure connection to the Raspberry Pi.

Before the connection is established, PuTTY displays a **Security Alert** dialog box warning that states that the Raspberry Pi's digital fingerprint (or host key) has not been registered and there is *no guarantee that the server is the computer you think it is*. The alert is normal and expected for the first connection to a new computer. Clicking on **Yes** clears the alert and adds the Raspberry Pi to PuTTY's list of known hosts.

After the security warning has been cleared, the PuTTY Terminal window is opened and we are prompted for the username (`login as:`) and password to use when logging in to the Raspberry Pi. After entering the username and password, a welcome message and the time of last login are displayed, which is followed by a command prompt.

There's nothing more that needs to be done in this recipe. Therefore, we will use the `exit` command to close the connection.

There's more...

Whenever the Raspberry Pi is reinstalled, it will create a new digital fingerprint. This new fingerprint will not be recognized by PuTTY the first time it is used. When PuTTY tries to connect to the newly reinstalled Raspberry Pi, PuTTY will display a warning that states that there has been a **POTENTIAL SECURITY BREACH** (see the following screenshot).

If you have just reinstalled your Raspberry Pi, do not panic. The Raspberry Pi's new digital fingerprint has not yet been recognized by PuTTY. Simply click on the **Yes** button to accept the new fingerprint.

If you didn't just reinstall your Raspberry Pi and this warning pops up, you may very well have a security breach. Therefore, check your network connections and ensure that there is no possibility of a man-in-the-middle attack:

See also

> ▶ **PuTTY** (`http://www.chiark.greenend.org.uk/~sgtatham/putty/`): PuTTY is a free SSH client for Windows. It is also a telnet client and an xterm emulator.

> ▶ **Man-in-the-middle attack** (`https://en.wikipedia.org/wiki/Man-in-the-middle_attack`): Wikipedia has more information about the man-in-the-middle attack, where the attacker secretly relays and possibly alters the communication between two parties who believe that they are directly communicating with each other.

Changing the login password (passwd)

This recipe shows how to change the login password.

Once remote access to the Raspberry Pi has been enabled, anyone on the local network who knows the correct username and password will be able to log in remotely. To prevent unauthorized access to the Raspberry Pi, the default installation password should be changed immediately after the installation is complete.

The `raspi-config` utility can be used to change the login password. However, this recipe uses the `passwd` command. The `passwd` command is a standard GNU utility that is available with most Linux distributions and can generally be used even when `raspi-config` is not available.

Changing the login password frequently will inhibit unauthorized access to the Raspberry Pi. You should use this recipe on a regular basis to protect access to your Raspberry Pi.

After completing this recipe, you will be able to change your login password.

Getting ready

The following ingredients are required for this recipe:

> ▶ You will require an initial setup or a basic networking setup for the Raspberry Pi that has been powered on. You also need to be logged in as the user `pi` (refer to the recipes in *Chapter 1, Installation and Setup,* for instructions for how to boot and log in and the previous recipes in this chapter for instructions for how to log in remotely).

> ▶ A network connection is an optional requirement.

If the Raspberry Pi has remote access enabled, this recipe can be completed remotely using SSH or PuTTY (refer to the *Remote access (SSH)* and *Remote access (PuTTY)* recipes).

How to do it...

Perform the following steps to change the login password:

1. Use the `passwd` command to change the password for the user `pi`, as follows:

   pi@raspberrypi ~ $ **passwd**

   ```
   Changing password for pi.
   (current) UNIX password:
   Enter new UNIX password:
   Retype new UNIX password:
   passwd: password updated successfully

   pi@raspberrypi ~ $
   ```

2. Enter the (current) Unix password, which is the password that was used during the login.

   > The passwords will not be displayed when they are entered.

3. Enter the new password.
4. Enter the new password a second time for verification.
5. The command responds with `passwd: password updated correctly`.
6. The login password has been changed successfully!

How it works...

The `passwd` command first prompts for the current login password to ensure that the user who's attempting to change the password is really authorized to do so.

The password is not displayed as it is typed to protect the password from being overseen. If the current password is not entered correctly, the user will be asked to retype the password.

Once the user has been authorized, the command prompts for a new Unix password. Again, the new password is not displayed. The command prompts you to retype the new Unix password to ensure that the password was entered correctly. If the two password entries differ, you will be asked to type them again.

After the new password has been entered correctly, you are notified with a message that states this: `password updated successfully`. Changing the login password on a regular basis will help prevent unauthorized access to the Raspberry Pi.

See also

> ▶ **passwd - change user password** (`http://manpages.debian.net/cgi-bin/ man.cgi?query=passwd`): The Debian manual page for `passwd` has details about the command and its use.

Adding a user (useradd)

This recipe shows how to add a new user login to your Raspberry Pi.

Creating separate logins for different users (or for different purposes) helps improve the security of the Raspberry Pi and organize the use of the Raspberry Pi's filesystem by giving each user a home directory in which they can organize their files.

After completing this recipe, you will be able to add a new user to the Raspberry Pi.

Getting ready

The following ingredients are required for this recipe:

> ▶ You will need an initial setup or a basic networking setup for the Raspberry Pi that has been powered on. You also need to be logged in as the user `pi` (refer to the recipes in *Chapter 1, Installation and Setup*, to learn how to boot and log in and the previous recipes in this chapter to understand how to log in remotely).
>
> ▶ A network connection is an optional requirement.

If the Raspberry Pi has remote access enabled, this recipe can be completed remotely using SSH or PuTTY (refer to the *Remote access (SSH)* and *Remote access (PuTTY)* recipes).

How to do it...

Perform the following steps to add a new user:

1. Use `ls` to display the users who already have home directories, as follows:

    ```
    pi@raspberrypi ~ $ ls -l /home

    total 8
    drwxr-xr-x 3 pi      pi      4096 Jun 28 05:00 pi

    pi@raspberrypi ~ $
    ```

2. Execute the `adduser` command to add the user whose username is `golden`, as follows:

```
pi@raspberrypi ~ $ sudo adduser golden

Adding user `golden' ...
Adding new group `golden' (1002) ...
Adding new user `golden' (1001) with group `golden' ...
Creating home directory `/home/golden' ...
Copying files from `/etc/skel' ...

Enter new UNIX password:
Retype new UNIX password:

passwd: password updated successfully
Changing the user information for golden
Enter the new value, or press ENTER for the default

    Full Name []: Rick Golden
    Room Number []: rick@golden-garage.net
    Work Phone []: +1 (650) 555-1212
    Home Phone []: +1 (650) 555-1212
    Other []:

Is the information correct? [Y/n] Y
```

3. The `adduser` command prompts for a new Unix password, but it does not display it as it is being typed. Therefore, it asks you to retype the new UNIX password so that the hidden password can be verified.

4. After the password is entered, you are prompted for the new user's full name, room number, work phone, and other information. None of these entries is mandatory. All of them can be left blank.

5. When the user information for the new user has been completely entered, the command asks `Is the information correct? [Y/n]`. Type *Y* and then press the *Enter* key to add the new user to the Raspberry Pi.

6. Use `ls` to show the new user's home directory, as follows:

   ```
   pi@raspberrypi ~ $ ls -l /home

   total 8
   drwxr-xr-x 2 golden golden 4096 Jun 29 04:12 golden
   drwxr-xr-x 3 pi     pi     4096 Jun 28 05:00 pi

   pi@raspberrypi ~ $
   ```

7. Finally, log out and log back in as the new user!

How it works...

First, the current users' home directories are listed. There is only one user home directory in the list, namely the home directory of the user whose username is `pi`.

The new user, `golden`, is added to the system. The new user is given a password and user information. When all the new user information is entered, the information is accepted and considered to be correct and the new user with `golden` as the username is created.

After the new user is added, the users' home directories are listed again. This time, there are two user home directories listed, namely `golden` and `pi`.

Finally, we can log out and log back in as `golden`.

See also

▶ **useradd - create a new user or update default new user information**

(`http://manpages.debian.net/cgi-bin/man.cgi?query=useradd`): The Debian manual page for `useradd` lists in detail the features and options of the `useradd` command as well as provides background information about how users and groups are managed on the Raspbian Linux distribution.

Giving a user sudo privileges (id and usermod)

This recipe shows how to add a user to the privileged `sudo` group.

When users are created, they are given an ordinary set of user privileges by default. The user can log in to the Raspberry Pi, create and delete files in their own user directory, and execute any command that does not require super-user privileges. If you'd like a new user to execute special commands such as `shutdown`, `reboot`, and `raspi-config`, you'll need to add the user to the `sudo` user group.

After completing this recipe, you'll be able to give an ordinary user super-user privileges by adding the user to the `sudo` user group.

Getting ready

The following ingredients are used in this recipe:

▶ You will require an initial setup or a basic networking setup for the Raspberry Pi that has been powered on. You also need to be logged in as the user `pi` (refer to the recipes in *Chapter 1, Installation and Setup*, to learn how to boot and log in and the previous recipes in this chapter to understand how to log in remotely)

▶ A network connection is an optional requirement.

If the Raspberry Pi has remote access enabled, this recipe can be completed remotely by using SSH or PuTTY (refer to the *Remote access (SSH)* and *Remote access (PuTTY)* recipes).

How to do it...

Perform the following steps to add a user to the `sudo` group:

1. Use the `id` command to see the groups to which the user whose username is `golden` currently belongs, as follows:

   ```
   pi@raspberrypi ~ $ id golden

   uid=1001(golden) gid=1002(golden) groups=1002(golden)

   pi@raspberrypi ~ $
   ```

2. Then, use the `usermod -a -G` command to add the user whose username is `golden` to the `sudo` user group, as follows:

   ```
   pi@raspberrypi ~ $ sudo usermod -a -G sudo golden

   pi@raspberrypi ~ $
   ```

3. Use the `id` command to validate that the user has indeed been added to the `sudo` group:

   ```
   pi@raspberrypi ~ $ id golden

   uid=1001(golden) gid=1002(golden) groups=1002(golden),27(sudo)

   pi@raspberrypi ~ $
   ```

4. Now, the user whose username is `golden` is a member of the `27(sudo)` group and can execute commands and modify files that require super-user privileges!

How it works...

First, the `id` command lists the groups for which the uses – chose username is `golden` – is currently a member.

Then, the `usermod` command is used to add (`-a`) the `sudo` group (`-G sudo`) to the user.

Finally, the `id` command is used once again to see which groups `golden` is a member of.

Now, the user whose username is `golden` can execute commands that require super-user privileges by using the `sudo` command as a prefix. The first recipe in this chapter, *Executing command with privileges*, has more information on the `sudo` command and its use.

See also

- **id - print real and effective user and group IDs** (`http://manpages.debian.net/cgi-bin/man.cgi?query=id`): The Debian manual page for `id` lists the command options.
- **usermod - change user password** (`http://manpages.debian.net/cgi-bin/man.cgi?query=usermod`): The Debian manual page for `usermod` has details about this command and its use.

3
Maintenance

In this chapter, we will cover the following topics:

- ▶ Updating the operating system (`apt-get`)
- ▶ Upgrading Raspbian from `wheezy` to `jessie` using `sources.list`
- ▶ Searching for software packages (`apt-cache`)
- ▶ Installing a package (`apt-get`)
- ▶ Package management (`aptitude`)
- ▶ Reading the built-in documentation (`man`)
- ▶ Reading the built-in documentation (`info`)

Introduction

The recipes in this chapter are for the basic maintenance of the Raspberry Pi.

The first few recipes show you how to update the Raspbian operating system and install new software packages, while the last two recipes show you how to access the documentation that is already built into the Raspberry Pi.

> The recipes in this chapter work for Debian-based operating systems such as PiNet, Raspbian (recommended by the Raspberry Pi Foundation), and Ubuntu MATE.
>
> Other operating systems, such as Pidora and RISC OS, have their own update and installation mechanisms. For instructions on how to update and install software on these operating systems, visit their respective websites. The *See Also* section at the end of this recipe has the needed reference links.

After completing the recipes in this chapter, you will be able to update the Raspberry Pi and better understand the built-in documentation.

Updating the operating system (apt-get)

This recipe shows how to update the Raspberry Pi using the `apt-get` command.

The Raspberry Pi and the operating systems that run on the Raspberry Pi, such as the Raspbian Linux distribution, are evolving at a rapid pace. Every week, if not everyday, there are new updates and security patches that can be downloaded and installed.

This recipe uses the Advance Packaging Tools command-line utility called `apt-get` to update the existing software on the Raspberry Pi to the latest version. This recipe does not install new software; it simply upgrades the software that has already been installed. The recipes named *Searching for software packages* and *Installing a package* show how to search for and install new software packages respectively.

After completing this recipe, you will be able to update the Raspbian operating system using `apt-get`, the advanced packaging tool.

Getting ready

Ingredients:

- ▶ You will need an *Initial Setup* or a *Basic Networking* setup for the Raspberry Pi that has been powered on. You also need to log in as the user with `pi` as their username (take a look at the recipes in *Chapter 1, Installation and Setup* to learn how to boot and log in and the recipes in *Chapter 2, Administration* to understand how to log in remotely).

- ▶ You will also require a network connection.

The Raspberry Pi will need access to the Internet to reach the update server(s) from which it will pull software updates and security fixes.

If the Raspberry Pi has remote access enabled, this recipe can be completed remotely using `SSH` or PuTTY (see the *Remote access* recipes in *Chapter 2, Administration*).

How to do it...

Perform the following steps to update the operating system of the Raspberry Pi:

1. Log in to the Raspberry Pi either directly or remotely.

2. Execute the `apt-get update` command to update the local package database, as follows:

```
golden@raspberrypi ~ $ sudo apt-get update
Get:1 http://mirrordirector.raspbian.org jessie InRelease [15.0 kB]
Get:2 http://archive.raspberrypi.org jessie InRelease [13.3 kB]
Get:3 http://mirrordirector.raspbian.org jessie/main armhf Packages [8,961 kB]
Get:4 http://archive.raspberrypi.org jessie/main Sources [31.2 kB]
Get:5 http://archive.raspberrypi.org jessie/ui Sources [5,197 B]
Get:6 http://archive.raspberrypi.org jessie/main armhf Packages [101 kB]
Get:7 http://archive.raspberrypi.org jessie/ui armhf Packages [7,639 B]
Ign http://archive.raspberrypi.org jessie/main Translation-en_GB
Ign http://archive.raspberrypi.org jessie/main Translation-en
Ign http://archive.raspberrypi.org jessie/ui Translation-en_GB
Ign http://archive.raspberrypi.org jessie/ui Translation-en
Get:8 http://mirrordirector.raspbian.org jessie/contrib armhf Packages [37.5 kB]
Get:9 http://mirrordirector.raspbian.org jessie/non-free armhf Packages [70.2 kB]
Get:10 http://mirrordirector.raspbian.org jessie/rpi armhf Packages [1,356 B]
Ign http://mirrordirector.raspbian.org jessie/contrib Translation-en_GB
Ign http://mirrordirector.raspbian.org jessie/contrib Translation-en
Ign http://mirrordirector.raspbian.org jessie/main Translation-en_GB
Ign http://mirrordirector.raspbian.org jessie/main Translation-en
Ign http://mirrordirector.raspbian.org jessie/non-free Translation-en_GB
Ign http://mirrordirector.raspbian.org jessie/non-free Translation-en
Ign http://mirrordirector.raspbian.org jessie/rpi Translation-en_GB
Ign http://mirrordirector.raspbian.org jessie/rpi Translation-en
Fetched 9,243 kB in 37s (245 kB/s)
Reading package lists... Done

pi@raspberrypi ~ $
```

3. Execute the `apt-get -y dist-upgrade` command to upgrade the system, as follows:

   golden@raspberrypi ~ $ **sudo apt-get dist-upgrade -y**

   ```
   Reading package lists... Done
   Building dependency tree
   Reading state information... Done
   Calculating upgrade... Done
   ```

4. The upgradable list of packages is calculated in the following way:

   ```
   The following packages will be upgraded:
     cups-bsd cups-client cups-common fuse libcups2 libcupsimage2 libfuse2
     libsqlite3-0 libssl1.0.0 openssl raspi-config
   11 upgraded, 0 newly installed, 0 to remove and 0 not upgraded.
   Need to get 3,877 kB of archives.
   After this operation, 455 kB disk space will be freed.
   ```

5. A status message is displayed as each package is downloaded, as follows:

   ```
   Get:1 http://mirrordirector.raspbian.org/raspbian/ jessie/main libssl1.0.0
   armhf 1.0.1e-2+rvt+deb7u17 [1,053 kB]
   Get:2 http://archive.raspberrypi.org/debian/ jessie/main raspi-config all
   20150131-4 [13.2 kB]
   …
   ```

   ```
   Get:11 http://mirrordirector.raspbian.org/raspbian/ jessie/main openssl
   armhf 1.0.1e-2+rvt+deb7u17 [702 kB]
   Fetched 3,877 kB in 3s (1,060 kB/s)
   ```

6. After the upgradable packages have been downloaded, they are preconfigured and prepared for installation:

   ```
   Preconfiguring packages ...
   (Reading database ... 77851 files and directories currently installed.)
   Preparing to replace libssl1.0.0:armhf 1.0.1e-2+rvt+deb7u16 (using .../
   libssl1.0.0_1.0.1e-2+rvt+deb7u17_armhf.deb) ...
   Unpacking replacement libssl1.0.0:armhf ...
   Preparing to replace libsqlite3-0:armhf 3.7.13-1+deb7u1 (using .../
   libsqlite3-0_3.7.13-1+deb7u2_armhf.deb) ...
   Unpacking replacement libsqlite3-0:armhf ...
   …
   ```

7. After the packages have been preconfigured and prepared for installation, they are installed:

```
Processing triggers for man-db ...
Processing triggers for initramfs-tools ...
Setting up libssl1.0.0:armhf (1.0.1e-2+rvt+deb7u17) ...
Setting up libsqlite3-0:armhf (3.7.13-1+deb7u2) ...
Setting up libcups2:armhf (1.5.3-5+deb7u6) ...
Setting up libcupsimage2:armhf (1.5.3-5+deb7u6) ...
Setting up cups-common (1.5.3-5+deb7u6) ...
Setting up cups-client (1.5.3-5+deb7u6) ...
Setting up cups-bsd (1.5.3-5+deb7u6) ...
Setting up libfuse2:armhf (2.9.0-2+deb7u2) ...
Setting up fuse (2.9.0-2+deb7u2) ...
udev active, skipping device node creation.
update-initramfs: deferring update (trigger activated)
Setting up openssl (1.0.1e-2+rvt+deb7u17) ...
Setting up raspi-config (20150131-4) ...

golden@raspberrypi ~ $
```

8. When the `apt-get dist-upgrade` command is completed, the currently upgradeable software on the Raspberry Pi will be completely installed and configured, and all the current security fixes will also be applied.

9. To ensure that the Raspberry Pi is using all the upgradable packages, reboot the system. Use the `reboot` command to reboot the Raspberry Pi, as follows:

```
pi@raspberrypi ~ $ sudo reboot

Broadcast message from root@raspberrypi (pts/0) (Sun Jul  5 12:24:10 2015):
The system is going down for reboot NOW!

pi@raspberrypi ~ $

Connection to 192.168.2.8 closed by remote host.
Connection to 192.168.2.8 closed.

golden-macbook:~ rick$
```

10. When the Raspberry Pi has rebooted, the upgrade is complete!

How it works...

After logging in to the Raspberry Pi, the `apt-get` update command is used to update the local package database, which is a local copy of the currently available software packages.

After the local package database has been updated, the `apt-get dist-upgrade` command is used to determine which packages are currently upgradable, download the upgradeable packages, and preconfigure and install the packages.

When the `apt-get dist-upgrade` command is complete, the Raspberry Pi is rebooted to ensure that it is using all the newly upgraded packages and security fixes.

There's more...

The Raspbian Linux distribution, like most operating system distributions for the Raspberry Pi, is organized as a collection of software packages. Each software package contains one or more applications with their configuration files and support libraries. Each package is also labeled with its current version and its dependency on other software packages. The **Advanced Package Tool** (`apt`) and its supporting utilities, such as `apt-get`, are used to manage the software packages of the Raspbian Linux distribution.

See also

- ▸ **apt – Advance Package Tool** (`http://manpages.debian.net/cgi-bin/man.cgi?query=apt`): This is the Debian manual page for `apt`.
- ▸ **apt-get – APT package handling** (`http://manpages.debian.net/cgi-bin/man.cgi?query=apt-get`): This is the Debian man-page for `apt-get`.

Upgrading Raspbian from wheezy to jessie using sources.list

This recipe shows how to upgrade the Raspberry Pi 2 from the `jessie` version of the Raspbian Linux distribution to the `stretch` version.

Currently, there are three versions of the Raspbian operating system distribution that are available for the Raspberry Pi 2, namely `wheezy`, `jessie`, and `stretch`. The source of these distributions is located at `http://mirrordirector.raspbian.org/raspbian`.

The `wheezy` distribution is based on Debian 7, `jessie` is based on Debian 8, and `stretch` is based on Debian 9. The current `stable` version is `jessie`. The default `wheezy` version is considered to be the `oldstable` release. The next planned release, `testing`, is `stretch`.

> If you are planning on upgrading an operating system from one version to another, which includes upgrading from `jessie` to `stretch`, you should do so before installing another software package, as this will greatly simplify the overall upgrade.

The Raspberry Pi Foundation provides default images for both the `wheezy` and `jessie` versions of the operating system. The instructions in this recipe are for when you would like to keep your existing `wheezy` configuration but try upgrading to `jessie`. Alternatively, these instructions can be used when you would like to try out `stretch`, the next release of the Raspbian operating system.

Raspbian does not currently have a tool to upgrade a version of the operating system distribution. The only way to upgrade from one version to another, such as upgrading from `wheezy` to `jessie` (that is, from `old stable` to `stable`), is to follow the instructions in this recipe.

> This upgrade will modify more than a thousand software packages. The upgrade requires at least 4 hours!

Upgrading an operating system from one version to another is risky. Interrupting a version upgrade can leave the system in an unstable state. However, you may find the risk worthwhile if you would like to try out the newest operating features or upgrade an already configured operating system.

> There is not enough room to finish on an SD card smaller than 8 GB. It will take longer if you have installed additional packages before upgrading.

After completing this recipe, you will have upgraded Raspbian from one version to another: from `wheezy` to `jessie`, or from `jessie` to `stretch`.

Getting ready

Ingredients:

- You require an *Initial Setup* or a *Basic Networking* setup for the Raspberry Pi that has been powered on. You also need to be logged in as the user whose username is `pi` (have a look at the recipes in *Chapter 1, Installation and Setup* to learn how to boot and log in and the recipes in *Chapter 2, Administration* to understand how to log in remotely).
- A network connection is also required.

The Raspberry Pi will need access to the Internet to reach the update server(s) from which it will pull software updates and security fixes.

If the Raspberry Pi has remote access enabled, this recipe can be completed remotely using `ssh` or PuTTY (take a look at the *Remote access* recipes in *Chapter 2, Administration*).

> This recipe uses the `vi` text editor to modify configuration files. Some other text editor can be used instead. Another editor that is available on the Raspberry Pi is the `nano` text editor.
>
> A documentation on the use of editors can be found in the editors themselves (type **:help** in `vi` or press **<ctrl-g>** in `nano` to get help).

How to do it...

Perform the following steps to upgrade Raspbian Linux from one version to another:

1. Log in to the Raspberry Pi either directly or remotely.

2. Use vi (or another editor) to modify `/etc/apt/sources.list`. For an upgrade from wheezy to jessie, change the value in the third field of each line from wheezy to jessie. For an upgrade from jessie to `stretch`, change the value in the third field to `stretch`, as follows:

   ```
   pi@raspberrypi:~$ sudo vi /etc/apt/sources.list
   ```

   ```
   deb http://mirrordirector.raspbian.org/raspbian/ stretch main contrib non-
   free rpi
   # Uncomment line below then 'apt-get update' to enable 'apt-get source'
   #deb-src http://archive.raspbian.org/raspbian/ stretch main contrib non-
   free rpi
   ~
   ~
   ~
   "/etc/apt/sources.list" 3 lines, 234 characters
   ```

3. Use `vi` (or another editor) to modify `/etc/apt/sources.list.d/raspi.list`. For an upgrade from wheezy to jessie, change the value in the third field of each line from wheezy to jessie. For an upgrade from jessie to stretch, *do not change this file this time*:

   ```
   pi@raspberrypi:~$ sudo vi /etc/apt/sources.list.d/raspi.list
   ```

   ```
   deb http://archive.raspberrypi.org/debian/ jessie main
   # Uncomment line below then 'apt-get update' to enable 'apt-get source'
   ```

```
#deb-src http://archive.raspberrypi.org/debian/ jessie main
~
~
~
"/etc/apt/sources.list.d/raspi.list" 3 lines, 187 characters
```

4. If you are upgrading from `wheezy` to `jessie`, use the `rm` command to remove the `collabora.list` configuration file. If you are upgrading from `jessie` to `stretch`, this file does not exist. Therefore, you need to *skip this step*:

```
pi@raspberrypi ~ $ sudo rm /etc/apt/sources.list.d/collabora.list

pi@raspberrypi ~ $
```

5. Now, update the operating system, as described in the previous recipe (*Updating the operating system*).

> Be aware of the fact that this update can take longer than 4 hours!

How it works...

After logging in to the Raspberry Pi, the `sources.list` configuration for `apt` is changed.

The `/etc/apt/sources.list` file is modified so that it references the next version of Debian. For example, it is changed to `jessie` if the previous version is `wheezy`, and it is changed to `stretch` if the previous version is `jessie`.

The `/etc/apt/sources.list.d/raspi.list` file is only modified if the previous version is `wheezy`. The file should reference the Debian version, that is, `jessie` even if you are upgrading to `stretch`.

> At the time of writing this book, if you are upgrading from `jessie` to `stretch`, the `raspi.list` file requires no change. If you are using this recipe after Spring 2016, you'll need to check out the Debian repository at `http://archive.raspberrypi.org/debian/dists/` to check whether there is a `stretch` distribution folder. If there is a folder, update the third field of this file to `stretch`.

When upgrading from `wheezy` to `jessie`, the `collabora.list` configuration file is removed using the `rm` command. This file does not exist for the `jessie` version of the Raspbian operating system. Hence, this step can be skipped.

After the sources are changed, the previous recipe (*Updating the operating system*) is used to update the operating system.

There's more...

The `apt-get update` command is used to fetch the current software catalogs from the software distribution sites that are configured in the `/etc/apt/sources.list` file and those configured in the files located in the `/etc/apt/sources.list.d` directory.

The sources.list and sources.list.d

The `sources.list` file located in the `/etc/apt` directory points to the base operating system distribution from `raspbian.org`, and the files (`raspi.list`) located in the `/etc/apt/sources.list.d` directory point to the location of the additional Raspberry Pi packages.

In the following terminal session, the content of the source files for the `wheezy` version of the Raspbian Linux distribution are displayed using the `cat` command:

```
pi@raspberrypi ~ $ cat /etc/apt/sources.list

deb http://mirrordirector.raspbian.org/raspbian/ wheezy main contrib non-free rpi
# Uncomment line below then 'apt-get update' to enable 'apt-get source'
#deb-src http://archive.raspbian.org/raspbian/ wheezy main contrib non-free rpi

pi@raspberrypi ~ $ ls /etc/apt/sources.list.d/

collabora.list   raspi.list

pi@raspberrypi ~ $ cat /etc/apt/sources.list.d/collabora.list

deb http://raspberrypi.collabora.com wheezy rpi

pi@raspberrypi ~ $ cat /etc/apt/sources.list.d/raspi.list

deb http://archive.raspberrypi.org/debian/ wheezy main
# Uncomment line below then 'apt-get update' to enable 'apt-get source'
#deb-src http://archive.raspberrypi.org/debian/ wheezy main

pi@raspberrypi ~ $
```

Each of these configuration files describe the location of one or more software package repositories. The most preferred repository is listed first in each file. The entire `sources.list` file is preferred over the files in the `sources.list.d` directory.

The sources.list file format

The file format for each of these files is simple. Each line of the file describes a single collection of packages within a software distribution repository, providing the type of collection, the name of the collection, and the location of the collection's packages.

The first item in each line defines the type of the collection. For Debian-based distributions, such as the Raspbian Linux distribution, the definition is either `deb` or `deb-src`. The `deb-src` catalogs include source code as well as compiled binaries.

The second item in each line is the location of the root of the software distribution repository. The `sources.list` file points to the root of the `raspbian` operating system distribution that is located on the `mirrordirector.raspbian.org` website. The `collabora.list` file points to the software packages provided by Collabora that are located at the `raspberrypi.collabora.com` website. Furthermore, the `raspi.list` file points to the additional Raspberry Pi-specific packages that are provided by the Raspberry Pi Foundation and which are located on the `archive.raspberrypi.org` website.

The third item in each line is the name of the Debian operating system version that you want to use. All files should specify the same version. At the time of writing this book, `jessie` is considered the current stable release of Debian. A new release, named `stretch`, will soon be available.

The remainder of the line is a list of distribution components. The configuration file for the base distribution, which is named `source.list`, points to the Raspbian Linux distribution and has a number of components defined. Each of the secondary configuration files, namely `collabra.list` and `raspi.list`, points to a smaller distribution of Raspberry Pi-specific packages. Each secondary configuration file has only one component, namely `rpi` for `collabra.list` and `main` for `raspi.list`.

The standard package collections for the Debian operating system are as follows:

- ▶ `main`: This is the base distribution that is supported by the core team
- ▶ `contrib`: This contains the packages that are contributed to Debian but are supported outside of the core team
- ▶ `non-free`: This contains the packages that are not open source or have some rights restrictions and are also supported outside of the core team
- ▶ `rpi`: This contains Raspberry Pi-specific packages that are supported by the Raspberry Pi community
- ▶ `rpi2`: This contains the Raspberry Pi packages that are specific to the new Raspberry Pi 2 chipset and which are supported by the Raspberry Pi community

▸ **sources.list – Package resource list for APT** (`http://manpages.debian.net/cgi-bin/man.cgi?query=sources.list`) The Debian man-page for `sources.list` describes the format of the configuration file.

▸ **vim – VI improved** (`http://manpages.debian.net/cgi-bin/man.cgi?query=vi`): The Debian man-page for `vi` describes the basic use of the text editor.

▸ **cat – concatenate files and print on the standard output** (`http://manpages.debian.net/cgi-bin/man.cgi?query=cat`): The Debian man-page for cat describes how to print files to the standard output.

▸ **Debian – the universal operating system** (`https://www.debian.org/`): The Raspbian Linux operating system distribution is based on Debian.

▸ **Debian releases** (`https://www.debian.org/releases/`): The naming convention for Debian releases is explained here.

▸ **Raspberry Pi Foundation Forum**s (`https://www.raspberrypi.org/forums/`): You can report a bug, an error, or other software deficiency, or suggest an improvement on one of the Raspberry Pi Foundation's forums.

▸ **Pidora is Fedora Remix optimized for the Raspberry Pi** (`http://pidora.ca/`): Pidora is not a Debian-based operating system. It is based on Fedora, which is an open source version of the Red Hat Linux enterprise distribution.

▸ **RISC OS – a fast and easily customizable operating system for ARM devices** (`https://www.riscosopen.org/content/`): RISC OS is the original operating system for ARM devices that was designed in the 1980s.

▸ **Collabora (**`https://www.collabora.com/`): Collabora supports a number of open source projects, including contributions that are specifically for the Raspberry Pi.

Searching for software packages (apt-cache)

This recipe shows how to search for software packages using `apt-cache`.

The complete software catalog of the Raspbian Linux distribution contains a large number of prebuilt software packages that are ready to be downloaded and installed. With the `apt-cache` command, this large software catalog can be searched by using keywords.

This recipe specifically searches for the keyword "fortune" in the names of all the software packages of the Raspbian Linux distribution. Searches can be made for other software packages by replacing the "fortune" keyword with keywords that interest you.

After you've completed this recipe, you will be able to locate software packages by searching for keywords using the `apt-cache search` command.

Getting ready

Ingredients:

> ▸ You will need an *Initial Setup* or a *Basic Networking* setup for the Raspberry Pi that has been powered on. You also need to log in as the user whose username is `pi` (see the recipes in *Chapter 1, Installation and Setup* to learn how to boot and log in and the recipes in *Chapter 2, Administration* to know how to log in remotely).

> ▸ You will also require a network connection.

The Raspberry Pi will need access to the Internet to reach the update server(s) from which it will pull software updates and security fixes.

If the Raspberry Pi has remote access enabled, this recipe can be completed remotely using `ssh` or PuTTY (see the *Remote access* recipes in *Chapter 2, Administration*).

How to do it...

Perform the following steps to search the Raspbian Linux software packages:

1. Log in to the Raspberry Pi either directly or remotely.

2. Use the `apt-get update` command to update the software catalog, as described in the first recipe of this chapter (*Updating the operating system*), as follows:

   pi@raspberrypi ~ $ **sudo apt-get update**

3. Execute the `apt-cache search --names-only fortune` command. Searching the cache does not require super user privileges:

   pi@raspberrypi ~ $ **apt-cache search --names-only fortune**

   ```
   fortune-mod - provides fortune cookies on demand
   fortunes - Data files containing fortune cookies
   fortunes-min - Data files containing selected fortune cookies
   fortunes-off - Data files containing offensive fortune cookies
   fortune-zh - Chinese Data files for fortune
   fortunes-bg - Bulgarian data files for fortune
   fortunes-bofh-excuses - BOFH excuses for fortune
   fortunes-br - Data files with fortune cookies in Portuguese
   fortunes-cs - Czech and Slovak data files for fortune
   fortunes-de - German data files for fortune
   fortunes-debian-hints - Debian Hints for fortune
   ```

```
fortunes-eo - Collection of esperanto fortunes.
fortunes-eo-ascii - Collection of esperanto fortunes (ascii encoding).
fortunes-eo-iso3 - Collection of esperanto fortunes (ISO3 encoding).
fortunes-es - Spanish fortune database
fortunes-es-off - Spanish fortune cookies (Offensive section)
fortunes-fr - French fortunes cookies
fortunes-ga - Irish (Gaelige) data files for fortune
fortunes-it - Data files containing Italian fortune cookies
fortunes-it-off - Data files containing Italian fortune cookies, offensive
section
fortunes-mario - Fortunes files from Mario
fortunes-pl - Polish data files for fortune
fortunes-ru - Russian data files for fortune
libfortune-perl - Perl module to read fortune (strfile) databases


golden@raspberrypi ~ $
```

4. The command displays a list of packages with **fortune** in the package name.

How it works...

After logging in to the Raspberry Pi, the Raspbian Linux software catalog is updated using the first recipe in this chapter, namely *Updating the operating system*.

Once the software catalog has been updated, the `apt-cache search` command is used to search the software catalog for software packages that have the `fortune` keyword in their names (`--names-only`).

One of the packages returned by the search, **fortune-mod**, is a command-line utility that provides fortune cookies on demand.

The packages that begin with **fortunes-** contain collections of fortunes that the `fortune` command-line utility selects from when displaying fortune cookies.

There's more...

In this recipe, we searched the Raspbian Linux software catalog for packages that have the keyword "fortune" in their package names. The search was limited to the package names because the `--names-only` option was specified. When the `apt-cache` command is run without the `--names-only` option, the summaries of packages are also searched for the specified keyword.

The `apt-cache search` command takes a list of keywords as parameters. If more than one keyword is given, the results will be narrowed down to only those packages that contain all the keywords. Here is an example of how to search for German fortunes:

pi@raspberrypi:~$ **apt-cache search fortunes german**

fortunes-de - German data files for fortune

pi@raspberrypi:~$

Instructions on how to install the `fortune` package are in the next recipe.

See also

▶ **apt-cache – query the APT cache** (`http://manpages.debian.net/cgi-bin/man.cgi?query=apt-cache`) The `apt-cache` command can generate interesting output from the metadata in the local cache of the Debian software catalog. The Debian man-page for `apt-cache` describes the command and its options.

Installing a package (apt-get)

This recipe shows how new software packages are installed using the `apt-get install` command.

In addition to updating the software package catalog and upgrading the already installed software packages, the `apt-get` command can also be used to install new software packages.

In this recipe, the `fortune-mod` software package is installed using the `apt-get install` command. Other software packages can be installed using this same recipe; just replace the `fortune-mod` package with the software package that you would like to install.

It is always a good idea to first update the software catalog using the `apt-get update` command and then upgrade the existing software packages using the `apt-get dist-upgrade` command before you begin installing new software packages (go through the *Updating the operating system* recipe for more information).

After completing this recipe, you will be able to install new software packages using the `apt-get install` command.

Getting ready

Ingredients:

- ▸ You require an *Initial Setup* or a *Basic Networking* setup for the Raspberry Pi that has been powered on. You also need to be logged in as the user whose username is `pi` (have a look at the recipes in *Chapter 1, Installation and Setup* to know how to boot and log in and the recipes in *Chapter 2, Administration* to learn how to log in remotely).

- ▸ A network connection is also required.

The Raspberry Pi will need access to the Internet to reach the update server(s) from which it will pull software updates and security fixes.

If the Raspberry Pi has remote access enabled, this recipe can be completed remotely using `ssh` or PuTTY (see the *Remote access* recipes in *Chapter 2, Administration*).

How to do it...

Perform the following steps to install a software package:

1. Log in to the Raspberry Pi either directly or remotely.

2. Use the `apt-get update` command to update the software catalog, as described in the first recipe of this chapter (*Updating the operating system*):

   ```
   golden@raspberrypi ~ $ sudo apt-get update
   ```

3. Use the `apt-get install -y` command to install the `fortune-mod` software package. The `-y` option for the command answers 'yes' automatically to all the installation questions:

   ```
   golden@raspberrypi:~$ sudo apt-get install -y fortune-mod
   ```

4. The command calculates the package dependencies and the additional space that will be used by the package and its configuration files:

   ```
   Reading package lists... Done
   Building dependency tree
   Reading state information... Done
   The following extra packages will be installed:
     fortunes-min librecode0
   Suggested packages:
     fortunes x11-utils
   The following NEW packages will be installed:
     fortune-mod fortunes-min librecode0
   ```

```
0 upgraded, 3 newly installed, 0 to remove and 0 not upgraded.
Need to get 599 kB of archives.
After this operation, 1,588 kB of additional disk space will be used.
```

5. The command then downloads the necessary software packages, namely **fortunes-mod**, **fortunes-min**, and **librecode0**:

```
Get:1 http://ftp.debian.org/debian/ jessie/main librecode0 armhf 3.6-21
[477 kB]
Get:2 http://ftp.debian.org/debian/ jessie/main fortune-mod armhf
1:1.99.1-7 [47.4 kB]
Get:3 http://ftp.debian.org/debian/ jessie/main fortunes-min all 1:1.99.1-
7 [74.3 kB]
Fetched 599 kB in 2s (252 kB/s)
```

6. The downloaded files are unpacked and preconfigured:

```
Selecting previously unselected package librecode0:armhf.
(Reading database ... 19391 files and directories currently installed.)
Preparing to unpack .../librecode0_3.6-21_armhf.deb ...
Unpacking librecode0:armhf (3.6-21) ...
Selecting previously unselected package fortune-mod.
Preparing to unpack .../fortune-mod_1%3a1.99.1-7_armhf.deb ...
Unpacking fortune-mod (1:1.99.1-7) ...
Selecting previously unselected package fortunes-min.
Preparing to unpack .../fortunes-min_1%3a1.99.1-7_all.deb ...
Unpacking fortunes-min (1:1.99.1-7) ...
```

7. Then, the software packages and their dependencies are installed and the execution of command is completed:

```
Processing triggers for man-db (2.7.0.2-5) ...
Setting up librecode0:armhf (3.6-21) ...
Setting up fortune-mod (1:1.99.1-7) ...
Setting up fortunes-min (1:1.99.1-7) ...
Processing triggers for libc-bin (2.19-18) ...


golden@raspberrypi:~$
```

8. Finally, the `fortune` command is tested to check whether it works:

```
golden@raspberrypi:~$ fortune

You single-handedly fought your way into this hopeless mess.
```

```
golden@raspberrypi:~$ fortune

Your best consolation is the hope that the things you failed to get
weren't
really worth having.

golden@raspberrypi:~$ fortune

Q:      How many hardware engineers does it take to change a light bulb?
A:      None.  We'll fix it in software.


Q:      How many system programmers does it take to change a light bulb?
A:      None.  The application can work around it.


Q:      How many software engineers does it take to change a light bulb?
A:      None.  We'll document it in the manual.


Q:      How many tech writers does it take to change a light bulb?
A:      None.  The user can figure it out.


golden@raspberrypi:~$
```

How it works...

After logging in to the Raspberry Pi, the Raspbian Linux software catalog is updated using the first recipe in *Chapter 3*, *Updating the operating system*.

Once the software catalog is updated, the `fortune-mod` software package is installed using the `apt-get install` command.

The command first calculates the package dependencies, determining which other packages need to be installed prior to the installation of the **fortune-mod** package.

The `apt-get install` command continues by downloading the `fortunes-mod` package and the two packages that it is dependent upon (`fortune-min` and `librecode0`).

Then, the command unpacks and preconfigures the three packages. Finally, the `apt-get install` command installs the software packages. After the installation is complete, the `fortune` command is tested.

There's more...

The `apt-get install` command uses the same local software catalog as that of the `apt-cache search` command. Both commands rely on the `apt-get update` command to download the updated package information.

See also

▸ **fortune – sample lines from a file** (`http://manpages.debian.net/cgi-bin/man.cgi?query=fortune`) The Debian man-page for the `fortune` command lists all of its options.

Package management (aptitude)

This recipe uses the `aptitude` frontend to find and install the `pianobar` application.

There are a number of frontends for the Advance Package Tool (apt) that provide a feature-rich user interface. Behind the scenes, these frontends still call the `apt-get` command and the `apt-cache` command. However, they combine the functionality of all the `apt` tools into a single user interface.

> If you do not already have the `aptitude` application installed on your Raspberry Pi, use the instructions in the previous recipe (*Installing a package*) to install the `aptitude` software package and its dependencies.

After completing this recipe, you will be able to use the `aptitude` application to find and install software packages.

Getting ready

Ingredients:

▸ You require an *Initial Setup* or a *Basic Networking* setup for the Raspberry Pi that has been powered on. You also need to be logged in as the user whose username is `pi` (take a look at the recipes in *Chapter 1, Installation and Setup* to learn how to boot and log in and the recipes in *Chapter 2, Administration* to understand how to log in remotely)

▸ A network connection is also required.

The Raspberry Pi will need access to the Internet to reach the update server(s) from which it will pull new software packages, software updates, and security fixes.

If the Raspberry Pi has remote access enabled, this recipe can be completed remotely using `ssh` or PuTTY (take a look at the *Remote access* recipes in *Chapter 2, Administration*).

How to do it...

Perform the following steps to manage software packages using `aptitude`:

1. Log in to the Raspberry Pi either directly or remotely.

2. Execute the `aptitude` command. This command is privileged and needs to be run as a privileged user:

   ```
   golden@raspberrypi:~$ sudo aptitude
   ```

3. The main screen of the `aptitude` application is displayed:

   ```
   Actions  Undo  Package  Resolver  Search  Options  Views  Help
   C-T: Menu  ?: Help  q: Quit  u: Update  g: Download/Install/Remove Pkgs
   aptitude 0.6.11
   --- New Packages (1)
   --- Installed Packages (317)
   --- Not Installed Packages (49041)
   --- Virtual Packages (7075)
   --- Tasks (216)


   These packages have been added to Debian since the last time you cleared the
   list of "new" packages (choose "Forget new packages" from the Actions menu to
   empty this list).


   This group contains 1 package.
   ```

4. Press **u** to update the local software package catalogue cache. The screen then displays the status messages that are being downloaded.

5. Type **/pianobar** to search for the `pianobar` package. Then, press the **<enter>** key to go to the first package that was found:

   ```
   Actions  Undo  Package  Resolver  Search  Options  Views  Help
   C-T: Menu  ?: Help  q: Quit  u: Update  g: Download/Install/Remove Pkgs
   aptitude 0.6.11
   p    pianobar-dbg                        <none>          2014.06.08-1+b
   p    pianobooster-dbg                    <none>          0.6.4b-2
   ```

```
p      pidgin-dbg                       <none>        2.10.11-1
p      pidgin-microblog-dbg             <none>        0.3.0-3
p      pidgin-mra-dbg                   <none>        20100304-1
p   ┌────────────────────────────────────────────────────────────────┐
p   |Search for:                                                      |
p   |pianobar                                                         |
co|            [ Ok ]                            [ Cancel ]          |
pi  └──────────────────────────────────        ────────────────────┘
```

Pandora, supporting all important features the official Flash™ client has:

* Create, delete, rename stations and add more music

* Rate and temporary ban tracks as well as move them to another station

* "Shared stations"

6. Press **n** until the **pianobar** package is selected. Each time the '**n**' key is pressed, the search for the `pianobar` package continues to the next package. The search will loop past the last package that matches `pianobar` and continue with the first package that matches.

7. Press **+** to select the package for installation. The letter "i" appears next to the package name to indicate the package that has been selected for installation:

```
Actions   Undo   Package   Resolver   Search   Options   Views   Help
C-T: Menu   ?: Help   q: Quit   u: Update   g: Download/Install/Remove Pkgs
aptitude 0.6.11             Will use 59.7 MB of disk space DL Size: 18.8 MB
pi     pianobar                    +119 kB   <none>      2014.06.08-1+b
p      picard                                <none>      1.2-2+b8
p      plait                                 <none>      1.6.2-1
p      playmidi                              <none>      2.4debian-10
p      pmidi                                 <none>      1.6.0-5
p      pms                                   <none>      0.42-1
p      poc-streamer                          <none>      0.4.2-3
p      pocketsphinx                          <none>      0.8-5
p      pocketsphinx-hmm-en-hub4wsj           <none>      0.8-5
p      pocketsphinx-hmm-en-tidigits          <none>      0.8-5
console based player for Pandora radio
pianobar is a cross-platform console client for the personalized web radio
Pandora, supporting all important features the official Flash™ client has:

* Create, delete, rename stations and add more music
* Rate and temporary ban tracks as well as move them to another station
* "Shared stations"
```

8. Press **g** to preview the installation of the selected package(s). The list of dependent packages is displayed:

```
Actions  Undo  Package  Resolver  Search  Options  Views  Help
C-T: Menu  ?: Help  q: Quit  u: Update  g: Download/Install/Remove Pkgs
              Packages                          Preview
aptitude 0.6.11          Will use 59.7 MB of disk space DL Size: 18.8 MB
--\ Packages being automatically installed to satisfy dependencies (55)
piA  libao-common            +49.2 kB  <none>        1.1.0-3
piA  libao4                  +113 kB   <none>        1.1.0-3
piA  libavcodec56            +7,131 kB <none>        6:11.4-1~deb8u
piA  libavfilter5            +324 kB   <none>        6:11.4-1~deb8u
piA  libavformat56           +1,254 kB <none>        6:11.4-1~deb8u
piA  libavresample2          +131 kB   <none>        6:11.4-1~deb8u
piA  libavutil54             +226 kB   <none>        6:11.4-1~deb8u
piA  libdrm-freedreno1       +75.8 kB  <none>        2.4.58-2
piA  libdrm-nouveau2         +84.0 kB  <none>        2.4.58-2

These packages are being installed because they are required by another package
you have chosen for installation.


This group contains 55 packages.


If you select a package, an explanation of its current state will appear in this
space.
```

9. Press **g** a second time to complete the installation.

10. The `aptitude` application downloads the selected software package, **pianobar**, and its dependencies. Then, it clears the screen and runs the `apt-get install` command to complete the installation. Press the **<enter>** key after the installation is complete to return to `aptitude`:

```
Setting up libao-common (1.1.0-3) ...
Setting up libao4 (1.1.0-3) ...
Setting up pianobar (2014.06.08-1+b1) ...
Setting up va-driver-all:armhf (1.4.1-1) ...
Processing triggers for libc-bin (2.19-18) ...
Processing triggers for systemd (215-17+deb8u1) ...
Press Return to continue.
```

11. After returning to `aptitude`, press **q** and then **y** to quit.

How it works...

After logging in to the Raspberry Pi, the `aptitude` application is started.

When the `aptitude` application is started, the application first takes a moment to initialize and then the application's main screen is displayed.

The main screen has a toolbar at the top of the screen with a list of menu items, a list of common commands (including **?: Help** and **q: Quit** – press '**?**' for help and '**q**' to quit), and the version of the application, which is **aptitude 0.6.11**.

The application is navigated and controlled using the following command keys:

- ▸ For help using the application, press **?** (question mark)
- ▸ Navigate the packages using the arrow keys
- ▸ Update the package cache by pressing **u** (the lowercase letter u)
- ▸ Select the updated packages by pressing **U** (the uppercase letter U)
- ▸ Search for packages by pressing **/** (slash)
- ▸ To go to the next package that was found, press **n** (the lowercase letter n)
- ▸ To go to the previous package that was found, press **p** (the lowercase letter p)
- ▸ Select individual packages by pressing **+** (plus) to select; press **-** (minus) to deselect the highlighted package
- ▸ Install the selected packages by pressing **g** (the lowercase letter g)
- ▸ Activate the menus by pressing **<ctrl-T>**
- ▸ Quit the application by pressing **q**

After the application has finished initializing, press **u** (the lowercase letter u) to update the package cache. The **Downloading** status messages are displayed as the local software package cache is downloaded and updated.

After the cache update is complete, type **/pianobar**. Pressing **/** starts the search mode, and **pianobar** is the search string. As the search string is typed, aptitude incrementally searches for the string. Press the **<enter>** key to complete the search phrase and select the first package that is found.

If the **pianobar** package is not selected, press **n** to go to the next package that matches the search string, or press **p** to go to the previous package that matches the search string.

When the **pianobar** package is selected, press **+** to select the package. If you have incorrectly selected a package, press **-** to deselect the package.

With the **pianobar** package selected, press **g** to calculate the dependent packages and prepare the installation of the selected package and its dependents.

Press **g** once again to install the **pianobar** package and its dependents. The **aptitude** application then starts the **apt-get install** command and begins installing the **pianobar** package and its dependents.

The display fills with installation messages from the apt-get install command (refer to the *Installing a package* recipe for more information about the apt-get install command). When the installation is complete, you will be asked to **Press Return to continue**, press the **<enter>** key to continue.

Finally, press **q** to quit the **aptitude** application and **y** to accept that you are quitting.

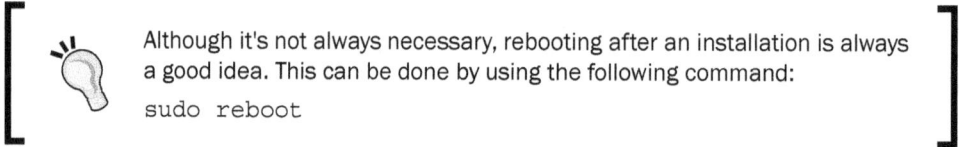

> Although it's not always necessary, rebooting after an installation is always a good idea. This can be done by using the following command:
>
> sudo reboot

There's more...

The aptitude software package manager is a software application that combines the functionality of the apt-cache and apt-get commands with a sophisticated terminal user interface that can still be used remotely with commands such as ssh.

The terminal-based user interface provided by the aptitude application simplifies searching for and installing software packages. By using simple keystrokes, software packages can be located, installed, and updated.

The aptitude application's terminal user interface is useful for interactive use. However, a command-line interface will be better for scripts and automation.

The command line interface

The aptitude application also has a set of commands that can be used as an alternative frontend to the functionality provided by the apt-cache and apt-get commands (refer to the recipes named *Searching for software packages* and *Installing a package* for instructions on using the apt-cache and apt-get commands to locate and install software packages).

The aptitude update command can be used to update the software package catalog. It provides the same functionality that the apt-get update command provides:

```
pi@raspberrypi ~ $ sudo aptitude update

Hit http://archive.raspberrypi.org jessie InRelease
Hit http://mirrordirector.raspbian.org stretch InRelease
Hit http://archive.raspberrypi.org jessie/main Sources

...
```

The `aptitude full-upgrade` command can be used to fully upgrade the already installed software packages. It provides a functionality that is similar to that of the `apt-get dist-upgrade` command:

```
pi@raspberrypi ~ $ sudo aptitude full-upgrade

The following NEW packages will be installed:
  raspberrypi-sys-mods{a}
The following packages will be upgraded:
  bluej dhcpcd5 epiphany-browser epiphany-browser-data fonts-opensymbol
  gir1.2-gdkpixbuf-2.0 gir1.2-gtk-3.0 gstreamer1.0-omx krb5-locales
  libfreetype6 libfreetype6-dev libgdk-pixbuf2.0-0 libgdk-pixbuf2.0-common

...
```

The `aptitude search` command can be used to search for software packages, as follows:

```
pi@raspberrypi ~ $ sudo aptitude search pianobar

p   pianobar                      - console based player for Pandora radio
p   pianobar-dbg                  - console based player for Pandora radio - d

pi@raspberrypi ~ $
```

The `aptitude install` command is used to install software packages. This is the same functionality as that of the `apt-get install` command:

```
pi@raspberrypi ~ $ sudo aptitude install pianobar

The following NEW packages will be installed:
  libao-common{a} libao4{a} libavfilter5{a} libpiano0{a} pianobar
0 packages upgraded, 5 newly installed, 0 to remove and 0 not upgraded.
Need to get 246 kB of archives. After unpacking 546 kB will be used.
Do you want to continue? [Y/n/?]

...
```

More information on the command-line use of the `aptitude` software package manager can be found in the `aptitude` manual pages (`man aptitude`).

See also

▸ **aptitude – high-level interface to the package manage**r (http://manpages. debian.net/cgi-bin/man.cgi?query=aptitude) The Debian man-page for aptitude has details about the command and its options.

▸ **pianobar – personalized online radio client** (http://6xq.net/projects/ pianobar/) The pianobar application is an open source, console-based client for Pandora.

Reading the built-in documentation (man)

This recipe shows how the man command can be used to display built-in documentation.

The Raspbian Linux distribution comes with a large amount of local documentation that is built into the system. There are three primary sources of built-in documentation, namely the man-pages, the Info documents, and the /usr/share/docs directory.

This recipe uses the man command to display the man-page documentation for the fortune command.

The next recipe in this chapter shows how to use the info command to navigate through documentation stored as info-pages.

[Instructions to install the fortune command can be found in the recipe named *Installing a package* that was discussed earlier in this chapter.]

After completing this recipe, you will able to use the man command to read the man-page documentation, which is a built-in feature of the Raspbian Linux distribution.

Getting ready

Ingredients:

▸ You need an *Initial Setup* or a *Basic Networking* setup for the Raspberry Pi that has been powered on. You also need to be logged in as the user whose username is pi (refer to the recipes in *Chapter 1, Installation and Setup* to know how to boot and log in and the recipes in *Chapter 2, Administration* to learn how to log in remotely).

▸ A network connection is an optional requirement.

The Raspberry Pi does not need access to the Internet for this application.

If the Raspberry Pi has remote access enabled, this recipe can be completed remotely using `ssh` or PuTTY (see the *Remote access* recipes in *Chapter 2, Administration*).

How to do it...

Perform the following steps to read the built-in documentation using `man`:

1. Log in to the Raspberry Pi either directly or remotely.

2. Execute the `man` command to read the built-in documentation for the `fortune` command:

   pi@raspberrypi:~$ **man fortune**

3. The man-page for the fortune command is displayed, which looks like this:

```
FORTUNE(6)                    UNIX Reference Manual                    FORTUNE(6)


NAME
        fortune - print a random, hopefully interesting, adage


SYNOPSIS
        fortune [-acefilosuw] [-n length] [ -m pattern] [[n%] file/dir/all]


DESCRIPTION
        when  fortune  is run with no arguments it prints out a random epigram.
        Epigrams are divided into several categories, where   each   category   is
        sub-divided  into those which are potentially offensive and those which
        are not.


   Options
        The options are as follows:


        -a      Choose from all lists of maxims, both offensive and  not.   (See
                the -o option for more information on offensive fortunes.)


        -c      Show the cookie file from which the fortune came.


        -e      Consider  all  fortune files to be of equal size (see discussion
                below on multiple files).

Manual page fortune(6) line 1 (press h for help or q to quit)
```

4. Press **<space>** to page through the manual. Press **h** for a list of the key commands used for reading and searching. Press **q** to quit reading the man-page.

How it works...

After logging in to the Raspberry Pi, the man command is used to display the built-in documentation for the fortune command.

There's more...

Most command-line utilities have a man-page. There are man-pages for configuration files and software libraries too. All the man-pages can be accessed via the man command.

For more information, use the man command to read its own man page, that is, by using the man man command.

It is possible to search the library of man pages using the apropos command. The apropos command searches the man pages database for keywords and returns a list of man pages. The man command also has an apropos form, namely man -k.

Here is a short terminal session that uses the apropos command to search for the keyword "music":

```
pi@raspberrypi:~$ apropos music

pianobar (1)          - console pandora.com music player

pi@raspberrypi:~$
```

> The pianobar console music player can be installed using the aptitude package management application (refer to the recipe named *Package Management*).

See also

▸ **apropos - search the manual page names and descriptions**(http://manpages. debian.net/cgi-bin/man.cgi?query=apropos) The Debian man-page for apropos has information about the command and its options.

> ▸ **man – an interface to the on-line reference manuals** (http://manpages. debian.net/cgi-bin/man.cgi?query=man) The Debian man-page for man can be found online or locally on the Raspberry Pi.

Reading the built-in documentation (info)

This recipe shows how the info command is used to read info-pages.

Info-pages are yet another source of documentation that has already been installed with the base Raspbian Linux distribution. The info command is used to display documentation stored as info-pages.

After completing this recipe, you will be able to use the info command to read the built-in documentation that has been stored as info-pages.

Getting ready

Ingredients:

> ▸ You need an *Initial Setup* or a *Basic Networking* setup for the Raspberry Pi that has been powered on. You also need to be logged in as the user whose username is pi (refer to the recipes in *Chapter 1, Installation and Setup* to learn how to boot and log in and the recipes in *Chapter 2, Administration* to know how to log in remotely).

> ▸ A network connection is an optional requirement.

The Raspberry Pi does not need access to the Internet for this application.

If the Raspberry Pi has remote access enabled, this recipe can be completed remotely using ssh or PuTTY (refer to the *Remote access* recipes in *Chapter 2, Administration*).

How to do it...

Perform the following steps to read the built-in documentation using info:

1. Log in to the Raspberry Pi either directly or remotely.
2. Execute the info command, as follows:
   ```
   pi@raspberrypi:~$ info
   ```

3. The main screen of the info-page is displayed, which looks like this:

```
File: dir,      Node: Top      This is the top of the INFO tree


   This (the Directory node) gives a menu of major topics.
   Typing "q" exits, "?" lists all Info commands, "d" returns here,
   "h" gives a primer for first-timers,
   "mEmacs<Return>" visits the Emacs manual, etc.


   In Emacs, you can click mouse button 2 on a menu item or cross reference
   to select it.


 * Menu:


Basics
 * Common options: (coreutils)Common options.
 * Coreutils: (coreutils).        Core GNU (file, text, shell) utilities.


-----Info: (dir)Top, 174 lines --Top---------------------------------------------
```

4. Press the spacebar to page through the documentation. This is the easiest way to read the file from top to bottom.

5. Use the arrow keys to put the cursor next to the ***** symbol of a menu item and then press the **<enter>** key to jump to that location in the file.

6. Press **h** (the lowercase letter h) to learn more about the `info` command. Press **H** (the uppercase letter H) to start a tutorial on how to use `info`.

7. Press **q** to quit.

How it works...

After logging in to the Raspberry Pi, the `info` application is started.

There's more...

The `info` command reads specially formatted files and info-pages and displays them in a text browser. Info-pages are well-structured with menu hierarchies to navigate through documentation by concepts. They look very much like web pages. The root of all the info-pages is displayed when the `info` command is entered without parameters: `info`.

Coreutils – the most common Raspbian Linux utilities

The `Coreutils` section of the info-pages documentation covers the most common command-line utilities that are used in the Raspbian Linux distribution, including common options that should be understood by all applications:

```
File: coreutils.info,  Node: Common options,  Next: Output of entire files,  Pr\
ev: Introduction,  Up: Top


2 Common options
****************


Certain options are available in all of these programs.  Rather than
writing identical descriptions for each of the programs, they are
described here.  (In fact, every GNU program accepts (or should accept)
these options.)


   Normally options and operands can appear in any order, and programs
act as if all the options appear before any operands.  For example,
'sort -r passwd -t :' acts like 'sort -r -t : passwd', since ':' is an
option-argument of '-t'.  However, if the 'POSIXLY_CORRECT' environment
variable is set, options must appear before operands, unless otherwise
specified for a particular command.


   A few programs can usefully have trailing operands with leading '-'.
With such a program, options must precede operands even if
'POSIXLY_CORRECT' is not set, and this fact is noted in the program
description.  For example, the 'env' command's options must appear
before its operands, since in some cases the operands specify a command


--zz-Info: (coreutils.info.gz)Common options, 73 lines --Top--------------------
```

In the info-pages, there is documentation on file permissions, access modes, and other concepts that are useful when you wish to manage the Raspberry Pi. Unlike man-pages, the info-pages documentation goes beyond just a summary; there exists a list of options to also explain the concepts behind the commands and their intended use.

Ironically, the info-page for the `info` command is not included by default with the Raspbian Linux distribution. Instead, use the `man info` command to read more about the `info` command.

Searching for info

You can search the info-pages using the -k option of the info command. Try searching for (-k) both man and info for keywords such as "permission", "access", or "download" when you cannot remember the name of a command.

Here is what you get when you search the Info pages for 'permissions':

golden@raspberrypi:~$ **info -k permissions**

```
"(coreutils)chmod invocation" -- access permissions, changing
"(coreutils)Setting Permissions" -- adding permissions
"(coreutils)chmod invocation" -- changing access permissions
"(coreutils)Copying Permissions" -- copying existing permissions
"(coreutils)Umask and Protection" -- giving away permissions
"(coreutils)Setting Permissions" -- group, permissions for
"(coreutils)Multiple Changes" -- multiple changes to permissions
"(coreutils)Setting Permissions" -- other permissions
"(coreutils)Setting Permissions" -- owner of file, permissions for
"(coreutils)install invocation" -- permissions of installed files, setting
"(coreutils)chmod invocation" -- permissions, changing access
"(coreutils)Copying Permissions" -- permissions, copying existing
"(coreutils)touch invocation" -- permissions, for changing file timestamps
"(coreutils)What information is listed" -- permissions, output by 'ls'
"(coreutils)chmod invocation" -- recursively changing access permissions
"(coreutils)Setting Permissions" -- removing permissions
"(coreutils)Setting Permissions" -- setting permissions
"(coreutils)Setting Permissions" -- subtracting permissions
"(coreutils)chmod invocation" -- symbolic links, permissions of
"(gnupg1)GPG Esoteric Options" -- preserve-permissions
"(wget)FTP Options" -- file permissions
```

golden@raspberrypi:~$

You already have a lot of detailed information about Linux, Debian, and the Raspbian Linux operating system that is installed on your Raspberry Pi. The info command gives you access to the information stored as info-pages.

See also

▶ **info – read Info documents** (`http://manpages.debian.net/cgi-bin/man.cgi?query=info`. The Debian man-page for `info` describes the command and its options.

4
File Sharing

In this chapter, we will cover:

- ▶ Mounting USB disks (`pmount`)
- ▶ Accessing another computer's files (`smbclient`)
- ▶ Sharing folders from other computers (`mount.cifs`)
- ▶ Auto-mounting USB disks at boot (`/etc/fstab`)
- ▶ Auto-mounting a shared folder at boot
- ▶ Creating a file server (Samba)
- ▶ Sharing an attached USB disk (Samba)

Introduction

The Raspberry Pi recipes in this chapter are for sharing files with other computers on the same local network.

The chapter begins with a recipe for mounting USB disks that are attached to the Raspberry Pi. The next recipes show how files are exchanged with other computers using the SMB (CIFS) protocol. Then, there are two recipes showing how disks can be automatically mounted during boot. The chapter ends with a couple of recipes for setting up the Raspberry Pi as a file server.

After completing the recipes in this chapter, you will be able to automatically mount local USB disks and exchange files between the Raspberry Pi and other computers using the SMB (CIFS) protocol.

Mounting USB disks (pmount)

This recipe installs and applies `pmount`, a command that mounts USB disks attached directly to the Raspberry Pi in the same manner as the desktop file manager.

If a disk is connected to the Raspberry Pi via a USB port when using the Raspberry Pi's **graphical user interface** (**GUI**), the desktop file manager will ask the user's permission to mount the disk. However, when using a Raspberry Pi remotely (or when the Raspberry Pi has been booted in text mode), there is no GUI to ask if a file should be mounted.

This recipe does not rely on the Raspberry Pi GUI or the desktop file manager to mount a disk. Instead, the command-line utility `pmount` is used to mount a USB drive in the same way that the GUI would—in the `/media` directory.

Once you've completed this recipe, you will be able to use both large USB storage devices and small USB flash drives to exchange files with other computers without relying on the Raspberry Pi graphical user interface or the desktop file manager.

Getting ready

Here are the ingredients used in this recipe:

- An initial setup or basic networking setup for the Raspberry Pi that has been powered on. You have also logged in as the user `pi` (see the recipes in *Chapter 1, Installation and Setup*, for how to boot and log in and the recipes in *Chapter 2, Administration*, for how to log in remotely).
- A powered USB hub (recommended).
- At least one USB disk drive.

This recipe does not require the desktop GUI and could either be run from the text-based console or from within an LXTerminal.

If the Raspberry Pi's Secure Shell server is running, this recipe can be completed remotely using a Secure Shell client (see the *Remote Access (SSH)* recipe in *Chapter 2, Administration*).

The examples in this recipe use two USB drives: a 32 GB flash drive and a 500 GB disk.

> Beware! The Raspberry Pi has power limits.
>
> The Raspberry Pi does not have enough internal power to reliably power a large USB disk that has been directly connected to the Raspberry Pi's USB ports.
>
> To ensure that the Raspberry Pi continues to function optimally, you should attach any device that requires power (including USB disks) indirectly to the Raspberry Pi via a powered USB hub.
>
> A powered USB hub provides enough power to run several large USB drives without draining extra power from the Raspberry Pi.
>
> If you see a large colorful square glowing in the top-right corner of the GUI, it is a warning that your Raspberry Pi does not have enough power.

How to do it...

The steps to mount USB disks are as follows:

1. Log in to the Raspberry Pi either directly or remotely.

2. Use `apt-get` to install the `pmount` command.

   pi@raspberrypi ~ $ **sudo apt-get install pmount**

   [sudo] password for pi:

3. The `apt-get install` command downloads and installs `pmount`.

   Reading package lists... Done

   Building dependency tree

   Reading state information... Done

   Suggested packages:

     cryptsetup

   The following NEW packages will be installed:

     pmount

   0 upgraded, 1 newly installed, 0 to remove and 0 not upgraded.

   Need to get 98.0 kB of archives.

   After this operation, 727 kB of additional disk space will be used.

   Get:1 http://mirrordirector.raspbian.org/raspbian/ wheezy/main pmount armhf 0.9.23-2 [98.0 kB]

   Fetched 98.0 kB in 1s (93.3 kB/s)

   Selecting previously unselected package pmount.

   (Reading database ... 89035 files and directories currently installed.)

```
Unpacking pmount (from .../pmount_0.9.23-2_armhf.deb) ...
Processing triggers for man-db ...
Setting up pmount (0.9.23-2) ...


pi@raspberrypi ~ $
```

4. Connect one or more USB disks to the Raspberry Pi. The example includes two disks: a 32 GB flash drive and a 500 GB disk.

5. Use the `fdisk -1` command to list the disks that are currently attached to the Raspberry Pi.

   pi@raspberrypi ~ $ **sudo apt-get install pmount**

6. The `fdisk` command displays information about the disks that are attached to the Raspberry Pi.

```
Disk /dev/mmcblk0: 31.9 GB, 31914983424 bytes
4 heads, 16 sectors/track, 973968 cylinders, total 62333952 sectors
Units = sectors of 1 * 512 = 512 bytes
Sector size (logical/physical): 512 bytes / 512 bytes
I/O size (minimum/optimal): 512 bytes / 512 bytes
Disk identifier: 0x0009bf4f
```

Device Boot	Start	End	Blocks	Id	System
/dev/mmcblk0p1 (LBA)	8192	122879	57344	c	W95 FAT32
/dev/mmcblk0p2	122880	62333951	31105536	83	Linux

```
Disk /dev/sda: 128 MB, 128974848 bytes
2 heads, 63 sectors/track, 1999 cylinders, total 251904 sectors
Units = sectors of 1 * 512 = 512 bytes
Sector size (logical/physical): 512 bytes / 512 bytes
I/O size (minimum/optimal): 512 bytes / 512 bytes
Disk identifier: 0x002d7aa3
```

Device Boot	Start	End	Blocks	Id	System
/dev/sda1 *	32	251903	125936	6	FAT16

```
Disk /dev/sdb: 500.1 GB, 500107862016 bytes
```

```
255 heads, 63 sectors/track, 60801 cylinders, total 976773168 sectors
Units = sectors of 1 * 512 = 512 bytes
Sector size (logical/physical): 512 bytes / 512 bytes
I/O size (minimum/optimal): 512 bytes / 512 bytes
Disk identifier: 0x002317d5


   Device Boot      Start         End      Blocks   Id  System
/dev/sdb1            2048   976773167   488385560    7  HPFS/NTFS/exFAT
```

7. The command output in the preceding example shows three disks:

    ❑   /dev/mmcblk0: The 31.9 GB SD card (the boot disk) has two partitions:
        /dev/mmcblk0p1 and /dev/mmcblk0p2

    ❑   /dev/sda: The 128 MB flash drive has one partition

    ❑   /dev/sdb: The 500.1 GB disk also has one partition

8. Use the freshly installed pmount command to mount the primary partition of the
   flash drive (/dev/sda1) and the primary partition of the USB disk (/dev/sdb1).
   The sudo command is not required.

   ```
   pi@raspberrypi ~ $ ls -l /media
   total 0

   pi@raspberrypi ~ $ pmount /dev/sda1
   pi@raspberrypi ~ $ pmount /dev/sdb1

   pi@raspberrypi ~ $ ls -l /media
   total 20
   drwx------ 4 pi pi 16384 Dec 31  1969 sda1
   drwxr-xr-x 6 pi pi  4096 May 30 12:23 sdb1

   pi@raspberrypi ~ $
   ```

9. The preceding command output shows the contents of the /media directory before
   and after the pmount command is used to mount the two disks. After the pmount
   command is executed, each disk appears in the /media directory.

10. The df -h command can also be used to display a list of the currently mounted disks
    with their mount points. In the following command output, the two disks, /dev/sda1
    and /dev/sdb1, are shown mounted on /media/sda1 and /media/sdb1:

    ```
    pi@raspberrypi ~ $ df -h
    Filesystem      Size  Used Avail Use% Mounted on
    rootfs           30G  4.2G   24G  15% /
    ```

```
/dev/root          30G   4.2G   24G   15%  /
devtmpfs          484M      0  484M    0%  /dev
tmpfs              98M   252K   98M    1%  /run
tmpfs             5.0M      0  5.0M    0%  /run/lock
tmpfs             195M      0  195M    0%  /run/shm
/dev/mmcblk0p1     56M    19M   37M   34%  /boot
/dev/sdb1         459G   172G  264G   40%  /media/sdb1
/dev/sda1         123M    71M   53M   58%  /media/sda1


pi@raspberrypi ~ $
```

How it works...

After logging in to the Raspberry Pi, the `pmount` command is installed, the two disk drives are attached, and the command `fdisk -l` is used to display the partition tables of the disks attached to the Raspberry Pi. In the example, three disks are displayed:

- `/dev/mmcblk0` is the boot disk
- `/dev/sda` is the 128 MB flash drive
- `/dev/sdb` is the 500 GB disk

The flash drive has one partition (`/dev/sda1`) and so does the disk (`/dev/sdb1`). Within disk partitions, is where files are stored.

The `pmount` command is used to mount disk partitions. The disk partitions are mounted in the `/media` directory. The `ls -l` command is used before and after the disks are mounted to show where the disk partitions appear once they have been mounted.

The mount points in the `/media` directory are given names that correspond to the disk partitions that have been mounted there. The disk partition of the flash drive, `/dev/sda1`, is mounted on `/media/sda1` and the disk partition of the 500 GB disk, `/dev/sdb1`, is mounted on `/media/sdb1`.

Finally, the `df -h` command is used to demonstrate another way of seeing where the disk partitions have been mounted. The `df` command also shows the amount of free disk space that is available on each of the mounted disks. The `-h` option tells `df` to display the size of each disk in bytes, instead of in disk blocks. The 500 GB disk is 40% full; it has 264 GB available. The flash drive is 58% full with only 53 MB available.

There's more...

Let's learn something more about the disks.

Device files

As each disk or disk partition is mounted, a device file is created for it and stored in the /dev directory. The names of each of these device files are assigned sequentially as the disks are mounted.

The assigned names of USB drives all begin with the characters sd. The first USB disk drive is assigned the device file /dev/sda, the second /dev/sdb, and so on.

The assigned names of the SD card drives begin with mmcblk, and a digit is added for each unique device starting with 0 (zero). The only SD card drive in the Raspberry Pi (the boot disk) has its device file located at /dev/mmcblk0.

For each disk partition discovered in a disk's partition table, a device file is also created. Each of these disk partition device files has the same name as the disk's device file with a digit attached corresponding to its location in the partition table.

In the example, the 32 GB SD card is assigned the device file /dev/mmcblk0. It has two partitions: /dev/mmcblk0p1 and /dev/mmcblk0p2. If the SD card had yet another partition, the third partition's device file would be /dev/mmcblk0p3.

When a disk has a partition table, each partition needs to be mounted separately. Use the pmount command with the partition's device file, not the disk device file. The 500 GB disk in the example has one partition that is mounted with the command pmount /dev/sdb1.

When a disk has no partition table, use the pmount command with the device file assigned to the disk drive.

Mount points

When disk partitions are mounted, by default a mount point is created for each partition in the /media directory. The name of the default mount point is the same as the name of the device file used to mount the disk partition.

The only partition of the 128 MB flash drive was assigned the device file /dev/sda1, so by default its mount point is /media/sda1. The 500 GB disk also has one partition, /dev/sdb1, mounted at /media/sdb1.

To create a mount point under the /media directory with a name other than the default name, you need to pass the desired mount point as a second parameter of the pmount command, as in the following example:

```
pi@raspberrypi ~ $ pmount /dev/sdb1 mydisk


pi@raspberrypi ~ $ ls -l /media
total 20
drwx------ 4 pi  pi 16384 Dec 31  1969 sda1
drwxr-xr-x 6 pi  pi  4096 May 30 12:23 mydisk

pi@raspberrypi ~ $
```

Unmounting disks

Use the pumount command to unmount the disks (there is no n in the command name). After the disks are unmounted, their mount points are deleted from the /media directory.

```
pi@raspberrypi ~ $ ls -l /media
total 20
drwx------ 4 pi  pi 16384 Dec 31  1969 sda1
drwxr-xr-x 6 pi  pi  4096 May 30 12:23 mydisk

pi@raspberrypi ~ $ pumount /dev/sda1

pi@raspberrypi ~ $ ls -l /media
total 4
drwxr-xr-x 6 pi  pi 4096 May 30 12:23 mydisk

pi@raspberrypi ~ $ pumount /media/mydisk

pi@raspberrypi ~ $ ls -l /media
total 0

pi@raspberrypi ~ $
```

As shown in the preceding example, the pumount command accepts either the disk device (/dev/sda1) or the mount point (/media/mydisk).

The plugdev group

Use of the `pmount` command does not require super user privileges. However, it does require some privileges. The privilege to execute the `pmount` command is reserved for members of the system group `plugdev`. Users who are not in the group `plugdev` cannot execute the `pmount` command.

Here is an example of how to add a user to the `plugdev` group:

```
pi@raspberrypi ~ $ groups golden
golden : golden sudo

pi@raspberrypi ~ $ adduser golden plugdev

pi@raspberrypi ~ $ groups golden
golden : golden sudo plugdev

pi@raspberrypi ~ $
```

> On Raspbian, the default user, `pi`, is already a member of the `plugdev` group.

Other mount commands

The system command `mount` requires super user privileges. During the boot process, the mount command is used to automatically mount disks like the SD card from which the Raspberry Pi boots. The next recipe shows how to configure the Raspberry Pi to automatically mount attached drives when it boots.

The file manager included with the Raspberry Pi desktop, PCManFM, will also mount disks in the `/media` directory. However, the PCManFM file manager uses the disk's label instead of the disk's device name as the name of the mount point.

Disk performance

A Class 10 SD card has a transfer rate of 10 MB per second, yet an external hard disk can transfer data to the computer at 300 MB/sec. The hard disk is almost 30x faster than an SD card!

Even though SD cards can be purchased in increasingly large sizes, they are not the best choice for high-speed performance. Even the Ultra High Speed SD cards at 30 MB/sec are 10x slower than a hard disk. Most of the recipes in this book will perform better if the data that they depend on is stored on an external hard disk.

The Raspberry Pi's power is limited

External disks and flash drives that have no power supply of their own draw power from the Raspberry Pi's USB connection. The power needed by devices without their own power supply is taken from the Raspberry Pi. The Raspberry Pi's power is limited; it cannot reliably support larger USB devices if the devices have no power supply of their own.

The amount of power needed by an external USB device could easily exceed the amount of power that is available from the Raspberry Pi. If too much power is drawn from the Raspberry Pi, other USB devices, including the network interface (which internally uses the USB bus), may cease to function properly or they may cease to function at all.

For best performance and reliability, it is recommended that all USB devices, including external disk drives and flash drives, be connected *indirectly* to the Raspberry Pi via a powered USB hub instead of being connected to the Raspberry Pi directly.

A powered USB hub is the power source for all of the USB devices that are connected to it. Only data is transferred to the Raspberry Pi. A powered USB hub does not draw power from the Raspberry Pi. Instead, it protects the Raspberry Pi from the power drain of other devices. By connecting USB devices *indirectly* via a powered USB hub, the Raspberry Pi can perform optimally and reliably.

See also

- **Hard disk drive** (http://en.wikipedia.org/wiki/Hard_disk_drive): This Wikipedia article has more information about disk drives.

- **USB flash drive** (http://en.wikipedia.org/wiki/USB_flash_drive): This Wikipedia article provides detailed information about USB drives.

- **SD cards** (http://en.wikipedia.org/wiki/Secure_Digital): This Wikipedia article is about the **Secure Digital** (**SD**) card format.

- **mount (Unix)** (http://en.wikipedia.org/wiki/Mount_(Unix)): This Wikipedia article is about the mount command.

- **df – report filesystem disk space usage** (http://manpages.debian.net/cgi-bin/man.cgi?query=df): The Debian man page for df has more information about the command and its options.

- **fdisk – partition table manipulator for Linux** (http://manpages.debian.net/cgi-bin/man.cgi?query=fdisk): The Debian man page for fdisk has more information about the command.

- **pmount – mount arbitrary hotpluggable devices as normal user** (http://manpages.debian.net/cgi-bin/man.cgi?query=pmount): The Debian man page for pmount has more information about the command.

▶ **pumount – unmount arbitrary hotpluggable devices** (http://manpages. debian.net/cgi-bin/man.cgi?query=pumount): The Debian man page for pumount has more information about the command.

▶ **udev – Linux dynamic device management** (http://manpages.debian.net/ cgi-bin/man.cgi?query=udev): The Debian man page for udev explains in more detail how devices are mounted.

Accessing another computer's files (smbclient)

The goal of this recipe is to transfer files between the Raspberry Pi and other computers using the command smbclient.

This recipe shows how to list the available network shared folders, to copy individual files, and how to copy entire directories of files from a computer with shared folders to the Raspberry Pi using the smbclient command.

After completing this recipe, you will be able to list the available file shares on the local network and transfer files directly between another computer and the Raspberry Pi using the SMB (CIFS) protocol.

Getting ready...

Here are the ingredients for this recipe:

▶ An initial setup or basic networking setup for the Raspberry Pi that has been powered on. You have also logged in as the user pi (see the recipes in *Chapter 1, Installation and Setup*, for how to boot and log in and the recipes in *Chapter 2, Administration*, for how to log in remotely).

▶ A network connection.

▶ A client PC connected to the same network as the Raspberry Pi.

This recipe does not require the desktop GUI and could either be run from the text-based console or from within an LXTerminal.

If the Raspberry Pi's Secure Shell server is running, this recipe can be completed remotely using a Secure Shell client (see the recipe *Remote access (SSH)* in *Chapter 2, Administration*).

The examples in this recipe will connect the Raspberry Pi to a local network computer, golden-mackbook, and a home file server, terragolden. Configuration for other computers using the SMB (CIFS) protocol will be similar.

How to do it...

The steps to accessing another computer's files are as follows:

1. Log in to the Raspberry Pi either directly or remotely.

2. Use the command `apt-get install` to download and install the `smbclient` software package.

   pi@raspberrypi ~ $ **sudo apt-get install smbclient**

3. Use the command `smbclient` to list the services (`-L`) on the home file server, `terragolden`. No password is required (`-N`) for guest access.

   pi@raspberrypi ~ $ **smbclient -N -L terragolden**

4. A list of SMB (CIFS) services from the home file server, `terrgolden`, is displayed.

   ```
   Anonymous login successful
   Domain=[GOLDEN] OS=[Unix] Server=[Samba 3.2.5]

           Sharename       Type        Comment
           ---------       ----        -------
           IPC$            IPC         IPC Service (Golden Family Media Drive)
           backups         Disk
           livemusic       Disk
           photos          Disk
           public          Disk


   Anonymous login successful
   Domain=[GOLDEN] OS=[Unix] Server=[Samba 3.2.5]

           Server              Comment
           ---------           -------
           TERRAGOLDEN         Golden Family Media Drive

           Workgroup           Master
           ---------           -------
           GOLDEN


   pi@raspberrypi ~ $
   ```

5. Use the command `smbclient` to list the services (`-L`) on the home computer, golden-macbook. A valid username (`-U`) and password is required for access.

    pi@raspberrypi ~ $ **smbclient –U golden -L golden-macbook --signing=off**

    Enter golden's password:

6. A list of SMB (CIFS) services from the golden-macbook is displayed.

    ```
    Domain=[GOLDEN-MACBOOK] OS=[Darwin] Server=[@(#)PROGRAM:smbd
    PROJECT:smbx-276.92.2]


    Sharename       Type        Comment
    ---------       ----        -------
    IPC$            IPC
    Macintosh HD    Disk
    xfer            Disk
    golden          Disk


    pi@raspberrypi ~ $
    ```

7. Now, use the `mkdir` command to create a new directory (`xfer`) on the Raspberry Pi, use the `cd` command to switch to the new directory, and then use the `ls` command to show that there are no files in the newly created directory (`~/xfer`).

    pi@raspberrypi ~ $ **mkdir xfer**

    pi@raspberrypi ~ $ **cd xfer**

    pi@raspberrypi ~/xfer $ **ls -l**
    total 0

    pi@raspberrypi ~/xfer $

8. Use the `smbclient` command to begin a conversation with the home file server, `terragolden`, about files in the file share `livemusic`.

    pi@raspberrypi ~/xfer $ **smbclient -N //teragolden/livemusic**
    smb: \>

9. The command prompt, `smb: \>`, is displayed showing that the `smbclient` command is ready to converse with `terragolden`.

10. Use the `ls` command to list the files and folders in the `livemusic` share of `terragolden`.

    ```
    smb: \> ls
    ```

.	D	0	Fri Oct 28 15:45:43 2011
..	D	0	Tue Oct 9 22:03:55 2012
catalog.txt	A	5119	Mon Jul 24 18:04:30 2017
dso040424	D	0	Wed Mar 9 19:46:22 2011
dtb2005-03-04	D	0	Wed Mar 9 19:43:35 2011
franti2010-06-11.flac16	D	0	Fri Mar 25 08:43:13 2011
garaj2005-04-10_16bit_64kb_mp3	D	0	Wed Mar 9 19:50:28 2011
JackJohnson2010-07-17	D	0	Mon Mar 14 14:04:25 2011
JasonMraz-FarmAid	D	0	Thu Apr 28 16:03:48 2011
JasonMrazGrandRex_vbr_mp3	D	0	Thu Apr 28 16:04:59 2011
jgb2008-07-19_64kb_mp3	D	0	Wed Mar 9 19:41:06 2011
jj2010-12-13.aud.flac16	D	0	Wed Mar 2 11:46:06 2011
MF2010-10-06_Nak30016BitFlac	D	0	Fri Mar 25 10:31:05 2011
mFranti2006-11-13	D	0	Wed Mar 9 19:55:00 2011
mfs2005-01-15	D	0	Wed Mar 9 19:48:50 2011
particle2010-04-15	D	0	Fri Mar 25 09:13:14 2011
particle2010-10-30	D	0	Fri Mar 25 08:45:00 2011
skb2005-10-01matrix_64kb_mp3	D	0	Mon Mar 14 14:12:01 2011
Soulive2011-03-08	D	0	Fri Mar 25 08:33:21 2011
Soulive2011-03-10	D	0	Fri Mar 25 08:34:11 2011
tenaciousd2005-09-22.flac16_64kb	D	0	Wed Mar 9 20:32:06 2011
um2007-04-21	D	0	Wed Mar 9 19:47:59 2011
ymsb2001-02-02	D	0	Wed Mar 9 09:23:13 2011
ymsb2007-06-22	D	0	Wed Mar 9 19:50:18 2011
.DS_Store	AH	6148	Fri Oct 28 15:45:43 2011
._.DS_Store	AH	4096	Fri Oct 28 15:45:43 2011

```
        59356 blocks of size 16777216. 4490 blocks available
```

```
smb: \>
```

11. Use the `get` command to download the `catalog.txt` file from `terragolden` to the Raspberry Pi.

    smb: \> **get catalog.txt**

    getting file \catalog.txt of size 5119 as catalog.txt (208.3 KiloBytes/
    sec) (average 208.3 KiloBytes/sec)

    smb: \>

12. Now, use the `mget` command to download an entire directory of files, `particle2010-04-15`, from `terragolden` to the Raspberry Pi. The `mget` command first requires that the `tarmode`, `recurse`, and `prompt` options are set.

    smb: \> **tarmode**

    tarmode is now full, system, hidden, noreset, verbose

    smb: \> **recurse**

    smb: \> **prompt**

    smb: \> **mget particle2010-04-15**

    getting file \particle2010-04-15\particle2010-04-15.ffp of size 594 as
    particle2010-04-15.ffp (11.8 KiloBytes/sec) (average 11.8 KiloBytes/sec)

    getting file \particle2010-04-15\particle2010-04-15t01.flac of size
    70373980 as particle2010-04-15t01.flac (8086.2 KiloBytes/sec) (average
    8039.9 KiloBytes/sec)

    getting file \particle2010-04-15\particle2010-04-15t02.flac of size
    58391723 as particle2010-04-15t02.flac (8070.1 KiloBytes/sec) (average
    8053.6 KiloBytes/sec)

    getting file \particle2010-04-15\particle2010-04-15t03.flac of size
    100964559 as particle2010-04-15t03.flac (4672.9 KiloBytes/sec) (average
    6110.7 KiloBytes/sec)

    getting file \particle2010-04-15\particle2010-04-15t04.flac of size
    82562641 as particle2010-04-15t04.flac (8648.2 KiloBytes/sec) (average
    6624.5 KiloBytes/sec)

    getting file \particle2010-04-15\particle2010-04-15t05.flac of size
    115649970 as particle2010-04-15t05.flac (5859.4 KiloBytes/sec) (average
    6398.7 KiloBytes/sec)

    getting file \particle2010-04-15\particle2010-04-15t06.flac of size
    57681372 as particle2010-04-15t06.flac (4870.3 KiloBytes/sec) (average
    6168.8 KiloBytes/sec)

    getting file \particle2010-04-15\particle2010-04-15t07.flac of size
    46807245 as particle2010-04-15t07.flac (8770.2 KiloBytes/sec) (average
    6333.9 KiloBytes/sec)

    getting file \particle2010-04-15\text.txt of size 491 as text.txt (10.0
    KiloBytes/sec) (average 6346.5 KiloBytes/sec)

    smb: \>

13. Use the `quit` command to end the SMB (CIFS) conversation with the `terragolden` home file server and return to the Raspberry Pi command prompt.

```
smb: \> quit

pi@raspberrypi ~/xfer $
```

14. Use the `ls -l` command to display the contents of the current directory on the Raspberry Pi.

```
pi@raspberrypi ~/xfer $ ls -l

total 20
-rw------- 1 pi pi 13564 Jul 19 13:52 catalog.txt
drwxr-xr-x 2 pi pi  4096 Jul 19 13:45 particle2010-04-15

pi@raspberrypi ~/xfer $
```

How it works...

After logging in to the Raspberry Pi, the software distribution package `smbclient` is installed using the `apt-get install` command. For more information on how the `apt-get` command works, see *Chapter 3, Maintenance*.

> Your software distribution may already have `smbclient` installed.

The `smbclient` software distribution package contains the command-line application `smbclient`. This application is used to communicate with other computers using the SMB protocol.

After the software distribution package is installed, the `smbclient` command is used to list the available services on a home file server named `terragolden`. The `-N` option tells the command that no password is required for the remote computer, and the `-L` option tells the command to just list the available shares and printers.

For comparison, the `smbclient` command is also used to list the available services on another computer attached to the local network, golden-macbook. This time, a username (`-U golden`) and a password (no `-N` option) are required for access to the computer and the `smbclient` command also requires the `--signing=off` option to turn off a security feature that the computer does not support.

Before the `smbclient` command is used to start a conversation with `terragolden`, a transfer directory (`xfer`) is created using the `mkdir` command to receive the transferred files and its (empty) contents are displayed using the `ls -l` command. The `-l` option tells the `ls` command to use the long listing format that includes a total count of files (`0`).

The command `smbclient -N //terragolden/livemusic` is used to start a conversation between the Raspberry Pi and the remote computer, `terragolden`, using the file share named `livemusic`. The command prompt changes to `smb: \>` telling the user that the conversation has begun.

The `ls` command of `smbclient` is used to list the files on the home file server. The command `dir` could be used instead and will return the same result as the `ls` command.

The command `get catalog.txt` is used to transfer the file `catalog.txt` from the file server to the Raspberry Pi. The `smbclient` command reports that the file transferred has a size of 5119 bytes and was transferred at a rate of 208.3 KB per second.

After the `catalog.txt` file has been transferred, three options are set to prepare for a multi-file transfer. The `tarmode` option is reset to its default setting to ensure that all files are transferred. The `recurse` option is toggled so that the upcoming `mget` command will copy subdirectories as well as files. And the `prompt` option is toggled so that the upcoming `mget` command does not prompt for validation before transferring each file.

Once the transfer options have been set, the `mget` command is used to transfer the `particle2010-04-15` directory of files to the Raspberry Pi. As each file is transferred, the size of the file and its rate of transfer are displayed.

After all of the files have been transferred, the `quit` command is used to tell the `smbclient` application that the conversation with the remote computer, `terragolden`, is now over.

The command prompt returns to `pi@raspberrypi ~ $` showing that the conversation is complete.

There's more...

The `smbclient` application has its own rich set of commands for communicating with remote computers via the SMB protocol.

help

The `help` command can be used to list the commands available from the `smb: \>` prompt.

```
smb: \> help
?               allinfo         altname     archive     blocksize
cancel          case_sensitive  cd          chmod       chown
close           del             dir         du          echo
```

exit	get	getfacl	geteas	hardlink
help	history	iosize	lcd	link
lock	lowercase	ls	l	mask
md	mget	mkdir	more	mput
newer	open	posix	posix_encrypt	posix_open
posix_mkdir	posix_rmdir	posix_unlink	print	prompt
put	pwd	q	queue	quit
readlink	rd	recurse	reget	rename
reput	rm	rmdir	showacls	setea
setmode	stat	symlink	tar	tarmode
translate	unlock	volume	vuid	wdel
logon	listconnect	showconnect	..	!

```
smb: \> help help
HELP help:
    [command] give help on a command


smb: \>
```

Each of the smbclient application's commands has its own help page displayed using the help command. Type help followed by a command name to display more information about the command.

Changing remote directories

The cd command in smbclient can be used to change directories on the remote computer in the same way cd is used to change directories on the Raspberry Pi. Notice that the current remote directory path is reflected in the smbclient command prompt.

```
smb: \> ls golden/stuff/astrology
  .                              D        0  Wed Jun 29 22:20:25 2011
  ..                             D        0  Wed Oct 26 13:49:49 2011
  astrolog data                 DR        0  Mon Dec 12 07:13:40 2005
  ephall-astrolog               DR        0  Mon Jan 10 08:01:24 2005
  ephcom-1.0                    DR        0  Thu Apr  7 00:39:03 2005
  experiments                   DR        0  Mon Jan 10 21:45:51 2005
  jpl                           DR        0  Fri Mar  4 03:48:43 2005
  SwissEphemeris                DR        0  Thu Apr  7 06:03:14 2005
```

```
zodiac                          DR        0  Thu Apr  7 00:34:28 2005

        59356 blocks of size 16777216. 4490 blocks available
```

smb: \ > cd **golden/stuff/astrology/zodiac**

```
smb: \golden\stuff\astrology\zodiac\> ls
    .                           DR        0  Thu Apr  7 00:34:28 2005
    ..                          D         0  Wed Jun 29 22:20:25 2011
    .classpath                  AHR     236  Thu Apr  7 00:33:05 2005
    .project                    AHR     382  Thu Apr  7 00:33:05 2005
    classes                     DR        0  Wed Apr 20 10:14:10 2005
    src                         DR        0  Thu Apr  7 00:34:28 2005

        59356 blocks of size 16777216. 4490 blocks available


smb: \golden\stuff\astrology\zodiac\>
```

Fetching a single file

If the location of a file on the remote computer is already known, it can be fetched directly with a single `smbclient` command.

pi@raspberrypi ~/xfer $ **smbclient -N //terragolden -c 'get /livemusic/Seeed/03-seed-aufstehen.mp3'**

```
getting file \livemusic\Seeed\03-seed-aufstehen.mp3 of size 650317 as \livemusic\
Seeed\03-seed-aufstehen.mp3 (10414.8 KiloBytes/sec) (average 10414.8 KiloBytes/
sec)


pi@raspberrypi ~/xfer $
```

/ versus \

Notice that the SMB (CIFS) protocol uses \ instead of / as a path separator.

The path separator is one of the major differences between the Windows operating system and Linux-based operating systems like Raspbian Linux, which is used by the Raspberry Pi.

Either character can be used within the `smbclient` application, if used consistently. However, it is much easier to use / as it is the path separator on the Raspberry Pi.

See also

- **cd – change the working directory** (http://manpages.debian.net/cgi-bin/man.cgi?query=cd): The Debian manual page for cd has more information about the command and its options.

- **smbclient – client to access SMB/CIFS resources on servers** (http://manpages.debian.net/cgi-bin/man.cgi?query=smbclient): The Debian manual page for smbclient has more information about the command.

Sharing folders from other computers (mount.cifs)

This recipe shows how to mount folders that have been shared from another computer.

Recent Linux kernels, including the kernel used by the Raspbian Linux distribution for the Raspberry Pi, have built-in support for mounting shared folders using the SMB (CIFS) protocol. This is the file sharing protocol used commonly by Windows computers and home file sharing devices. It is also used on OS X when sharing files.

This is the simplest recipe for mounting a shared folder from the command line on the Raspberry Pi.

Once you've completed this recipe, you will be able to share files with other computers on the same network using the SMB (CIFS) protocol.

> SMB and CIFS are synonyms for the same file sharing protocol.

Getting ready

Here are the ingredients for this recipe:

- An initial setup or basic networking setup for the Raspberry Pi that has been powered on. You have also logged in as the user pi (see the recipes in *Chapter 1, Installation and Setup*, for how to boot and log in and the recipes in *Chapter 2, Administration*, for how to log in remotely).

- A powered USB hub (recommended).

- At least one USB disk drive.

This recipe does not require the desktop GUI and could either be run from the text-based console or from within an LXTerminal.

If the Raspberry Pi's Secure Shell server is running, this recipe can be completed remotely using a Secure Shell client (see the recipe *Remote access (SSH)* in *Chapter 2, Administration*).

The examples in this recipe will connect the Raspberry Pi to a home file server named terragolden sharing one folder, livemusic, which is configured for guest access.

How to do it...

The steps to sharing folders from other computers are as follows:

1. Log in to the Raspberry Pi either directly or remotely.

2. Create a mount point for the shared folder using the mkdir command:

   pi@raspberrypi ~ $ **sudo mkdir /media/livemusic**

3. Use the mount command with the guest and uid=pi options (-o) to mount the remote file share //terragolden/livemusic on the local directory, /media/livemusic.

   pi@raspberrypi ~ $ **sudo mount -o guest,uid=pi //terragolden/livemusic / media/livemusic**

4. Use the ls -l command to list the files in the folder /media/livemusic.

   ```
   pi@raspberrypi ~ $ ls -l /media/livemusic
   total 0
   drwx------ 2 pi nogroup 0 Mar  9  2011 dso040424
   drwx------ 2 pi nogroup 0 Mar  9  2011 dtb2005-03-04
   drwxrwxrwx 2 pi nogroup 0 Mar 25  2011 franti2010-06-11.flac16
   drwx------ 2 pi nogroup 0 Mar  9  2011 garaj2005-04-10_16bit_64kb_mp3
   drwx------ 2 pi nogroup 0 Mar 14  2011 JackJohnson2010-07-17
   drwx------ 2 pi nogroup 0 Apr 28  2011 JasonMraz-FarmAid
   drwx------ 2 pi nogroup 0 Apr 28  2011 JasonMrazGrandRex_vbr_mp3
   drwx------ 2 pi nogroup 0 Mar  9  2011 JGB2007-06-15
   drwx------ 2 pi nogroup 0 Mar  9  2011 jgb2008-07-19_64kb_mp3
   drwx------ 2 pi nogroup 0 Mar  2  2011 jj2010-12-13.aud.flac16
   drwxrwxrwx 2 pi nogroup 0 Mar 25  2011 MF2010-10-06_Nak30016BitFlac
   drwx------ 2 pi nogroup 0 Mar  9  2011 mFranti2006-11-13
   drwx------ 2 pi nogroup 0 Mar  9  2011 mfs2005-01-15
   ```

```
drwxrwxrwx 2 pi nogroup 0 Mar 25  2011 particle2010-04-15
drwxrwxrwx 2 pi nogroup 0 Mar 25  2011 particle2010-10-30
drwx------ 2 pi nogroup 0 Mar 14  2011 skb2005-10-01matrix_64kb_mp3
drwx------ 2 pi nogroup 0 Mar 25  2011 Soulive2011-03-08
drwx------ 2 pi nogroup 0 Mar 25  2011 Soulive2011-03-10
drwx------ 2 pi nogroup 0 Mar  9  2011 tenaciousd2005-09-22.flac16_64kb
drwx------ 2 pi nogroup 0 Mar  9  2011 um2007-04-21
drwx------ 5 pi nogroup 0 Mar  9  2011 ymsb2001-02-02
drwx------ 2 pi nogroup 0 Mar  9  2011 ymsb2007-06-22

pi@raspberrypi ~ $
```

How it works...

After logging in to the Raspberry Pi, the `mkdir` command is used to create a mount point for the shared folder in the `/media` directory. A mount point is an empty directory (`/media/livemusic`) that serves as a placeholder in the filesystem.

Then, the file share, `//terragolden/livemusic`, from the home file server, `terragolden`, is mounted at the newly created mount point (`/media/livemusic`). The options to the `mount` command (`-o guest,uid=pi`) tell the command that the share is to be accessed without a username or password (`guest`) and that the mounted files will belong to the user `pi` (`uid=pi`).

Finally, the files in the mount point (`/media/livemusic`) are listed using the command `ls -l` to verify that they are indeed identical to the files on the home file server.

There's more...

Let's look at some other aspects related to the sharing of folders.

Protected shares require a username and a password

If a file share is password protected, then the options on the mount command need to be expanded to include `username=USER` and `password=PASS` options. `USER` and `PASS` should be replaced with the respective username and password of a user who has access to the file share.

```
pi@raspberrypi ~/xfer $ sudo mount -o uid=pi,user=golden //golden-macbook/xfer /
media/xfer
```

Password:

```
pi@raspberrypi /media/xfer $ ls -l /media/golden-macbook/
total 8200
drwxr-xr-x 2 pi root       0 Jul 17 16:58 Applications
drwxr-xr-x 2 pi root       0 Jul  9 09:33 bin
drwxr-xr-x 2 pi root       0 Aug 24  2013 cores
drwxr-xr-x 2 pi root       0 Jul 14 18:06 dev
-rwxr-xr-x 1 pi root       0 Mar 11 09:23 etc
-rwxr-xr-x 1 pi root       0 Mar 11 09:26 HGN.flag
drwxr-xr-x 2 pi root       0 Jul 14 18:06 home
drwxr-xr-x 2 pi root       0 Mar 27 10:35 Library
-rwxr-xr-x 1 pi root 8394688 Mar 18 16:20 mach_kernel
drwxr-xr-x 2 pi root       0 Jul 14 18:06 net
drwxr-xr-x 2 pi root       0 Aug 24  2013 Network
drwxr-xr-x 2 pi root       0 Mar 18 08:53 opt
drwxr-xr-x 2 pi root       0 Mar 11 09:35 private
drwxr-xr-x 2 pi root       0 Jul  9 09:33 sbin
drwxr-xr-x 2 pi root       0 Mar 11 09:30 System
-rwxr-xr-x 1 pi root       0 Mar 11 09:23 tmp
drwxr-xr-x 2 pi root       0 Mar 27 14:48 Users
drwxr-xr-x 2 pi root       0 Mar 11 09:23 usr
-rwxr-xr-x 1 pi root       0 Mar 11 09:23 var
drwxr-xr-x 2 pi root       0 Jul 19 11:18 Volumes

pi@raspberrypi /media/xfer $
```

Unmounting disks

Use the umount command to unmount the disks (there is no n in the command name).

```
pi@raspberrypi /media/xfer $ sudo umount /media/golden-macbook
pi@raspberrypi /media/xfer $ ls -l /media/golden-macbook
total 0

pi@raspberrypi /media/xfer $
```

After the disks are unmounted, the mount points remain under the /media directory; however, they are once again empty. The command umount is privileged (use sudo).

▸ **Filesystem** (http://en.wikipedia.org/wiki/Filesystem): The Wikipedia article on filesystems explains the differences in more detail.

▸ **Server Message Block** (http://en.wikipedia.org/wiki/Server_Message_Block): The Wikipedia article on the **Server Message Block** (**SMB**) protocol discusses the protocol's use and its history.

▸ **Uniform Naming Convention** (http://en.wikipedia.org/wiki/Uniform_Naming_Convention): The Wikipedia article on the **Uniform Naming Convention** (**UNC**) protocol shows how it supports the SMB (CIFS) protocol.

▸ **mount – mount a filesystem** (http://manpages.debian.net/cgi-bin/man.cgi?query=mount): The Debian manual page for mount explains the command and its options.

▸ **mount.cifs – mount using the CIFS filesystem** (http://manpages.debian.net/cgi-bin/man.cgi?query=mount.cifs): The Debian manual page for mount.cifs explains the command in more detail.

▸ **umount – unmounts filesystems** (http://manpages.debian.net/cgi-bin/man.cgi?query=umount): The Debian manual page for umount shows the command and its options.

Auto-mounting USB disks at boot (/etc/fstab)

This recipe shows how to configure the Raspberry Pi so that it automatically mounts attached USB disk drives during the boot process.

The goal of this recipe is to mount the example disks at boot time with the same configuration that is used by the command pmount.

The first few steps of this recipe use the pmount and mount commands to discover the correct filesystem table configuration parameters for two example disk drives. Once the correct configuration parameters are discovered, the filesystem table configuration file (/etc/fstab) is updated so that the disks are mounted when the Raspberry Pi boots.

This recipe does not provide details on the meaning of each configuration parameter. Instead, the recipe reuses the same configuration that is used by the pmount command. More detail on the configuration parameters can be found in the man pages for the mount command.

After completing this recipe, the Raspberry Pi will mount USB disk drives at boot time with a configuration that is consistent with the pmount utility.

Getting ready

Here are the ingredients for this recipe:

- An initial setup or basic networking setup for the Raspberry Pi that has been powered on. You have also logged in as the user pi (see the recipes in *Chapter 1, Installation and Setup*, for how to boot and log in and the recipes in *Chapter 2, Administration*, for how to log in remotely).
- A Powered USB hub (recommended).
- At least one USB disk drive.

This recipe does not require the desktop GUI and could either be run from the text-based console or from within an LXTerminal.

If the Raspberry Pi's Secure Shell server is running, this recipe can be completed remotely using a Secure Shell client (see the recipe *Remote access (SSH)* in *Chapter 2, Administration*).

The examples in this recipe use two USB drives: a 128 MB flash drive and a 500 GB disk.

The pmount command should already be installed (see the recipe *Mounting USB disks*).

> Be careful! A broken /etc/fstab may prevent the system from booting. Make sure that you've tested the configuration before rebooting!

How to do it...

The steps to auto-mount USB disks at boot are as follows:

1. Log in to the Raspberry Pi either directly or remotely.
2. Use the pmount command to mount the 128 MB flash drive's primary partition /dev/sda1 in the /media directory at the mount point thumbdrive.
   ```
   pi@raspberrypi /media/xfer $ pmount /dev/sda1 thumbdrive
   ```
3. Use the pmount command to mount the 500 GB disk's primary partition /dev/sdb1 in the /media directory at the mount point bigdisk.
   ```
   pi@raspberrypi /media/xfer $ pmount /dev/sdb1 bigdisk
   ```
4. Show that the disks are mounted with the ls -l command.
   ```
   pi@raspberrypi ~ $ ls -l /media
   total 20
   drwxr-xr-x 6 pi pi  4096 May 30 12:23 bigdisk
   ```

```
drwx------ 4 pi pi 16384 Dec 31  1969 thumbdrive

pi@raspberrypi ~ $
```

5. Display the configuration used to mount the two disks with the `mount` command.

```
pi@raspberrypi ~ $ mount
```

6. The `mount` command displays the filesystem table, including the mount parameters needed for each disk (or disk partition).

```
/dev/root on / type ext4 (rw,noatime,data=ordered)

devtmpfs on /dev type devtmpfs (rw,relatime,size=494800k,nr_
inodes=123700,mode=755)

tmpfs on /run type tmpfs (rw,nosuid,noexec,relatime,size=99820k,mode=755)

tmpfs on /run/lock type tmpfs (rw,nosuid,nodev,noexec,relatime,size=5120k)

proc on /proc type proc (rw,nosuid,nodev,noexec,relatime)

sysfs on /sys type sysfs (rw,nosuid,nodev,noexec,relatime)

tmpfs on /run/shm type tmpfs (rw,nosuid,nodev,noexec,relatime,size=19962
0k)

devpts on /dev/pts type devpts (rw,nosuid,noexec,relatime,gid=5,mode=620,p
tmxmode=000)

/dev/mmcblk0p1 on /boot type vfat (rw,relatime,fmask=0022,dmask=0022,codep
age=437,iocharset=ascii,shortname=mixed,errors=remount-ro)

/dev/sda1 on /media/thumbdrive type vfat (rw,nosuid,nodev,noexec,relatime
,uid=1001,gid=1004,fmask=0177,dmask=0077,codepage=437,iocharset=iso8859-
1,shortname=mixed,quiet,utf8,errors=remount-ro)

/dev/sdb1 on /media/bigdisk type ext4 (rw,nosuid,nodev,noexec,relatime,err
ors=remount-ro,data=ordered)

pi@raspberrypi ~ $
```

7. After the disk configuration parameters have been displayed, use the `pumount` command to unmount the two disks.

```
pi@raspberrypi ~ $ pumount /media/thumbdrive
pi@raspberrypi ~ $ pumount /media/bigdisk

pi@raspberrypi ~ $ ls -l /media
total 0
```

8. Make a copy of the current filesystem configuration with the `cp` command. Files can only be created in (or copied into) the `/etc` directory by a privileged user (so use `sudo`).

```
pi@raspberrypi ~ $ sudo cp /etc/fstab /etc/fstab.orig
```

9. Use the `vi` command to edit the filesystem configuration table `fstab`.

    pi@raspberrypi ~ $ **sudo vi /etc/fstab**

10. The vi editor displays the contents of the `/etc/fstab` configuration file. Instructions for using the editor can be found in the vi man pages. See the recipe *Reading the built-in documentation* in *Chapter 2, Administration.*

    ```
    proc                /proc         proc    defaults           0    0
    /dev/mmcblk0p1  /boot         vfat    defaults           0    2
    /dev/mmcblk0p2  /             ext4    defaults,noatime  0    1
    # a swapfile is not a swap partition, so no using swapon|off from here on,
    use   dphys-swapfile swap[on|off]   for that
    ~

    ~

    ~

    "/etc/fstab" 4 lines, 322 characters
    ```

11. Add the configuration parameters for each disk to the bottom of the configuration file. The parameters for each disk can be copied from the output of the `mount` command.

    > Each disk configuration should be a single line with fields separated by spaces or tabs. The example does not fit the page width.

    ```
    proc                /proc         proc    defaults           0    0
    /dev/mmcblk0p1  /boot         vfat    defaults           0    2
    /dev/mmcblk0p2  /             ext4    defaults,noatime  0    1
    # a swapfile is not a swap partition, so no using swapon|off from here on,
    use   dphys-swapfile swap[on|off]   for that
    /dev/sda1          /media/thumbdrive  vfat   rw,nosuid,nodev,noexec,relatime,u
    id=1001,gid=1004,fmask=0177,dmask=0077,codepage=437,iocharset=iso8859-1,sh
    ortname=mixed,quiet,utf8,errors=remount-ro 0 2
    /dev/sdb1          /media/bigdisk  ext4      rw,nosuid,nodev,noexec,relatime,er
    rors=remount-ro,data=ordered 0 2
    ~

    ~

    "/etc/fstab" 6 lines, 605 characters
    ```

12. After entering the configuration parameters for each disk, save the file and exit the editor.

    pi@raspberrypi ~ $

13. Before the disks can be mounted, they need to have mount points. Create mount points using the `mkdir` command.

```
pi@raspberrypi ~ $ sudo mkdir /etc/thumbdrive
pi@raspberrypi ~ $ sudo mkdir /etc/bigdisk

pi@raspberrypi ~ $ ls -l /media
total 8
drwxr-xr-x 2 root root 4096 Jul 19 19:14 bigdisk
drwxr-xr-x 2 root root 4096 Jul 19 19:15 thumbdrive

pi@raspberrypi ~ $ ls -l /media/thumbrioe/
total 0

pi@raspberrypi ~ $ ls -l /media/bigdisk/
total 0
```

14. Use the `mount -a` command to mount all of the configured disks.

```
pi@raspberrypi ~ $ sudo mount -a

pi@raspberrypi ~ $ ls -l /media
total 20
drwxr-xr-x 6 pi staff   4096 May 30 12:23 bigdisk
drwx------ 4 pi pi     16384 Dec 31  1969 thumbdrive

pi@raspberrypi ~ $ ls -l /media/bigdisk/
total 24
drwxrwsr-x 11 pi pi  4096 Apr 26  2012 archive
drwxrws--- 20 pi pi  4096 Jan 23  2010 Live
drwx------  2 pi pi 16384 Oct  4  2010 lost+found

pi@raspberrypi ~ $ ls -l /media//thumbdrive/
total 71278
-rw------- 1 pi pi 72988392 Mar  7 00:34 docker.tgz

pi@raspberrypi ~ $
```

15. Use the `reboot` command to reboot the system, then log back in and use the `ls -l` command to display the contents of the two mount points `/media/thumdrive` and `/media/bigdisk`.

```
pi@raspberrypi ~ $ sudo reboot

Broadcast message from root@raspberrypi (pts/2) (Sun Jul 19 18:40:55
2015):
The system is going down for reboot NOW!
pi@raspberrypi ~ $ Connection to 192.168.2.7 closed by remote host.
Connection to 192.168.2.7 closed.

golden-macbook:~ golden$ ssh pi@raspberrypi.local
Linux raspberrypi 3.18.11-v7+ #781 SMP PREEMPT Tue Apr 21 18:07:59 BST
2015 armv7l


The programs included with the Debian GNU/Linux system are free software;
the exact distribution terms for each program are described in the
individual files in /usr/share/doc/*/copyright.

Debian GNU/Linux comes with ABSOLUTELY NO WARRANTY, to the extent
permitted by applicable law.
Last login: Sun Jul 19 18:44:50 2015 from 192.168.2.1

pi@raspberrypi ~ $ ls -l /media
total 20
drwxr-xr-x 6 pi staff   4096 May 30 12:23 bigdisk
drwx------ 4 pi pi     16384 Dec 31  1969 thumbdrive

pi@raspberrypi ~ $ ls -l /media/bigdisk
total 24
drwxrwsr-x 11 pi staff  4096 Apr 26  2012 archive
drwxrws--- 20 pi staff  4096 Jan 23  2010 Live
drwx------  2 pi staff 16384 Oct  4  2010 lost+found

pi@raspberrypi ~ $ ls -l /media/thumbdrive
```

```
total 71278
-rw------- 1 pi pi 72988392 Mar  7 00:34 docker.tgz


pi@raspberrypi ~ $
```

16. The disks are now mounted automatically at boot!

How it works...

After logging in to the Raspberry Pi, two example disks are mounted using the personal mount command, pmount (see the recipe *Mounting USB disks* for more information on the pmount command).

The 128 MB flash drive (/dev/sda1) is mounted at /media/thumbdrive.

The 500 GB disk (/dev/sdb1) is mounted at /media/bigdisk.

The system mount command is used to display the filesystem table configuration parameters of all the disks attached to the Raspberry Pi including the bigdisk and the thumbdrive.

After the configuration parameters are displayed, the two USB disks (/dev/sda1 and /dev/sdb1) are unmounted using the pumount command. The /media directory is once again empty.

Before any changes are made to the filesystem configuration, the cp command is used to create a backup copy of /etc/fstab.

The vi editor is then used to add the configuration parameters for each disk to the bottom of the filesystem table configuration file (/etc/fstab).

Before the disks can be mounted, they first need to have mount points within the filesystem. The mkdir command is used to create a mount point for each of the USB disks at /media/ thumbdrive and /media/bigdisk.

Once the mount points have been created, the mount all disks command, mount -a, is used to mount the example disks.

After the disks are mounted, the contents of the disks are displayed by using the ls -l command.

Everything looks good, so the Raspberry Pi is rebooted using the reboot command.

When the Raspberry Pi is finished rebooting, the user logs back in to the Raspberry Pi using the ssh command.

Finally, the `ls -l` command is used once again to list the contents of the two disks' mount points, `/media/thumbdrive` and `/media/bigdisk`.

The disks have been mounted successfully during boot!

There's more...

We will look at how we can recover from an error.

Error recovery

If the `mount` command displays an error, edit the `/etc/fstab` file again and look for typos and extra spaces. Correct any errors and try again.

If there are still errors, replace the configuration file with its original version using the following command:

```
pi@raspberrypi ~ $ sudo cp -f /etc/fstab.orig /etc/fstab
```

The fstab file format

Each line of the `fstab` configuration file is used to configure where one disk (or disk partition) is mounted. Each line has six fields separated by blanks (or tabs):

  ▶ The first field is the device file. The device file is assigned automatically to each disk and can be discovered using the `fdisk -l` command (see the previous recipe). The 128 MB `thumbdrive` has one partition; its mountable device file is `/dev/sda1`. The 500 GB disk also has one partition with the mountable device file `/dev/sdb1`.

  ▶ The second field is the mount point. Mount points can be located anywhere in the filesystem; however, current convention is to locate them in the `/media` directory. The mount point for the 128 MB flash drive is `/media/thumbdrive`. The mount point for the 500 GB disk is `/media/bigdisk`.

  ▶ The third field is the type of filesystem on the device. The 128 MB flash drive has the `vfat` filesystem and the 500 GB drive has an `ext4` filesystem.

  ▶ The fourth field is a comma-separated list of configuration parameters. They should be copied from the parenthetical list of parameters in the output of the `mount` command. There should be no spaces in this field and no parentheses.

  ▶ The fifth field is a dump flag. It is usually zero (`0`), indicating that the filesystem does not need to be dumped. Both disks have `0` in this field.

  ▶ The sixth field selects the boot phase in which the disk will be mounted. The disk mounted as the root filesystem (`/`) is mounted in phase one; all other disks should be mounted in phase two. The example disks will not be mounted as the root filesystem, so they both have `2` in this field.

For the 128 MB flash drive, the configuration parameters are as follows:

- ▶ **The device file**: `/dev/sda1`
- ▶ **The mount point**: `/media/thumbdrive`
- ▶ **The filesystem type**: `vfat`
- ▶ **The mount options**: `rw,nosuid,nodev,noexec,relatime,uid=1001,gid=100
  4,fmask=0177,dmask=0077,codepage=437,iocharset=iso8859-1,shortn
  ame=mixed,quiet,utf8,errors=remount-ro`
- ▶ **Dump option**: (0)
- ▶ **Boot phase**: (2)

For the 500 GB USB disk, the configuration parameters are as follows:

- ▶ **The device file**: `/dev/sdb1`
- ▶ **The mount point**: `/media/bigdisk`
- ▶ **The filesystem type**: `ext4`
- ▶ **The mount options**: `rw,nosuid,nodev,noexec,relatime,errors=remount-
  ro,data=ordered`
- ▶ **Dump option**: (0)
- ▶ **Boot phase**: (2)

See also

- ▶ **fstab – static information about the filesystems** (`http://manpages.debian.
  net/cgi-bin/man.cgi?query=fstab`): The Debian manual page for the `fstab`
  command has detailed information about the command and its options.

Auto-mounting a shared folder at boot

The goal of this recipe is to mount a shared folder from another computer at boot time.

The previous recipe showed how to configure `/etc/fstab` for mounting USB disks. This recipe shows how a similar configuration can be used to auto-mount a Windows share at boot time (or any other set of files shared using the SMB (CIFS) protocol).

At home or at the office, it is common for a local network to have some form of **Networked Attached Storage** (**NAS**) available to network users as shared folders using the SMB (CIFS) protocol. This recipe shows how the Raspberry Pi can be configured to automatically mount a shared folder at boot time.

After completing this recipe, a shared folder from another computer will be attached to the root filesystem every time the Raspberry Pi boots.

Getting ready

Here are the ingredients:

- ▶ An initial setup or basic networking setup for the Raspberry Pi that has been powered on. You have also logged in as the user pi (see the recipes in *Chapter 1, Installation and Setup*, for how to boot and log in and the recipes in *Chapter 2, Administration*, for how to log in remotely).
- ▶ A network connection.
- ▶ A client PC connected to the same network as the Raspberry Pi.

This recipe does not require the desktop GUI and could either be run from the text-based console or from within an LXTerminal.

If the Raspberry Pi's Secure Shell server is running, this recipe can be completed remotely using a Secure Shell client (see the recipe *Remote access (SSH)* in *Chapter 2, Administration*).

The examples in this recipe will connect the Raspberry Pi to a home file-sharing device named terragolden. This file server has several shares available, including backups. The shared folder is configured for guest access so no username or password is required.

Configuration for other computers using the SMB (CIFS) protocol will be similar.

How to do it...

The steps for auto-mounting shared folders at boot are as follows:

1. Log in to the Raspberry Pi either directly or remotely.

2. Use the cp command to make a backup copy of the /etc/fstab configuration file named /etc/fstab.orig. Files can only be created in (or copied into) the /etc directory by a privileged user (so use sudo).

   pi@raspberrypi ~ $ **sudo cp /etc/fstab /etc/fstab.orig**

3. Execute the command:

   nano /etc/fstab

   Edit the filesystem configuration table fstab. The file fstab may only be modified by a privileged user (use sudo).

4. Use the vi command to edit the filesystem configuration table fstab.

   pi@raspberrypi ~ $ **sudo vi /etc/fstab**

5. The vi editor displays the contents of the /etc/fstab configuration file. Instructions for using the editor can be found in the vi man pages. See the recipe *Reading the built-in documentation* in *Chapter 2, Administration*.

```
proc                /proc          proc     defaults         0      0
/dev/mmcblk0p1  /boot          vfat     defaults         0      2
/dev/mmcblk0p2  /              ext4     defaults,noatime 0      1
# a swapfile is not a swap partition, so no using swapon|off from here on,
use  dphys-swapfile swap[on|off]  for that
//terragolden/backups /media/backups cifs guest,uid=pi 0 2
~

~

"/etc/fstab" 4 lines, 322 characters
```

6. For the example home file server, the configuration is as follows:

   ❑ The network location is //terragolden/backups

   ❑ The mount point is /media/backups

   ❑ The filesystem type is cifs

   ❑ The mount options are guest,uid=pi

   ❑ The dump option is 0

   ❑ The boot phase is 2

7. After entering the configuration parameters for file share, save the file and exit the editor.

   ```
   pi@raspberrypi ~ $
   ```

8. Before the file share can be mounted, it needs to have a mount point. Create a mount point at /media/backups using the mkdir command.

   ```
   pi@raspberrypi ~ $ sudo mkdir /etc/backups

   pi@raspberrypi ~ $ ls -l /media
   total 4
   drwxr-xr-x 2 root root 4096 Jul 19 19:15 backups

   pi@raspberrypi ~ $ ls -l /media/thumbdrive/
   total 0

   pi@raspberrypi ~ $ ls -l /media/bigdisk/
   total 0
   ```

9. Use the `mount -a` command to mount all of the configured disks.

    ```
    pi@raspberrypi ~ $ sudo mount -a

    pi@raspberrypi ~ $ ls -l /media
    total 0
    drwxrwxrwx 14 pi 254 0 Jul 24  2017 backups

    pi@raspberrypi ~ $ ls -l /media/backups
    total 3072
    drwxrwxrwx 44 pi nogroup      0 Oct 28  2011 0 - live music
    drwxr-xr-x  9 pi nogroup      0 Oct 26  2011 1 - family video
    drwxr-xr-x  4 pi nogroup      0 Oct  1  2011 3 - golden studios
    drwxrwxrwx  5 pi nogroup      0 Mar 29  2012 8 - software
    drwxrwxrwx  2 pi nogroup      0 May 19  2011 9 - virtual machines
    drwxrwxrwx  8 pi nogroup      0 May 11  2011 Alex
    drwxrwxrwx 21 pi nogroup      0 Jan 20  2012 Barbara
    drwxrwxrwx  4 pi nogroup      0 Feb 19 19:53 Michael
    drwxrwxrwx  2 pi nogroup      0 May 19  2011 Patrick
    drwxr-xr-x 30 pi nogroup      0 Apr  2  2012 Richard
    drwxr-xr-x  4 pi nogroup      0 Dec 10  2011 xfer

    pi@raspberrypi ~ $
    ```

10. Use the `reboot` command to reboot the system.

    ```
    pi@raspberrypi ~ $ sudo reboot
    Broadcast message from root@raspberrypi (pts/2) (Sun Jul 19 18:40:55
    2015):
    The system is going down for reboot NOW!
    ```

11. Log back in to the Raspberry Pi and then use the `ls -l` command to display the contents of the file share /media/backups.

    ```
    pi@raspberrypi ~ $ ls -l /media/backups
    total 3072
    drwxrwxrwx 44 pi nogroup      0 Oct 28  2011 0 - live music
    drwxr-xr-x  9 pi nogroup      0 Oct 26  2011 1 - family video
    drwxr-xr-x  4 pi nogroup      0 Oct  1  2011 3 - golden studios
    drwxrwxrwx  5 pi nogroup      0 Mar 29  2012 8 - software
    ```

```
drwxrwxrwx  2 pi nogroup       0 May 19  2011 9 - virtual machines
drwxrwxrwx  8 pi nogroup       0 May 11  2011 Alex
drwxrwxrwx 21 pi nogroup       0 Jan 20  2012 Barbara
drwxrwxrwx  4 pi nogroup       0 Feb 19 19:53 Michael
drwxrwxrwx  2 pi nogroup       0 May 19  2011 Patrick
drwxr-xr-x 30 pi nogroup       0 Apr  2  2012 Richard
drwxr-xr-x  4 pi nogroup       0 Dec 10  2011 xfer

pi@raspberrypi ~ $
```

12. The remote file share is now mounted automatically at boot!

How it works...

After logging in to the Raspberry Pi, a backup is made of the filesystem table configuration file `/etc/fstab`. The configuration file is copied to `/etc/fstab.orig`.

The vi editor is used to add the configuration parameters for the shared folder to the bottom of the configuration file.

The configuration used in the example is as follows:

- ▸ The first field is the network location: `//terragolden/xfer`. The second field is the mount point: `/media/backups`.
- ▸ The third field is the type of filesystem: `cifs`. This is the protocol used by the file server to share folders.
- ▸ The fourth field is a comma-separated list of options: `guest,uid=pi`. Additional options include `user=` and `password=` for specifying the username and password when a shared folder is protected.
- ▸ The fifth field is a dump flag. It is set to zero (`0`), indicating that the shared folder does not need to be dumped at boot.
- ▸ The sixth field selects the boot phase in which the disk will be mounted. The disk mounted as the root filesystem (`/`) is mounted in phase one; all other disks should be mounted in phase two (`2`).

Once the filesystem table configuration file (`/etc/fstab`) has been updated, the configuration is tested before rebooting the system. The `mount all disks` command, `mount -a`, is used to mount the example disks.

If there is no error, the system can be rebooted.

If the mount command displays an error, edit the `/etc/fstab` file again and look for typos and extra spaces. Correct any errors and try again.

If there are still errors, replace the configuration file with its original version using the following command:

```
pi@raspberrypi ~ $ sudo cp -f /etc/fstab.orig /etc/fstab
```

See also

> ▶ **Network Attached Storage** (http://en.wikipedia.org/wiki/Network_Attached_Storage): Here is an interesting Wikipedia article on **Network Attached Storage** (**NAS**).

Creating a file server (Samba)

This recipe shows how the Raspberry Pi can be configured to become a file server on the local network.

The Raspberry Pi, with attached file storage, functions well as a file server. Such a file server could be used as a central location for sharing files and documents, for storing backups of other computers, and for storing large media files, such as photo, music, and video files.

This recipe installs and configures samba and samba-common-bin. The Samba software distribution package, samba, contains a server for the SMB (CIFS) protocol used by modern computers for setting up *shared drives* or *shared folders*. The samba-common-bin package contains a small collection of utilities for managing access to shared files.

The recipe includes setting a file sharing password for the logged-in user and providing read/write access to the files in the user's home directory. However, it does not set up a new file share or show how to share a USB disk. The next recipe shows how to do that.

After completing this recipe, other computers on the local network can exchange files with the Raspberry Pi.

Getting ready

Here are the ingredients for this recipe:

> ▶ An initial setup or basic networking setup for the Raspberry Pi that has been powered on. You have also logged in as the user pi (see the recipes in *Chapter 1, Installation and Setup*, for how to boot and log in and the recipes in *Chapter 2, Administration*, for how to log in remotely).
>
> ▶ A network connection.
>
> ▶ A client PC connected to the same network as the Raspberry Pi.

This recipe does not require the desktop GUI and could either be run from the text-based console or from within an LXTerminal.

If the Raspberry Pi's Secure Shell server is running, this recipe can be completed remotely using a Secure Shell client (see the recipe *Remote access (SSH)* in *Chapter 2, Administration*).

How to do it...

The steps to creating a file server are as follows:

1. Log in to the Raspberry Pi either directly or remotely.

2. Use the `apt-get install` command to install the software packages samba and samba-common-bin.

```
pi@raspberrypi ~ $ sudo apt-get install -y samba samba-common-bin

Reading package lists... Done
Building dependency tree
Reading state information... Done
The following extra packages will be installed:
  tdb-tools
Suggested packages:
  openbsd-inetd inet-superserver smbldap-tools ldb-tools ctdb
The following NEW packages will be installed:
  samba samba-common-bin tdb-tools
0 upgraded, 3 newly installed, 0 to remove and 0 not upgraded.
Need to get 6,119 kB of archives.
After this operation, 36.1 MB of additional disk space will be used.
Get:1 http://mirrordirector.raspbian.org/raspbian/ wheezy/main samba armhf
2:3.6.6-6+deb7u5 [3,356 kB]
Get:2 http://mirrordirector.raspbian.org/raspbian/ wheezy/main samba-
common-bin armhf 2:3.6.6-6+deb7u5 [2,737 kB]
Get:3 http://mirrordirector.raspbian.org/raspbian/ wheezy/main tdb-tools
armhf 1.2.10-2 [25.9 kB]
Fetched 6,119 kB in 2s (2,236 kB/s)
Preconfiguring packages ...
Selecting previously unselected package samba.
(Reading database ... 89348 files and directories currently installed.)
Unpacking samba (from .../samba_2%3a3.6.6-6+deb7u5_armhf.deb) ...
Selecting previously unselected package samba-common-bin.
Unpacking samba-common-bin (from .../samba-common-bin_2%3a3.6.6-6+deb7u5_
armhf.deb) ...
```

```
Selecting previously unselected package tdb-tools.
Unpacking tdb-tools (from .../tdb-tools_1.2.10-2_armhf.deb) ...
Processing triggers for man-db ...
Setting up samba (2:3.6.6-6+deb7u5) ...
Generating /etc/default/samba...
Adding group `sambashare' (GID 110) ...
Done.
update-alternatives: using /usr/bin/smbstatus.samba3 to provide /usr/bin/
smbstatus (smbstatus) in auto mode
[ ok ] Starting Samba daemons: nmbd smbd.
Setting up samba-common-bin (2:3.6.6-6+deb7u5) ...
update-alternatives: using /usr/bin/nmblookup.samba3 to provide /usr/bin/
nmblookup (nmblookup) in auto mode
update-alternatives: using /usr/bin/net.samba3 to provide /usr/bin/net
(net) in auto mode
update-alternatives: using /usr/bin/testparm.samba3 to provide /usr/bin/
testparm (testparm) in auto mode
Setting up tdb-tools (1.2.10-2) ...
update-alternatives: using /usr/bin/tdbbackup.tdbtools to provide /usr/
bin/tdbbackup (tdbbackup) in auto mode


pi@raspberrypi ~ $
```

3. Use the `vi` command to edit the Samba configuration file (`/etc/samba/smb.conf`).

   pi@raspberrypi ~ $ **sudo vi /etc/samba/smb.conf**

4. The vi editor displays the contents of the `/etc/samba/smb.conf` file. Instructions for using the editor can be found in the vi man pages; see the recipe *Reading the built-in documentation* in *Chapter 2, Administration*.

```
#
# Sample configuration file for the Samba suite for Debian GNU/Linux.
#
#
# This is the main Samba configuration file. You should read the
# smb.conf(5) manual page in order to understand the options listed
# here. Samba has a huge number of configurable options most of which
# are not shown in this example
#
"/etc/samba/smb.conf" 333 lines, 12173 characters
```

5. Change the security = user line. Uncomment the line. (Remove the hash, #, from the beginning of the line.)

```
# "security = user" is always a good idea. This will require a Unix
account
# in this server for every user accessing the server. See
# /usr/share/doc/samba-doc/htmldocs/Samba3-HOWTO/ServerType.html
# in the samba-doc package for details.
security = user
```

6. Change the read only = yes line to be read only = no.

```
[homes]
    comment = Home Directories
    browseable = no


# By default, the home directories are exported read-only. Change the
# next parameter to 'no' if you want to be able to write to them.
    read only = no
```

7. Save (:w) and exit (:q) the vi editor.

8. Use the /etc/init.d/samba initialization script to tell the Samba server to reload its configuration file.

```
pi@raspberrypi ~ $ sudo /etc/init.d/samba reload
[ ok ] Reloading /etc/samba/smb.conf: smbd only.
```

9. Use the smbpasswd -a command to create an SMB (CIFS) password for the logged-in user, pi. Enter the password (twice).

```
pi@raspberrypi ~ $ sudo smbpasswd -a pi
New SMB password:
Retype new SMB password:
Added user pi.


pi@raspberrypi ~ $
```

10. The Raspberry Pi is now accessible as a file server!

11. From a Windows computer, use **Map network drive** to mount the Raspberry Pi as a network disk.

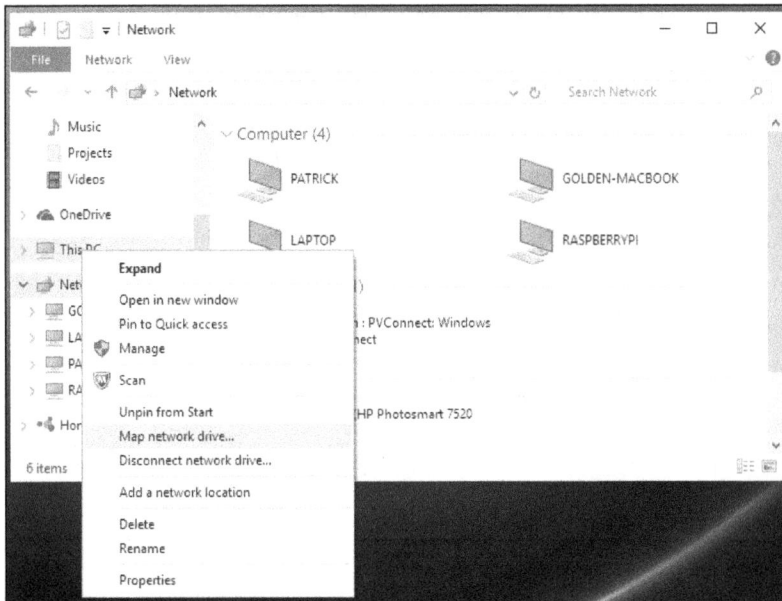

The above screenshot shows the mapping of a network drive to the Raspberry Pi on Windows 7.

12. Enter the UNC address \\raspberrypi\pi as the network folder. Choose an appropriate drive letter. The following example uses the R: drive. Select **Connect using different credentials**. Click on **Finish**.

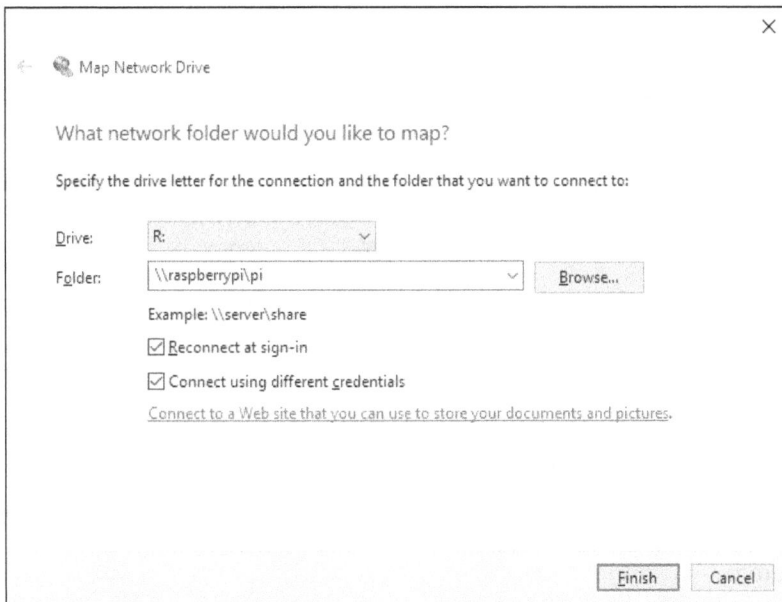

The above screenshot finishes mapping a network drive to the Raspberry Pi.

13. Log in using the newly configured SMB (CIFS) password (from step 7).

In the screenshot, a dialog box is displayed for logging in to the Raspberry Pi with the SMB (CIFS) username and password.

14. The Raspberry Pi is now accessible as a Windows share! Only the home directory of the user `pi` is accessible at this point. The next recipe configures a USB disk for use as a shared drive.

How it works...

After logging in to the Raspberry Pi, the recipe installs two software distribution packages: samba and samba-common-bin, using the `apt-get install` command.

The samba package contains an implementation of the **Server Message Block (SMB)** protocol (also known as the **Common Internet File System, CIFS**). For sharing files and printers, Microsoft Windows computers use the SMB (CIFS) protocol.

After the packages are installed, the Samba configuration file `/etc/samba/smb.conf` is updated. The file is updated to turn on user security (`security = user`) and to enable writing files to user home directories (`readonly = no`).

After the configuration file is updated, the Samba server is told to reload its configuration using the server's initialization file, `/etc/init.d/samba`.

At this point, the Raspberry Pi should be visible to other machines on the local network that are using the SMB protocol. However, the passwords for the authorized users have not yet been configured.

The `smbpasswd` command is used to add (`-a`) the user `pi` to the list of users authorized to share files with the Raspberry Pi using the SMB protocol. The passwords for file sharing are managed separately from the login passwords used to log in to the Raspberry Pi either directly or remotely.

After the password has been added for the user `pi`, the Raspberry Pi should be accessible from any machine on the local network that is configured for the SMB protocol.

The last steps of the recipe configure access to the Raspberry Pi from a Windows 7 PC using a mapped network drive. The UNC name for the file share, `\\raspberrypi\pi`, could also be used to access the share directly from Windows Explorer.

There's more...

This is a very simple configuration for sharing files. It enables file sharing for users with a login to the Raspberry Pi. However, it only permits the files in the user home directories to be shared. The next recipe describes how to add a new file share.

In addition to the SMB protocol server `smbd`, the Samba software distribution package also contains a NetBIOS name server, `nmbd`. The NetBIOS name server provides naming services to computers using the SMB protocol. The `nmbd` server broadcasts the configured name of the Raspberry Pi, `raspberrypi`, to other computers on the local network.

In addition to file sharing, a Samba server could also be used as a **Primary Domain Controller** (**PDC**)—a central network server that is used to provide logins and security for all computers on a LAN. More information on using the samba package as a PDC can be found in the following links.

See also

- **Samba (software)** (`http://en.wikipedia.org/wiki/Samba_(software)`): A Wikipedia article on the Samba software suite.

- **nmbd – NetBIOS over IP naming service** (`http://manpages.debian.net/cgi-bin/man.cgi?query=nmbd`): The Debian manual page for `nmbd`.

- **samba – a Windows SMB/CIFS file server for Unix** (`http://manpages.debian.net/cgi-bin/man.cgi?query=samba`): The Debian man page for samba.

- **smb.conf – the configuration file for the Samba suite** (`http://manpages.debian.net/cgi-bin/man.cgi?query=smb.conf`): The Debian manual page for `smb.conf`.

- **smbd – server to provide SMB/CIFS services to clients** (`http://manpages.debian.net/cgi-bin/man.cgi?query=smbd`): The Debian manual page for `smbd`.

- ▶ **smbpasswd – change a user's SMB password** (`http://manpages.debian.net/cgi-bin/man.cgi?query=smbpasswd`): The Debian manual page for `smbpasswd`.

- ▶ **System Initialization** (`http://www.debian.org/doc/manuals/debian-reference/ch04.en.html`): The *Debian Reference Manual* article on system initialization.

- ▶ **Samba.org** (`http://www.samba.org`): The Samba software website.

Sharing an attached USB disk (Samba)

This recipe extends the default Samba configuration to include sharing a USB disk.

The previous recipe showed how to install Samba and set up basic file sharing. However, the Samba configuration used only shared files that are in the user's home directory. Other directories on the Raspberry Pi are not yet accessible via the SMB (CIFS) protocol.

This recipe extends the Samba configuration used in the previous recipe to include a new file share definition that points to a USB hard disk mounted on the Raspberry Pi.

After completing this recipe, the Raspberry Pi can be used as a file server for any computer that shares its files via the SMB (CIFS) protocol (for example, Windows, Mac, and Linux computers).

Getting ready

Ingredients:

- ▶ An initial setup or basic networking setup for the Raspberry Pi that has been powered on. You have also logged in as the user `pi` (see the recipes in *Chapter 1, Installation and Setup*, for how to boot and log in and the recipes in *Chapter 2, Administration*, for how to log in remotely).

- ▶ A network connection (optional).

- ▶ A client PC connected to the same network as the Raspberry Pi (optional).

- ▶ A powered USB hub (recommended).

- ▶ At least one USB disk drive (the example uses a 500 GB USB disk).

This recipe does not require the desktop GUI and could either be run from the text-based console or from within an LXTerminal.

If the Raspberry Pi's Secure Shell server is running and it has a network connection, this recipe can be completed remotely using a Secure Shell client (see the preceding).

The example in this recipe uses a USB disk mounted at `/media/bigdisk` (see the recipe *Mounting USB disks* at the beginning of this chapter).

The example in this recipe also includes test access to the new file share from another computer on the local network, golden-macbook.

The Raspberry Pi should already have Samba installed (see the previous recipe).

How to do it...

The steps for sharing an attached USB disk are as follows:

1. Log in to the Raspberry Pi either directly or remotely.

2. Use the `ls -l` command to list the disk drives that have been mounted in the `/media` directory.

   ```
   pi@raspberrypi ~ $ ls -l /media
   total 4
   drwxr-xr-x  6 pi staff 4096 May 30 12:23 bigdisk

   pi@raspberrypi ~ $
   ```

3. Use the vi editor to edit the Samba configuration file, `/etc/samba/smb.conf`.

   ```
   pi@raspberrypi ~ $ vi /etc/samba/smb.conf
   ```

4. The vi editor displays the contents of the configuration file. Instructions for using the editor can be found in the vi man pages; see the recipe *Reading the built-in documentation* in *Chapter 2, Administration*.

   ```
   #
   # Sample configuration file for the Samba suite for Debian GNU/Linux.
   #
   #
   # This is the main Samba configuration file. You should read the
   # smb.conf(5) manual page in order to understand the options listed
   "/etc/samba/smb.conf" 333 lines, 12173 characters
   ```

5. Add a new share configuration to the bottom of the file:

   ```
   [bigdisk]
           comment = A really big disk!
           path = /media/bigdisk
           valid users = pi
           admin users = pi
           read only = No

   #======================= Share Definitions =======================

   [bigdisk]
   ```

```
    comment = A really big disk!
    path = /media/bigdisk
    valid users = pi
    admin users = pi
    read only = no


[homes]
    comment = Home Directories
    browseable = no


"/etc/samba/smb.conf" 340 lines, 12294 characters
```

6. Save and exit the vi editor.

7. Use the `/etc/init.d/samba reload` command to tell the Samba server to reload its configuration file.

```
pi@raspberrypi ~ $ sudo /etc/init.d/samba reload
[ ok ] Reloading /etc/samba/smb.conf: smbd only.


pi@raspberrypi ~ $
```

8. The file share `\\raspberrypi\bigdisk` is now accessible from the local network! Connect as the user `pi`.

```
golden-macbook:~ golden$ smbutil view //pi@raspberrypi
Password for 192.168.2.7:
Share                                Type    Comments
-------------------------------
print$                               Disk    Printer Drivers
pi                                   Disk    Home Directories
IPC$                                 Pipe    IPC Service (raspberrypi
server)
bigdisk                              Disk    A really big disk!


4 shares listed


golden-macbook:~ golden$
```

How it works...

After logging in to the Raspberry Pi, the recipe lists the disks that have been mounted in the /media directory. This is the directory used by the Raspberry Pi desktop (GUI) when auto-mounting USB disks. It is also the directory used by the pmount command (and the recipe auto-mounting USB disks at boot).

Then, the vi editor is used to modify the Samba configuration file, smb.conf. The configuration for a new share [bigdisk] is added to the file.

- ▸ [bigdisk] starts a new section in the config file and sets the name of the share: bigdisk

- ▸ Comment = A really big disk! defines a comment to display when users browse the share from another computer

- ▸ Path = /media/bigdisk is the location of the files on the Raspberry Pi

- ▸ valid users = pi declares that only the user pi can access the files

- ▸ admin users = pi gives the user pi administrative access to the files

- ▸ read only = no allows files to be written to and deleted from the share

After the configuration is saved and the vi editor has been exited, the Samba server is told to reload its configuration with the command /etc/init.d/samba reload.

Once the configuration file is reloaded, the Samba server is ready to share files from the /media/bigdata directory over the file share, bigdata, at the UNC address \\ raspberrypi\bigdata.

Finally, the smbutil command is used on another computer (golden-macbook) to validate that the new bigdisk share is accessible from the local network.

There's more...

The files in the new share are protected and require that users on other computers connect to the share using the Samba password of the pi user.

> Remember: the Samba password of a user is maintained separately from the login password.
>
> Use the smbpasswd command to create and manage Samba passwords (see the previous recipe, *Creating a file server for an example*).

5
Advanced Networking

In this chapter, we will cover:

- ▶ Configuring a static IP address
- ▶ Creating a firewall with `ufw`
- ▶ Remote access to a desktop session (`xrdp`)
- ▶ Remote access to the monitor (`x11vnc`)
- ▶ Installing a web server (`apache`, `lighttpd`, `nginx`)
- ▶ Installing a wiki (`mediawiki`)
- ▶ Creating a wireless access point with `hostapd`
- ▶ Installing a network trace utility
- ▶ Installing a network protocol analyzer
- ▶ Enabling the IPv6 network protocol

Introduction

The advanced networking recipes in this chapter are not specific to the Raspberry Pi. However, they demonstrate some of the advanced capabilities of the Raspberry Pi.

The recipes in this chapter should generally work with any Linux computer. The installation instructions, however, are specific to Linux operating systems that are Debian based, like the Raspbian Linux distribution used in this book.

After completing the recipes in this chapter, you will have configured a static IP address for your Raspberry Pi; learned to protect your Raspberry Pi with a firewall; connected to the Raspberry Pi desktop remotely; installed a web server and a wiki; set up a wireless access point; and analyzed network packets.

Configuring a static IP address

This recipe configures a Raspberry Pi so that it has a static IP address.

A static IP address, unlike the dynamic addresses provided by a **DHCP (Dynamic Host Configuration Protocol**) server, does not change. Network servers on a wired network connection (for example, web servers, wikis, and wireless access points) generally have static IP addresses to provide a consistent telephone-number-like reference for use by its network clients (for example, web browsers, mobile phones, and other Internet devices). Servers that have a static IP address are easier to find.

After completing this recipe, you will be able to configure a static network IP address.

Getting ready

Ingredients:

An Initial Setup or Basic Networking setup for the Raspberry Pi that has been powered on. You have also logged in as the user `pi`
(see the recipes in *Chapter 1, Installation and Setup* for how to boot and log in and the recipes in *Chapter 2, Administration* for how to log in remotely).

This recipe does not require the desktop GUI and could either be run from the text-based console or from within an `LXTerminal`.

If the Raspberry Pi's Secure Shell server is running, this recipe can be completed remotely using a Secure Shell client.

How to do it...

The steps to configuring a static IP address are:

1. Log in to the Raspberry Pi either directly or remotely.

2. Use the `hostname -I` command to display the Raspberry Pi's current IP address.

    ```
    pi@raspberrypi ~ $ hostname -I
    192.168.2.13

    pi@raspberrypi ~ $
    ```

3. Use the output of the `route` command filtered through the `awk` command to determine the IP address of the default network gateway.

```
pi@raspberrypi ~ $ route -n | awk '/^0/ { print $2 }'
192.168.2.1

pi@raspberrypi ~ $
```

Use the output of the route command filtered through the awk command to determine the network mask for the local network.

```
pi@raspberrypi ~ $ route -n | awk '/^[1-9]/ { print $3 }'
255.255.255.0

pi@raspberrypi ~ $
```

4. Use the `vi` command to edit the network interface configuration file (`/etc/network/interface`).

```
pi@raspberrypi ~ $ sudo vi /etc/network/interfaces
```

5. The `vi` editor displays the contents of the configuration file. Instructions for using the editor can be found in the `vi` manpages (see the recipe *Reading the built-in documentation* in *Chapter 2, Administration*).

```
auto lo
iface lo inet loopback

auto eth0
allow-hotplug eth0
iface eth0 inet manual

auto wlan0
allow-hotplug wlan0
iface wlan0 inet manual
wpa-conf /etc/wpa_supplicant/wpa_supplicant.conf

auto wlan1
allow-hotplug wlan1
iface wlan1 inet manual
wpa-conf /etc/wpa_supplicant/wpa_supplicant.conf

~
~
"/etc/network/interfaces" 17 lines, 295 characters
```

6. Change the word **manual** at the end of the line starting with `iface eth0` to `static`.

   ```
   iface eth0 inet static
   ```

7. Add the following lines after the line starting with `iface eth0` using the current IP address (`192.168.2.13`), the default network gateway (`192.168.2.1`), and network mask (`255.255.255.0`) from steps 2, 3 and 4:

   ```
       address 192.168.2.13
       netmask 255.255.255.0
       gateway 192.168.2.1
   ```

8. After editing, the file should look something like this:

   ```
   auto lo
   iface lo inet loopback

   auto eth0
   allow-hotplug eth0
   iface eth0 inet static
       address 192.168.2.13
       netmask 255.255.255.0
       gateway 192.168.2.1

   auto wlan0
   allow-hotplug wlan0
   iface wlan0 inet manual
   wpa-conf /etc/wpa_supplicant/wpa_supplicant.conf

   auto wlan1
   allow-hotplug wlan1
   iface wlan1 inet manual
   wpa-conf /etc/wpa_supplicant/wpa_supplicant.conf


   ~
   ~
   "/etc/network/interfaces" 20 lines, 370 characters
   ```

9. Save the file and exit the editor (`:wq`).

10. Finally, reboot the Raspberry Pi to use the new static IP address!

    ```
    pi@raspberrypi ~ $ sudo reboot

    Broadcast message from root@raspberrypi (pts/0) (Mon Aug 10 23:23:29
    2015):
    The system is going down for reboot NOW!
    pi@raspberrypi ~ $ Connection to 192.168.2.13 closed by remote host.
    Connection to 192.168.2.13 closed.
    ```

How it works...

After logging in to the Raspberry Pi, this recipe first discovers the necessary network configuration parameters needed to configure a static IP address, then it uses those parameters to modify the network interface configuration file.

The `hostname -I` command is used to display the Raspberry Pi's current IP address (`192.168.2.13`).

The output of the `route` command, filtered by the `awk` command, displays the IP address of the default network gateway (**192.168.2.1**) and the network mask of the local network (**255.255.255.0**). The output of **route** is piped (**|**) through `awk` so that **awk** can extract information specific to this recipe and discard the rest.

Unfiltered, the `route` command displays more information than is needed for this recipe.

```
pi@raspberrypi ~ $ route -n
Kernel IP routing table
Destination     Gateway         Genmask         Flags Metric Ref    Use Iface
0.0.0.0         192.168.2.1     0.0.0.0         UG    202    0        0 eth0
192.168.2.0     0.0.0.0         255.255.255.0   U     202    0        0 eth0

pi@raspberrypi ~ $
```

The `awk` command **'/^0/ { print $2 }'** limits its output to those lines beginning with a 0 (**/^0/**) and for those limited lines prints the second field (**$2**). The result is the IP address of the default gateway (**192.168.2.1**).

And the `awk` command **'/^[1-9]/ { print $3 }'** limits the output that has been piped (**|**) into it to those lines beginning with a digit other than zero (**/^[1-9]/**) and for those lines prints the third field (**$3**). The result is the network mask (**255.255.255.0**) for the local network.

More information about `awk` and the `awk` command language can be found in the `awk` manpages (see the recipe Reading the built-in documentation in *Chapter 2, Administration*).

After discovering the current IP address, the default gateway, and the network mask, the recipe modifies the network interface configuration file (`/etc/network/interfaces`) to include the discovered parameters.

The wired network interface (**iface eth0**) is set to **static** and the configuration parameters **address**, **gateway**, and **netmask** are added using the parameter values discovered earlier.

After the configuration file is saved, the Raspberry Pi is rebooted with its new IP address.

There's more...

In most networks, both at home and at work, (DHCP) servers are used to dynamically assign IP addresses to client computers and devices. Because the DHCP servers are responsible for IP address assignment, they usually need additional configuration to reserve static IP addresses so that they are not accidentally assigned to another client device or computer.

In order to configure the DHCP server, you will need the hardware address of the Raspberry Pi's wired network interface. The `ifconfig` command can be used to display a lot of useful network information. This combination of `ifconfig` and an `awk` filter can be used to display just the hardware address of the network interface.

```
pi@raspberrypi ~ $ ifconfig | awk '/^eth0/ { print $5 }'
b8:27:eb:3f:aa:0c

pi@raspberrypi ~ $
```

Connected Devices > Devices > Add Device

Connect a Device using a Reserved IP address.   more

Add Device with Reserved IP Address

Host Name:	raspberry-pi
MAC Address:	b8:27:eb:3f:aa:0c
Reserved IP Address:	192.168.2.13
Comments:	Raspberry Pi

SAVE   CANCEL

In the preceding screenshot, a local home network gateway is being configured, setting the **Reserved IP Address** to **192.168.2.13** for the exclusive use of the **raspberry-pi** computer.

The **MAC Address (b8:27:eb:3f:aa:0c)** is the unique number assigned to this specific Raspberry Pi's network interface.

After this configuration is saved, the IP address **192.168.2.13** will be reserved for the exclusive use of the **raspberry-pi** computer.

See also

▶ **Dynamic Host Configuration Protocol** (http://en.wikipedia.org/wiki/Dynamic_Host_Configuration_Protocol): This Wikipedia article describes the DHCP protocol, its history, and how it works.

▶ **hostname – show or set the system's hostname**(http://manpages.debian.net/cgi-bin/man.cgi?query=hostname): The Debian manpage for hostname describes the command and its options.

▶ **route – show/manipulate the IP routing table**(http://manpages.debian.net/cgi-bin/man.cgi?query=route): The Debian manpage for route describes the command and its options.

▶ **ifconfig – configure network interfaces** (http://manpages.debian.net/cgi-bin/man.cgi?query=ifconfig): The Debian manpage for ifconfig describes the command and its options.

▶ **interfaces – network interface configuration for ifup and ifdown** (http://manpages.debian.net/cgi-bin/man.cgi?query=interfaces): The Debian manpage for interfaces describes the configuration file and its parameters.

▶ **awk – pattern-directed scanning and processing language** (http://manpages.debian.net/cgi-bin/man.cgi?query=awk): The Debian manpage for awk describes the command and the awk command language.

Creating a firewall with ufw

This recipe uses a simple, yet powerful command-line tool (ufw) to configure a firewall.

This recipe can be used to completely block network access to the Raspberry Pi. It can also be used to configure the Uncomplicated Firewall (ufw) to allow access through the firewall to specific applications (for example, web servers).

After completing this recipe, you will be able to protect network access to your Raspberry Pi using a firewall.

Getting ready

Ingredients:

An Initial Setup or Basic Networking setup for the Raspberry Pi that has been powered on. You have also logged in as the user pi (see the recipes in *Chapter 1, Installation and Setup* for how to boot and log in and the recipes in *Chapter 2, Administration* for how to log in remotely).

This recipe does not require the desktop GUI and could either be run from the text-based console or from within an LXTerminal.

If the Raspberry Pi's Secure Shell server is running, this recipe can be completed remotely using a Secure Shell client.

How to do it...

The steps for creating a firewall with ufw are:

1. Log in to the Raspberry Pi either directly or remotely.

2. Use the apt-get install command to install the ufw software package.

```
pi@raspberrypi ~ $ sudo apt-get install ufw
Reading package lists... Done
Building dependency tree
Reading state information... Done
The following NEW packages will be installed:
  ufw
0 upgraded, 1 newly installed, 0 to remove and 0 not upgraded.
Need to get 166 kB of archives.
After this operation, 708 kB of additional disk space will be used.
Get:1 http://mirrordirector.raspbian.org/raspbian/ wheezy/main ufw all
0.31.1-2 [166 kB]
Fetched 166 kB in 2s (65.6 kB/s)
Preconfiguring packages ...
Selecting previously unselected package ufw.
(Reading database ... 83839 files and directories currently installed.)
Unpacking ufw (from .../archives/ufw_0.31.1-2_all.deb) ...
Processing triggers for man-db ...
Setting up ufw (0.31.1-2) ...

Creating config file /etc/ufw/before.rules with new version

Creating config file /etc/ufw/before6.rules with new version

Creating config file /etc/ufw/after.rules with new version

Creating config file /etc/ufw/after6.rules with new version

pi@raspberrypi ~ $
```

3. The `apt-get install` command downloads and installs `ufw`. The installation of `ufw` includes a default set of firewall rules.

4. Use the `ufw allow` command to add the `ssh` protocol to the list of allowed protocols in the firewall rules.

   ```
   pi@raspberrypi ~ $ sudo ufw allow ssh
   Rules updated

   pi@raspberrypi ~ $
   ```

5. Use the `ufw enable` command to turn on the firewall.

   ```
   pi@raspberrypi ~ $ sudo ufw enable
   Command may disrupt existing ssh connections. Proceed with operation
   (y|n)? y
   Firewall is active and enabled on system startup

   pi@raspberrypi ~ $
   ```

6. The firewall rules are enabled immediately and also on startup!

How it works...

After logging in to the Raspberry Pi, this recipe uses the `apt-get install` command to download and install the Uncomplicated Firewall (**ufw**).

Then, a firewall rule is defined to permit remote access to the Raspberry Pi using the Secure Shell (`ssh`) protocol (`ufw allow ssh`).

Finally, the firewall is turned on (`ufw enable`).

There's more...

The Uncomplicated Firewall (`ufw`) is a command-line tool for defining firewall rules. The `ufw` command is not actually a firewall. There is no extra firewall server installed. The Linux kernel can be used as a firewall.

The `ufw` command is just used to configure firewall rules. The rule definitions are stored in the `/etc/ufw` directory; however, those definition files should not be modified directly. Modifying those files correctly is the purpose of the `ufw` command.

Don't forget to enable remote access

In the preceding recipe, after the `ufw` command is installed and before the firewall is enabled, a new firewall rule, allow SSH access (`ufw`) `allow ssh`, is added to the rule definitions. Without this rule, the next attempt to connect remotely via `ssh` would fail.

```
golden-imac:~ golden$ ssh pi@192.168.2.13
ssh: connect to host 192.168.2.13 port 22: Operation timed out

golden-imac:~ golden$
```

In this example, the `ssh` command fails because there is no firewall rule permitting Secure Shell access to the Raspberry Pi.

Disabling the firewall

The firewall rules defined using `ufw` will not prevent a user from logging in locally using a keyboard and display connected directly to the Raspberry Pi.

If `ufw` is preventing remote access, log in directly to the Raspberry Pi and then use the command: `ufw disable` to disable the firewall rules.

```
pi@raspberrypi ~ $ sudo ufw disable
Firewall stopped and disabled on system startup

pi@raspberrypi ~ $
```

Allowing a file server through the firewall

If the Raspberry Pi has been set up as a file server (see *Chapter 4, File Sharing*), use the firewall rule `ufw allow cifs` to allow the SMB (CIFS) protocol through the firewall.

```
pi@raspberrypi ~ $ sudo ufw allow cifs
Rules updated

pi@raspberrypi ~ $
```

Allowing a web server through the firewall

Similarly, if the Raspberry Pi has been set up as a local web server (see the next recipe in this chapter), use the firewall rule `ufw allow http` to allow the HTTP protocol through the firewall.

```
pi@raspberrypi ~ $ sudo ufw allow http
Rules updated

pi@raspberrypi ~ $
```

Application rules

The Uncomplicated Firewall has predefined rules for a number of application protocols, in addition to network protocols. The applications currently recognized by `ufw` can be displayed with the command `ufw app list`.

```
pi@raspberrypi ~ $ sudo ufw app list
Available applications:
  AIM
  Bonjour
  CIFS
  DNS
  Deluge
  IMAP
  IMAPS
  IPP
  KTorrent
  Kerberos Admin
  Kerberos Full
  Kerberos KDC
  Kerberos Password
  LDAP
  LPD
  MSN
  MSN SSL
  Mail submission
  NFS
  OpenSSH
  POP3
  POP3S
  PeopleNearby
  SMTP
  SSH
  Socks
  Telnet
  Transmission
  Transparent Proxy
  VNC
  WWW
  WWW Cache
  WWW Full
  WWW Secure
  XMPP
  Yahoo
  qBittorent
  svnserve
pi@raspberrypi ~ $
```

Enable all the defined network connections for one of the preceding applications using the command `ufw allow` and disable them using the command `ufw deny`.

The `ufw app info` command will display the application's configuration.

```
pi@raspberrypi ~ $ sudo ufw app info "WWW Full"
Profile: WWW Full
Title: Web Server (HTTP,HTTPS)
Description: Web Server (HTTP,HTTPS)

Ports:
  80,443/tcp

pi@raspberrypi ~ $ sudo ufw allow "WWW Full"
Rule added

pi@raspberrypi ~ $
```

The preceding example shows that the application configuration for **"WWW Full"** includes both the **HTTP** port (**80**) and the **HTTPS** port (**443**). By using the **"WWW Full"** application profile, network access to both web server ports can be allowed (denied or rejected) using a single firewall rule.

Resetting the firewall rules

By default, the `ufw` rules deny all network access to the Raspberry Pi. However, also by default, the firewall rules are not enabled.

Use the command `ufw reset` to return the firewall rules to their defaults – no remote access at all with the firewall disabled.

After resetting the default rules, the firewall can then be re-enabled with the command `ufw enable`.

See also

  ▶ **Uncomplicated Firewall (ufw)** (http://en.wikipedia.org/wiki/
     Uncomplicated_Firewall): This Wikipedia article about the Uncomplicated
     Firewall explains how it works.

  ▶ **ufw – program for managing a netfilter firewall** (http://manpages.debian.
     net/cgi-bin/man.cgi?query=ufw): The Debian manpage for `ufw` describes the
     command and its options.

  ▶ **iptables – administration tool for IPv4 packet filtering and NAT** (http://
     manpages.debian.net/cgi-bin/man.cgi?query=iptables): The Debian
     manpage for `iptables` describes in more detail how to configure the Linux kernel's
     built-in firewall.

Remote access to a desktop session (xrdp)

This recipe enables remote access to a Raspberry Pi desktop session using `xrdp`.

Using `xrdp`, teachers, support engineers, and hobbyists can create a new desktop session on the Raspberry Pi remotely from another computer. The newly created desktop session is separate from the desktop session currently displayed on the monitor attached to the Raspberry Pi. This private session is perfect for installing updates or performing other background tasks that should not interrupt the desktop session currently displayed on the Raspberry Pi's monitor.

After completing this recipe, you will be able to use `xrdp` to create a new remote desktop session on the Raspberry Pi.

Getting ready

Ingredients:

An Initial Setup or Basic Networking setup for the Raspberry Pi that has been powered on. You have also logged in as the user `pi` (see the recipes in *Chapter 1, Installation and Setup* for how to boot and log in and the recipes in *Chapter 2, Administration* for how to log in remotely).

Running this application requires the desktop GUI. Use `raspi-config` to configure the Raspberry Pi to automatically boot with the desktop GUI (see Chapter 2, *Administration*).

The installation portion of this recipe does not require the desktop and can be run from the text-based console (or from within an LXTerminal).

If the Raspberry Pi's Secure Shell server is running, this recipe can be completed remotely using a Secure Shell client.

How to do it...

The steps for connecting to the Raspberry Pi desktop remotely are:

1. Log in to the Raspberry Pi either directly or remotely. If you are using the Raspberry Pi desktop, open an LXTerminal window.

2. Use the `apt-get install` command to install the `xrdp` software package.

    ```
    pi@raspberrypi ~ $ sudo apt-get install -y xrdp
    Reading package lists... Done
    Building dependency tree
    Reading state information... Done
    ```

The following extra packages will be installed:
  tightvncserver xfonts-base
Suggested packages:
  tightvnc-java
The following NEW packages will be installed:
  tightvncserver xfonts-base xrdp
0 upgraded, 3 newly installed, 0 to remove and 0 not upgraded.
Need to get 7,219 kB of archives.
After this operation, 11.5 MB of additional disk space will be used.
Get:1 http://mirrordirector.raspbian.org/raspbian/ wheezy/main
tightvncserver armhf 1.3.9-6.4 [786 kB]
Get:2 http://mirrordirector.raspbian.org/raspbian/ wheezy/main xfonts-base
all 1:1.0.3 [6,181 kB]
Get:3 http://mirrordirector.raspbian.org/raspbian/ wheezy/main xrdp armhf
0.5.0-2 [252 kB]
Fetched 7,219 kB in 3s (2,000 kB/s)
Selecting previously unselected package tightvncserver.
(Reading database ... 83956 files and directories currently installed.)
Unpacking tightvncserver (from .../tightvncserver_1.3.9-6.4_armhf.deb) ...
Selecting previously unselected package xfonts-base.
Unpacking xfonts-base (from .../xfonts-base_1%3a1.0.3_all.deb) ...
Selecting previously unselected package xrdp.
Unpacking xrdp (from .../xrdp_0.5.0-2_armhf.deb) ...
Processing triggers for man-db ...
Processing triggers for fontconfig ...
Setting up tightvncserver (1.3.9-6.4) ...
update-alternatives: using /usr/bin/tightvncserver to provide /usr/bin/
vncserver (vncserver) in auto mode
update-alternatives: using /usr/bin/Xtightvnc to provide /usr/bin/Xvnc
(Xvnc) in auto mode
update-alternatives: using /usr/bin/tightvncpasswd to provide /usr/bin/
vncpasswd (vncpasswd) in auto mode
Setting up xfonts-base (1:1.0.3) ...
Setting up xrdp (0.5.0-2) ...
[....] Generating xrdp RSA keys......
Generating 512 bit rsa key...

ssl_gen_key_xrdp1 ok

saving to /etc/xrdp/rsakeys.ini

done (done).

```
[ ok ] Starting Remote Desktop Protocol server : xrdp sesman.

pi@raspberrypi ~ $
```

3. The `apt-get install` command downloads and installs `xrdp`.
   Installation of the software package includes starting the `xrdp` service.

4. Use a **RDP** (**Remote Desktop Protocol**) client (such as Microsoft's Remote Desktop Connection) to connect to the Raspberry Pi using its IP address (**192.168.2.13**).

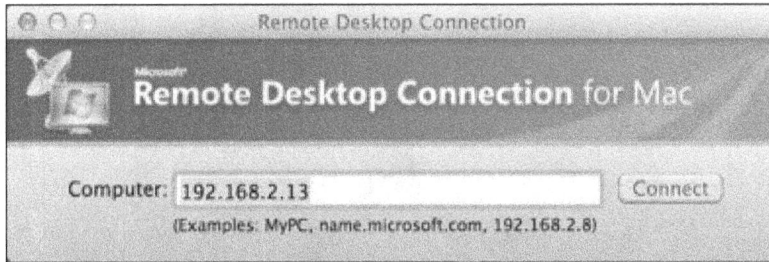

The preceding screenshot shows how to connect to the Raspberry Pi using Microsoft's Remote Desktop Connection for Mac.

5. Once connected, the `xrdp` session manager (`sesman`) displays a login screen.

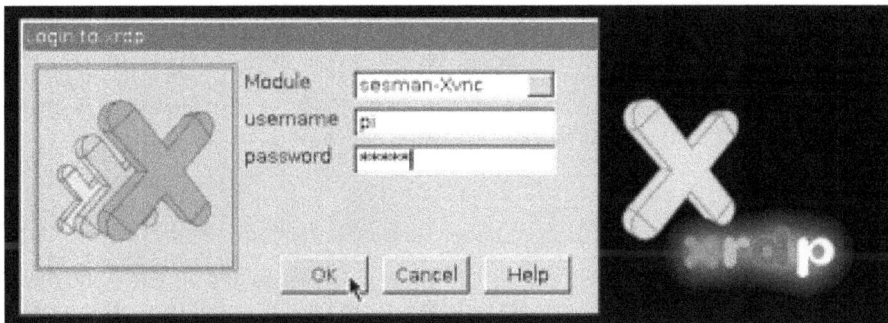

The preceding image shows how to start a remote desktop session with the Raspberry Pi using `xrdp`.

6. Log in to the `xrdp` session: Choose `sesman-Xvnc` as the Module. Use the same username (`pi`) and password (`raspberry`) that you use to log in via the console (or via ssh).

7. After a successful login, the Raspberry Pi desktop is displayed.

The preceding screenshot shows a remote connection to the Raspberry Pi desktop via an RDP connection (client resolution was set to 640x480).

How it works...

After logging in to the Raspberry Pi, the `xrdb` software package is downloaded and installed using `apt-get install`. The installation includes starting `xrdb` and the desktop session manager (`sesman`).

After `sesman` has started, a remote session to the Raspberry Pi can be created from another computer that has an RDP client installed.

The example in the recipe uses Microsoft's Remote Desktop Connection for Mac. The Microsoft RDP client prompts for the **Computer**. Enter the Raspberry Pi's IP address (**192.168.2.13**) to create a remote connection.

After the remote connection is made, an RDP session is created (**Login to xrdp**) by logging in to xrdp with the same username and password that is used to log in directly to the Raspberry Pi via ssh or directly via the GUI desktop.

Once the username and password have been entered correctly, a new desktop session is created. This new desktop session is not the same as the session running on the monitor connected directly to the Raspberry Pi. It is a new desktop session.

There's more...

The Remote Desktop Protocol (RDP) is a client-server protocol developed by Microsoft. The xrdp client is used to display the graphical user interface sent by an RDP server. The Microsoft RDP client (mstsc.exe) is included in every Windows version since XP.

The xrdp software package also includes the TightVNC server (tightvncsever) that communicates via the **Virtual Network Computing** (**VNC**) protocol – another graphical desktop sharing protocol. A number of open source and proprietary clients exist for both the RDP and VNC remote desktop protocols, including clients for mobile devices and tablet PCs.

The remote desktop connection displays the Raspberry Pi desktop in much the same way, as the desktop would be seen, if the Raspberry Pi were connected directly to a display. There are some exceptions.

No streaming video (or Minecraft)

The most noticeable limitation that a remote display has is not being able to display streaming video. Most video streaming applications stream directly to the video frame buffer, the part of memory that is shared with the display. So, the video is streamed directly to the display and bypasses the desktop. Because the video bypasses the desktop, it is also not sent to the remote desktop.

The Minecraft game for the Raspberry Pi also accesses the video frame buffer directly. So, like video streaming, Minecraft cannot be played through a remote desktop session.

It's not the display

Each remote desktop session is a separate desktop session. It is not the same desktop session that is displayed on the monitor directly connected to the Raspberry Pi.

See also

▶ **Remote Desktop Protocol** (http://en.wikipedia.org/wiki/Remote_Desktop_Protocol): This Wikipedia article describes the Remote Desktop Protocol (RDP).

> ▶ **Comparison of remote desktop software** (http://en.wikipedia.org/wiki/ Comparison_of_remote_desktop_software): This Wikipedia article compares remote desktop software.

> ▶ **xrdp – a Remote Desktop Protocol (RDP) server** (http://manpages.debian. net/cgi-bin/man.cgi?query=xrdp): The Debian manpage for xrdp has more details about the command and its options.

> ▶ **sesman – an xrdp(8) session manager** (http://manpages.debian.net/cgi- bin/man.cgi?query=sesman): The Debian manpage for sesman has more details about the command and its options.

> ▶ **xrdp – an open source remote desktop protocol (rdp) server** (http://www.xrdp. org/): The xrdp website has more details about this RDP server.

Remote access to the monitor (x11vnc)

This recipe enables remote access to the Raspberry Pi's monitor using xrdp.

Using x11vnc, teachers, support engineers, and hobbyists can access the desktop session currently displayed on the monitor attached to the Raspberry Pi. Teachers can use the remote desktop access to help students complete an assignment. Remote support engineers can help a Raspberry Pi user debug, install, or configure software. And, hobbyists can use xrdp to access the Raspberry Pi attached to the living room TV from another room.

After completing this recipe, you will be able to use xrdp to remotely access the desktop session currently displayed on the Raspberry Pi's monitor.

Getting ready

Ingredients:

An Initial Setup or Basic Networking setup for the Raspberry Pi that has been powered on. You have also logged in as the user pi (see the recipes in *Chapter 1, Installation and Setup* for how to boot and log in and the recipes in *Chapter 2, Administration* for how to log in remotely).

Running this application requires the desktop GUI. Use raspi-config to configure the Raspberry Pi to automatically boot with the desktop GUI (see *Chapter 2, Administration*).

The installation portion of this recipe does not require the desktop and can be run from the text-based console (or from within an LXTerminal).

If the Raspberry Pi's Secure Shell server is running, the installation portion of this recipe can also be completed remotely using a Secure Shell client (see ssh recipe in *Chapter 2, Administration*).

How to do it...

The steps for connecting to the Raspberry Pi desktop remotely are:

1. Log in to the Raspberry Pi either directly or remotely. If you are using the Raspberry Pi desktop, open an LXTerminal.

2. Use the `apt-get install` command to install the `x11vnc` package.

```
pi@raspberrypi ~ $ sudo apt-get install -y x11vnc
Reading package lists... Done
Building dependency tree
Reading state information... Done
The following extra packages will be installed:
  libvncserver0 tcl tk x11vnc-data
Suggested packages:
  libvncserver0-dbg
The following NEW packages will be installed:
  libvncserver0 tcl tk x11vnc x11vnc-data
0 upgraded, 5 newly installed, 0 to remove and 0 not upgraded.
Need to get 0 B/1,841 kB of archives.
After this operation, 3,192 kB of additional disk space will be used.
Selecting previously unselected package libvncserver0:armhf.
(Reading database ... 84404 files and directories currently installed.)
Unpacking libvncserver0:armhf (from .../libvncserver0_0.9.9+dfsg-1+deb7u1_
armhf.deb) ...
Selecting previously unselected package tcl.
Unpacking tcl (from .../archives/tcl_8.5.0-2.1_all.deb) ...
Selecting previously unselected package tk.
Unpacking tk (from .../archives/tk_8.5.0-2.1_all.deb) ...
Selecting previously unselected package x11vnc-data.
Unpacking x11vnc-data (from .../x11vnc-data_0.9.13-1_all.deb) ...
Selecting previously unselected package x11vnc.
Unpacking x11vnc (from .../x11vnc_0.9.13-1_armhf.deb) ...
Processing triggers for man-db ...
Processing triggers for desktop-file-utils ...
Setting up libvncserver0:armhf (0.9.9+dfsg-1+deb7u1) ...
Setting up tcl (8.5.0-2.1) ...
update-alternatives: using /usr/bin/tclsh-default to provide /usr/bin/
tclsh (tclsh) in auto mode
Setting up tk (8.5.0-2.1) ...
update-alternatives: using /usr/bin/wish-default to provide /usr/bin/wish
(wish) in auto mode
```

```
Setting up x11vnc-data (0.9.13-1) ...
Setting up x11vnc (0.9.13-1) ...

pi@raspberrypi ~ $
```

3. The `apt-get install` command downloads and installs `x11vnc`.

4. From a remote computer, use a Secure Shell tunnel (`ssh`) to start an instance of `x11vnc` running on the Raspberry Pi. It will continue to run while the connection is open.

```
golden-macbook:~ A601012$ ssh -t -L 5900:localhost:5900 pi@192.168.2.13
'x11vnc -q -localhost -display :0 -passwd pass1234'

pi@192.168.2.13's password:
The VNC desktop is: localhost:0
PORT=5900
```

5. Use a VNC client (such as TightVNC) to connect to the remote Raspberry Pi from the local machine (**127.0.0.1**) using the ssh tunnel.

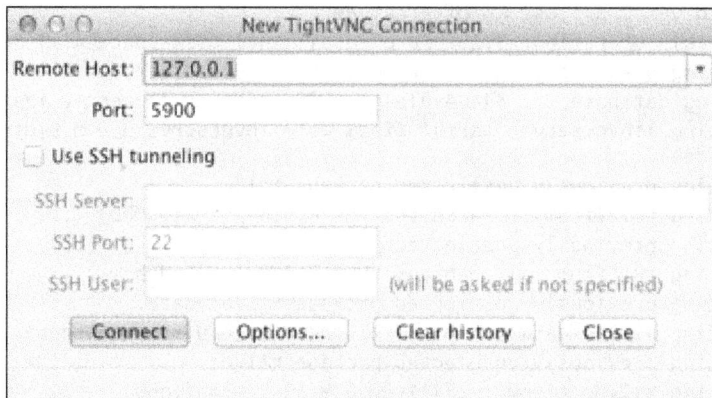

The preceding screenshot shows how to connect to the Raspberry Pi using TightVNC. The **Remote Host** is actually the local host (**127.0.0.1**) because of the `ssh` tunnel. The **Port** is the default VNC port (**5900**).

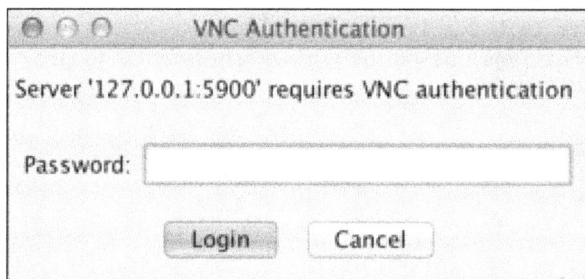

In the preceding screenshot, the TightVNC client asks for the user to enter the authentication password. Enter the password that was specified in the previous step (**pass1234**).

6. Once connected, TightVNC displays what is on the monitor.

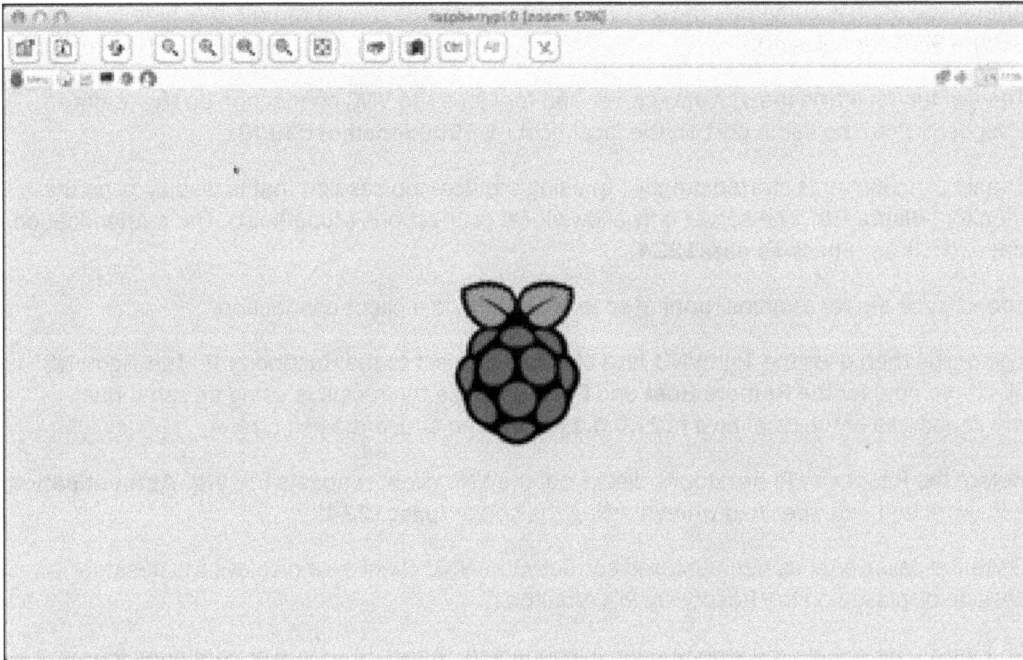

The preceding screenshot shows a remote connection to the Raspberry Pi desktop via a TightVNC client (client resolution is at 50 percent).

How it works...

After logging in to the Raspberry Pi, the `apt-get install` command is used to download and install the `x11vnc` software package.

After installation is complete, the `x11vnc` server is started from a remote machine using a Secure Shell tunnel (ssh).

The ssh tunnel starts the `x11vnc` server and forwards the VNC connection on the remote Raspberry Pi to the same port on the local host (**-L 5900:localhost:5900**).

The `x11vnc` server is started quietly (**-q**) using the desktop session that is displayed on the monitor (**-display :0**). The server only allows local connections (**-localhost**). The authentication password is set (**-passwd pass1234**).

The `x11vnc` server remains running so long as there is a client connection.

The recipe then uses the TightVNC Java client to connect to the Raspberry Pi. The TightVNC client prompts for the **Remote Host** and **Port**. Because the recipe is using an ssh tunnel, the IP address of the local host (**127.0.0.1**) is entered to use the ssh tunnel.

Before the Raspberry Pi desktop is displayed, the VNC client requests the **VNC Authentication** password that was specified when starting the server (**pass1234**).

Once the password has been entered correctly, the VNC client also displays the desktop session displayed on the Raspberry Pi's monitor.

So long as the remote desktop session is connected, the `x11vnc` server continues to run. As soon as the remote connection is closed, the `x11vnc` server quits.

There's more...

The VNC client displays the same desktop session that is being displayed on the Raspberry Pi's monitor. However, there are some exceptions.

No streaming video (or Minecraft)

Applications that write directly to the video frame buffer (for example, video streaming and Minecraft) are still not displayed over VNC (see the previous recipe for more info).

See also

▶ **Virtual Network Computing** (http://en.wikipedia.org/wiki/Vnc): This Wikipedia article about Virtual Network Computing (VNC) describes the history and capabilities of the VNC protocol.

- ▸ **x11vnc** (`https://en.wikipedia.org/wiki/X11vnc`): This Wikipedia article about x11vnc describes its use and configuration.

- ▸ **x11vnc** – allow VNC connections to real X11 displays (`http://manpages.debian.net/cgi-bin/man.cgi?query=x11vnc`): The Debian manpage for x11nvc describes the command and its options.

- ▸ **TightVNC Software** (`http://tightvnc.com/`): The TightVNC Software website has instructions on how to download and install a client.

Installing a web server (Apache, lighttpd, Nginx)

This recipe installs the Apache HTTP web server. Installation differences for the lighttpd and Nginx web servers are found at the end of this recipe.

The Apache web server is one of the most commonly used web servers on GNU Linux platforms like the Raspbian Linux distribution used by the Raspberry Pi. Apache is a mature, extensible web server that can be used to host a variety of applications; proxy access to websites internal and external; as well as host static web pages and images.

After completing this recipe, the Raspberry Pi will able to serve static and dynamic web pages from the SD card boot disk and from an external disk.

Getting ready

Ingredients:

An Initial Setup or Basic Networking setup for the Raspberry Pi that has been powered on. You have also logged in as the user pi (see the recipes in *Chapter 1, Installation and Setup* for how to boot and log in and the recipes in *Chapter 2, Administration* for how to log in remotely).

This recipe does not require the desktop GUI and could either be run from the text-based console or from within an LXTerminal.

If the Raspberry Pi's Secure Shell server is running, this recipe can be completed remotely using a Secure Shell client.

The examples in this recipe also use an external hard disk mounted at /media/bigdisk (see *Chapter 4, File Sharing* for more information).

The steps for installing the Apache web server are:

1. Log in to the Raspberry Pi either directly or remotely.

2. Use the `apt-get install` command to download and install the Apache HTTP web server (apache2).

```
pi@raspberrypi ~ $ sudo apt-get install -y apache2
Reading package lists... Done
Building dependency tree
Reading state information... Done
The following extra packages will be installed:
  apache2-mpm-worker apache2-utils apache2.2-bin apache2.2-common libapr1
  libaprutil1 libaprutil1-dbd-sqlite3 libaprutil1-ldap ssl-cert

...

Setting up apache2.2-common (2.2.22-13+deb7u5) ...
Enabling site default.
Enabling module alias.
Enabling module autoindex.
Enabling module dir.
Enabling module env.
Enabling module mime.
Enabling module negotiation.
Enabling module setenvif.
Enabling module status.
Enabling module auth_basic.
Enabling module deflate.
Enabling module authz_default.
Enabling module authz_user.
Enabling module authz_groupfile.
Enabling module authn_file.
Enabling module authz_host.
Enabling module reqtimeout.
Setting up apache2-mpm-worker (2.2.22-13+deb7u5) ...
[....] Starting web server: apache2apache2: Could not reliably determine
the server's fully qualified domain name, using 127.0.1.1 for ServerName
. ok
Setting up apache2 (2.2.22-13+deb7u5) ...
Setting up ssl-cert (1.0.32) ...

pi@raspberrypi ~ $
```

3. The `apt-get install` command downloads and installs `apache2`.

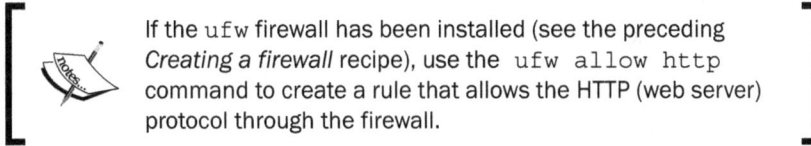

> If the `ufw` firewall has been installed (see the preceding *Creating a firewall* recipe), use the `ufw allow http` command to create a rule that allows the HTTP (web server) protocol through the firewall.

```
pi@raspberrypi ~ $ sudo ufw allow http
Rules updated

pi@raspberrypi ~ $
```

4. Use the web browser on another computer (or device) to test the HTTP connection to the Raspberry Pi.

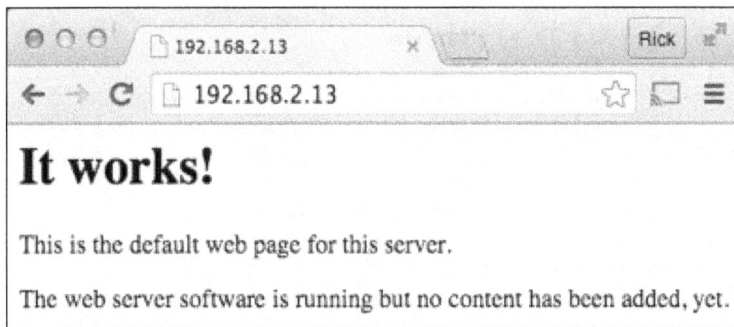

In the preceding image, a web browser on another computer is used to access the default web page of the Apache web server running on the Raspberry Pi. The web server works!

5. Use the command `ls -l` to list the contents of the web server's root directory, `/var/www`.

```
pi@raspberrypi ~ $ ls -l /var/www
total 4
-rw-r--r-- 1 root root 177 Aug 12 20:11 index.html

pi@raspberrypi ~ $
```

There is one file in the web server's root directory, **index.html**.

6. Use the command `ls -l` to list the contents of a website stored on an external disk, `/media/bigdisk/MyWebsite/`.

```
pi@raspberrypi ~ $ ls -l /media/bigdisk/MyWebsite/
total 4
-rw-r--r-- 1 root root 92 Aug 11 20:13 hello.html

pi@raspberrypi ~ $
```

There is one file in the directory on the external disk, `hello.html`.

7. Use the command `ln -s` to create a symbolic link from the external disk directory (`/media/bigdisk/MyWebsite`) to the web server's root directory (`/var/www/`).

```
pi@raspberrypi ~ $ ln -s /media/bigdisk/MyWebsite /var/www/MyWebsite

pi@raspberrypi ~ $ ls -l /var/www
total 4
-rw-r--r-- 1 root root 177 Aug 12 20:11 index.html
-rw-r--r-- 1 root root  24 Aug 12 20:48 MyWebsite -> /media/bigdisk/
MyWebsite

pi@raspberrypi ~ $ ls -l /var/www/MyWebiste/
total 4
-rw-r--r-- 1 root root 92 Aug 11 20:13 hello.html

pi@raspberrypi ~ $
```

The web server's root directory (`/var/www`) now has a symbolic link to the website stored on the external disk (`/media/bigdisk/MyWebsite`).

8. Use the web browser on another computer (or device) to test the HTTP connection to the Raspberry Pi. The website on the external disk is now accessible!

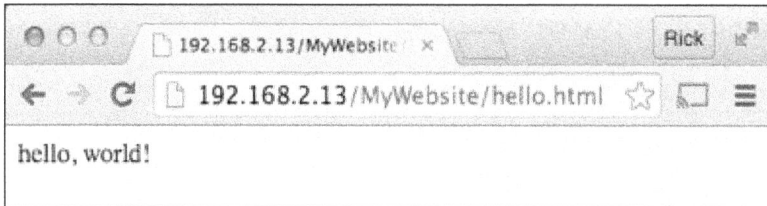

The preceding image shows how a web browser on another computer is used to access a web page stored on an external disk attached to the Raspberry Pi.

9. Use the `vi` command to create a dynamic web page (`timestamp`) in the `/usr/lib/cgi-bin` directory.

    `pi@raspberrypi ~ $ sudo vi /usr/lib/cgi-bin/timestamp`

10. Add the following lines to the new dynamic web page:

    ```
    #!/bin/sh

    echo "Content-Type: text/plain"
    echo ""
    echo $(date)
    ```

11. Save the file and exit (`:wq`).

12. Use the command `chmod a+rx` to make the dynamic web page `/usr/lib/cgi-bin/timestamp` executable.

    ```
    pi@raspberrypi ~ $ sudo chmod a+rx /usr/lib/cgi-bin/timestamp

    pi@raspberrypi ~ $ ls -l /usr/lib/cgi-bin
    total 4
    -rwxr-xr-x 1 root root 68 Aug 12 21:21 timestamp

    pi@raspberrypi ~ $
    ```

    The dynamic web page `/usr/lib/cgi-bin/timestamp` is now executable.

13. Use a web browser on another computer to display the dynamic web page (`http://192.168.2.13/cgi-bin/timestamp`). The dynamic web page displays the current time with each page refresh!

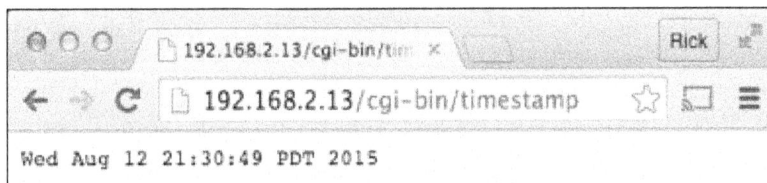

The preceding image shows the dynamic web page in action – with every page refresh, the timestamp is updated to the current time. The Raspberry Pi now displays dynamic pages!

14. Use the `ls -l` command to display the contents of the web server's log files directory (`/var/log/apache2/`).

```
pi@raspberrypi ~ $ ls -l /var/log/apache2/
total 8
-rw-r----- 1 root adm  1483 Aug 12 21:30 access.log
-rw-r----- 1 root adm   325 Aug 12 21:01 error.log
-rw-r--r-- 1 root root    0 Aug 12 20:11 other_vhosts_access.log
pi@raspberrypi ~ $
```

The preceding example shows how the `ls -l` command is used to display the contents of the Apache web server's log files directory.

How it works...

After logging in to the Raspberry Pi, this recipe begins by using the **apt-get install** command to download and install the Apache HTTP server software distribution meta package, `apache2`. The `apache2` software distribution includes the Apache HTTP server and supporting utilities.

The Apache HTTP server is started as soon as it is installed. However, if the Raspberry Pi has been protected with a firewall (see the *Creating a firewall* recipe in this chapter), the firewall will need to be configured to allow HTTP connections. The **ufw allow http** command adds a firewall rule that allows connections from other computers using the HTTP protocol.

After the firewall has been configured, a web browser on another computer is used to connect to the Raspberry Pi using the Raspberry Pi's IP address (`192.168.2.13`).

The easiest way to add files from an external disk to the web server, is to first mount the external disk in the `/media` directory (see *Chapter 4*, *File Sharing*) and then create a symbolic link to the external disk in the root directory of the web server (`/var/www`). A symbolic link does not copy files, it just points to where files are located.

In the example, a website directory on the external disk (`/media/bigdisk/MyWebsite`) is symbolically linked (**ln -s**) to the web server's root directory at `/var/www/MyWebsite`. The example website has only one file that is physically located on the external disk at `/media/bigdisk/MyWebsite/hello.html`. After the symbolic link is made, that file is also located symbolically at `/var/www/MyWebsite/hello.html` and can be reached from a web browser at the URL `http://192.168.2.13/MyWebsite/hello.html`.

The recipe continues by creating a simple dynamic web page that displays the current time. The **vi** editor is used to create the file `timestamp` in the `/usr/lib/cgi-bin/` directory. The directory is protected so the `sudo` command is used as a prefix to temporarily grant the user the privilege of creating and editing the file.

The `timestamp` dynamic web page uses the Bash scripting language (`#!/bin/bash`). The web page first outputs a header describing the content of the web page as plain text (**echo "Content-Type: text/plain"**) followed by a blank line (`echo ""`) to separate the HTTP response header from the content of the web page. The only line of the web page displays the current time by executing the GNU `date` utility (`echo "$(date)"`).

In order for the script to be called dynamically, the execution bit of the file's mode needs to be set with the `chmod` command (`chmod a+rx`). The file is located in a protected directory, so the `sudo` command is used again to temporarily grant privileges.

Viewing the dynamic web page (`http://192.168.2.13/cgi-bin/timestamp`) in the browser on another computer shows that the page is dynamic with each refresh of the browser.

Finally, the contents of the web server's log file directory (`/var/log/apache2/`) are displayed. Each request sent to the Apache HTTP web server is logged in the `access.log` file – one line per request. Error messages are appended to the end of the `error.log` file. If a dynamic web page does not display – or does not display properly, look at the end of the error log for a message describing the cause. All of the log files in this directory should be deleted (or archived) on a regular basis to free up disk space.

There's more...

Configuration files, static content, and dynamic pages

The configuration files for the server are located in the `/etc/apache` directory. However, there is no need to change the configuration as the default configuration is sufficient for serving static web pages from the `/var/www` directory and CGI-based dynamic web pages from the `/usr/lib/cgi-bin` directory.

The directory `/var/www` is the default location of static web pages, as well as static content like images, fonts, video, and sounds. Any file located under this directory can be displayed in a web browser using the URL of the Raspberry Pi plus the name of the file (or path to the file). Initially, there is only one file in this directory, `index.html`. In the example, it has the URL `http://192.168.2.13/index.html`. The `/var/www` directory is protected, so use the `sudo` command to add, modify, or delete files in this directory.

In the default Apache HTTP web server configuration, dynamic web pages use the Common Gate Interface (CGI) and are located in the `/usr/lib/cgi-bin` directory.

Other servers

The Apache HTTP web server is not the only web server that runs on the Raspberry Pi; however, it is perhaps the most famous and full-featured open source web server available today. Since 2009, more than 100 million websites have been hosted by Apache HTTP web servers. Although robust and complete, the Apache HTTP web server can also be resource heavy, consuming more memory and compute power than other servers.

lighttpd

The lighttpd web server is lighter on resources than Apache, and has the potential to scale to a higher number of requests per second.

Originally designed as a proof-of-concept to handle 10,000 parallel connections on one server, lighttpd has since become a popular web server.

The lighttpd web server can be installed with the command `apt-get install lighttpd`.

```
pi@raspberrypi ~ $ sudo apt-get install -y lighttpd
Reading package lists... Done
Building dependency tree
Reading state information... Done
The following extra packages will be installed:
  libfam0 libterm-readkey-perl libterm-readline-perl-perl spawn-fcgi

...
```

Although lighttpd does use `/var/www` as the root directory of the web server, it does not run CGI dynamic web pages by default.

The command `lighty-enable-mod cgi` is used to enable the lighttpd CGI module.

```
pi@raspberrypi ~ $ sudo lightly-enable-mod cgi
Enabling cgi: ok
Run /etc/init.d/lighttd force-reload to enable changes

pi@raspberrypi ~ $ sudo /etc/init.d/lighttd force-reload
[ ok ] Reloading web server configuration: lighttpd.

pi@raspberrypi ~ $
```

The preceding example shows how to use the command `lighty-enable-mod` to enable CGI dynamic web pages.

The lighttpd CGI module expects the `cgi-bin` directory to be located in the root directory of the web server instead of in the `/usr/lib` directory. The command `ln -s` can be used to create a symbolic link from the web server's root directory to the default location for dynamic web pages (`/usr/lib/cgi-bin`).

```
pi@raspberrypi ~ $ sudo ln -s /usr/lib/cgi-bin /var/www/cgi-bin

pi@raspberrypi ~ $
```

The lighthttp web server's configuration files are stored in the `/etc/lighttpd` directory, and its log files are written to the `/var/log/lighttpd` directory.

Nginx

Another popular modern web server is Nginx.

Using an event-driven approach to handling requests, Nginx can provide more predictable performance under high loads than the Apache web server. Nginx also has a number of options for deploying web applications including modular support for the popular web framework Ruby on Rails.

The Nginx web server can be installed with the command `apt-get install nginx`.

```
pi@raspberrypi ~ $ sudo apt-get install -y nginx
Reading package lists... Done
Building dependency tree
Reading state information... Done
The following extra packages will be installed:
  nginx-common nginx-full

...
```

The Nginx web server does not by default use the same root directory as the Apache HTTP or lighttpd web servers; instead, static web pages are by default stored in the `/usr/share/ngix/www` directory. The Nginx web server also does not support CGI; however, the Nginx web server can also produce dynamic web pages using FastCGI or Ruby Passenger.

The Nginx web server's configuration files are stored in the `/etc/nginx` directory, and its log files are written to the `/var/log/nginx` directory.

In addition to Apache, lighttpd, and Nginx, the Raspberry Pi can also run a number of lesser-known web servers including the AOL web server, monkey, and yaws.

```
pi@raspberrypi ~ $ apt-cache search httpd |grep -i server |grep -v '^lib'
aolserver4-core - AOL web server version 4 - core libraries
aolserver4-daemon - AOL web server version 4 - program files
apache2-mpm-event - Apache HTTP Server - event driven model
apache2-mpm-prefork - Apache HTTP Server - traditional non-threaded model
apache2-mpm-worker - Apache HTTP Server - high speed threaded model
boa - Lightweight and high performance web server
bozohttpd - Bozotic HTTP server
ebhttpd - specialized HTTP server to access CD-ROM books
lighttpd - fast webserver with minimal memory footprint
mathopd - Very small, yet very fast HTTP server
micro-httpd - really small HTTP server
mini-httpd - a small HTTP server
monkey - fast, efficient, small and easy to configure web server
```

```
mono-fastcgi-server - ASP.NET backend for FastCGI webservers - default version
mono-fastcgi-server2 - ASP.NET 2.0 backend for FastCGI webservers
mono-fastcgi-server4 - ASP.NET 4.0 backend for FastCGI webservers
nginx-extras - nginx web/proxy server (extended version)
nginx-full - nginx web/proxy server (standard version)
nginx-light - nginx web/proxy server (basic version)
nginx-naxsi - nginx web/proxy server (version with naxsi)
nginx-naxsi-ui - nginx web/proxy server - naxsi configuration front-end
ocsigen - web server and programming framework in OCaml
ocsigenserver - web server of the Ocsigen project
php5-cgi - server-side, HTML-embedded scripting language (CGI binary)
tntnet - modular, multithreaded web application server for C++
webfs - lightweight HTTP server for static content
yaws - High performance HTTP 1.1 webserver written in Erlang

pi@raspberrypi ~ $
```

In the preceding example, `apt-cache search` and `grep` are used to display a list of available HTTP web servers. Any of the listed web servers can be installed by using the `apt-get install` command (for example, `apt-get install monkey`).

See also

▶ **Apache HTTP Server Project** (`http://httpd.apache.org`): The Apache web server website is the complete reference for the web server.

▶ **lighttpd – fly light** (`http://www.lighttpd.net/`): The lighttpd website has detailed documentation for the web server.

▶ **Nginx** (`http://nginx.org/en`): The Nginx website has more information for the web server.

▶ **bash – GNU Bourne-Again SHell** (`http://manpages.debian.net/cgi-bin/man.cgi?query=bash`): The Debian manpage for `bash` is a reference for the Bash command language.

▶ **chmod – change file mode bits** (`http://manpages.debian.net/cgi-bin/man.cgi?query=chmod`): The Debian manpage for `chmod` details the command and its options.

▶ **date – print or set the system date and time** (`http://manpages.debian.net/cgi-bin/man.cgi?query=date`): The Debian manpage for `date` details the command and its options.

▶ **grep – print lines matching a pattern** (`http://manpages.debian.net/cgi-bin/man.cgi?query=grep`): The Debian manpage for `grep` details the command and its options.

- ► **ln -s – make links between files** (http://manpages.debian.net/cgi-bin/man.cgi?query=ln): The Debian manpage for ln -s details the command and its options.
- ► **AOL web server** (http://www.aolserver.com): The AOL web server website.

Installing a wiki (mediawiki)

This recipe installs and sets up the same wiki used by Wikipedia (MediaWiki).

Wikis are useful collaborative environments for teams that share a continuously evolving set of documentation. Each team member can contribute to the creation and editing of pages within the wiki. The resulting pages of documentation stored in the wiki are the result of a group effort and reflect the team's combined knowledge.

This recipe is used to install the MediaWiki. This is the same wiki software used by Wikipedia. The Wikipedia website is hosted by a cluster of high-powered servers so that it can continuously serve millions of users. This recipe uses a single Raspberry Pi that has more than enough power to manage a wiki for a team or small office of collaborators.

After completing this recipe, you will have a wiki that is ready for collaboration.

Getting ready

Ingredients:

An Initial Setup or Basic Networking setup for the Raspberry Pi that has been powered on. You have also logged in as the user pi (see the recipes in *Chapter 1, Installation and Setup* for how to boot and log in and the recipes in *Chapter 2, Administration* for how to log in remotely).

This recipe does not require the desktop GUI and could either be run from the text-based console or from within an LXTerminal.

If the Raspberry Pi's Secure Shell server is running, this recipe can be completed remotely using a Secure Shell client.

Once installed, the MediaWiki is accessed and configured from a web browser. Configuration does not need to be completed on the Raspberry Pi; it can be completed remotely from another computer on the same network as the Raspberry Pi.

For better performance, the video memory of the Raspberry Pi should be set as low as possible, so that there is more memory available for MediaWiki (see the recipe Configuring memory usage in *Chapter 2, Administration* for more information).

How to do it...

The steps for installing the MediaWiki wiki server are:

1. Log in to the Raspberry Pi either directly or remotely.

2. Use the `apt-get install` command to install the `mediawiki` software package.

```
pi@raspberrypi ~ $ sudo apt-get install -y mediawiki
Reading package lists... Done
Building dependency tree
Reading state information... Done
The following extra packages will be installed:
  apache2 apache2-mpm-prefork apache2-utils apache2.2-bin apache2.2-common
  heirloom-mailx javascript-common libaio1 libapache2-mod-php5 libapr1
  libaprutil1 libaprutil1-dbd-sqlite3 libaprutil1-ldap libdbd-mysql-perl
  libdbi-perl libhtml-template-perl libjs-jquery libjs-jquery-cookie
  libjs-jquery-form libjs-jquery-tipsy libmysqlclient16 libmysqlclient18
  libonig2 libqdbm14 lsof mediawiki-extensions-base mysql-client-5.5
  mysql-common mysql-server mysql-server-5.5 mysql-server-core-5.5
  php-wikidiff2 php5 php5-cli php5-common php5-mysql ssl-cert wwwconfig-
common
```

...

3. The `apt-get install` command downloads and installs MediaWiki.

> The installation of `mediawiki` includes `apache2`, `mysql`, and `php5`.
>
> The complete installation time will be at least 15 to 30 minutes.

4. During install, the `mysql` package will prompt for a new root password that should be used when managing the database. Enter a root password and repeat it on the next screen.

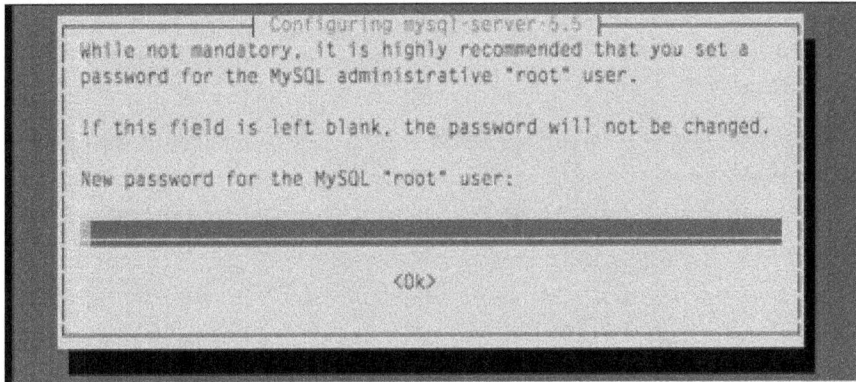

5. After accepting the root password for the `mysql` database (twice), the installation of `mediawiki` completes.

   ❑ Use the vi editor to edit the MediaWiki website configuration file (`/etc/mediawiki/apache.conf`).

   pi@raspberrypi ~ $ **sudo vi /etc/mediawiki/apache.conf**

6. The `vi` editor displays the contents of the configuration file. Instructions for using the editor can be found in the `vi` manpages (see the recipe *Reading the built-in documentation* in *Chapter 2, Administration*).

   ```
   # Uncomment this to add an alias.
   # This does not work properly with virtual hosts..
   #Alias /mediawiki /var/lib/mediawiki

   "/etc/mediawiki/apache.conf" 33 lines, 800 characters
   ```

7. Uncomment the `Alias` for the MediaWiki website by removing the # from the beginning of the line.

   ```
   Alias /mediawiki /var/lib/mediawiki
   ```

8. Save and close the file (`:wq`).

9. Use the `apachectl restart` command to restart the web server.

```
pi@raspberrypi ~ $ sudo apachectl restart
apache2: Could not reliably determine the server's fully qualified domain
name, using 127.0.1.1 for ServerName

pi@raspberrypi ~ $
```

10. Once the Apache web server has restarted, the configuration of MediaWiki continues in the web browser.

11. Open a web browser (possibly on another computer) and browse to the URL of the MediaWiki, (`http://192.168.2.13/mediawiki/`).

> The IP address (`192.168.2.13`) of your Raspberry Pi will be different. The `hostname -I` command can be used to display the IP address of the Raspberry Pi – see the *Remote access* recipes in *Chapter 2, Administration* for an example of using the `hostname -I` command.

MediaWiki 1.19.20+dfsg-2.3

LocalSettings.php not found.

Please set up the wiki first.

12. The MediaWiki initial configuration page is displayed in the browser. Click the set up the wiki link to continue.

MediaWiki 1.19.20+dfsg-2.3 installation

MediaWiki home
User's Guide
Administrator's Guide
FAQ

Read me
Release notes
Copying
Upgrading

Language

Your language:
? help
en – English

Wiki language:
? help
en – English

Continue →

- **Language**
- Existing wiki
- Welcome to MediaWiki!
- Connect to database
- Upgrade existing installation
- Database settings
- Name
- Options
- Install
- Complete!

- Restart installation

13. Choose the language to be used by MediaWiki. Click **Continue ->** for the next configuration page.

14. Once the language has been set, MediaWiki runs a number of tests to determine if (and how) it can be set up on the Raspberry Pi.

> The environment has been checked. You can install MediaWiki.

The preceding image shows a web page verifying that the Raspberry Pi is ready for MediaWiki.

15. The message "**The environment has been checked. You can install MediaWiki**." indicates MediaWiki is ready to be installed. (If you do not see this green message, click **Restart installation**.)

16. Scroll to the bottom of the page. Click **Continue ->** to accept the license and continue the installation.

Copyright and Terms

This wiki is powered by MediaWiki 🔒, copyright © 2001-2015 Magnus Manske, Brion Vibber, Lee Daniel Crocker, Tim Starling, Erik Möller, Gabriel Wicke, Ævar Arnfjörð Bjarmason, Niklas Laxström, Domas Mituzas, Rob Church, Yuri Astrakhan, Aryeh Gregor, Aaron Schulz, Andrew Garrett, Raimond Spekking, Alexandre Emsenhuber, Siebrand Mazeland, Chad Horohoe, Roan Kattouw, Trevor Parscal, Bryan Tong Minh, Sam Reed, Victor Vasiliev, Rotem Liss, Platonides, Antoine Musso and others 🔗.

This program is free software; you can redistribute it and/or modify it under the terms of the GNU General Public License as published by the Free Software Foundation; either version 2 of the License, or (at your option) any later version.

This program is distributed in the hope that it will be useful, but **without any warranty**; without even the implied warranty of **merchantability** or **fitness for a particular purpose**. See the GNU General Public License for more details.

You should have received a copy of the GNU General Public License along with this program; if not, write to the Free Software Foundation, Inc., 51 Franklin Street, Fifth Floor, Boston, MA 02110-1301, USA. or read it online 🔗.

← Back   Continue →

The screenshot shows the copyright agreement that must be accepted to continue.

17. Once the license agreement has been accepted, configuration continues with the MySQL settings.

18. Enter the password for the MySQL root user from Step 4.

19. After the database name and root password for MySQL have been entered, configuration continues with some additional database settings for web access.

20. Accept the defaults by clicking **Continue ->**.

MySQL settings

Database host:

? help

> localhost

--- Identify this wiki ---

Database name:

? help

> my_wiki

Database table prefix:

? help

--- User account for installation ---

Database username:

? help

> root

Database password:

? help

← Back   Continue →

The preceding screenshot shows how the MySQL database settings are entered.

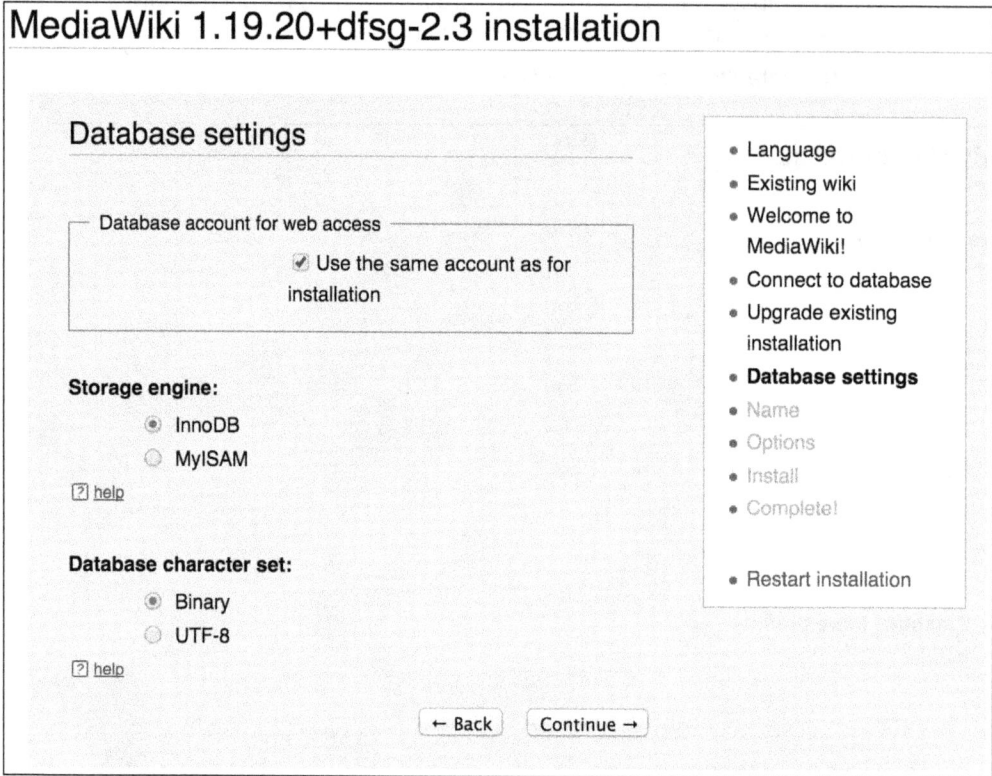

MediaWiki 1.19.20+dfsg-2.3 installation

Database settings

- Database account for web access

  ☑ Use the same account as for installation

Storage engine:

- ◉ InnoDB
- ○ MyISAM

? help

Database character set:

- ◉ Binary
- ○ UTF-8

? help

- Language
- Existing wiki
- Welcome to MediaWiki!
- Connect to database
- Upgrade existing installation
- **Database settings**
- Name
- Options
- Install
- Complete!

- Restart installation

← Back   Continue →

The preceding screenshot accepts the default database settings.

21. After the default database settings have been accepted, configuration continues by entering the name of the wiki and the username and password for the Administrator Account.

22. Enter a Name for the wiki. Enter a username and password for the MediaWiki Administrator Account. Click **Continue ->**.

Name

Name of wiki:

? help

My Raspberry Pi Wiki

Project namespace:

? help

- ⦿ Same as the wiki name: My_Raspberry_Pi_Wiki
- ○ Project
- ○ Other (specify)

```
  Administrator account
```

Your name:

? help

Admin

Password:

•••••

Password again:

•••••

E-mail address:

? help

admin@golden-garage.net

? help

☐ Subscribe to the release announcements mailing list 🔒.

- Language
- Existing wiki
- Welcome to MediaWiki!
- Connect to database
- Upgrade existing installation
- Database settings
- **Name**
- Options
- Install
- Complete!

- Restart installation

The preceding screenshot shows the web page used to enter the Name of the wiki and the username and password for the Administrator Account.

23. After the wiki Name and the MediaWiki Administrator username and password have been entered, scroll to the bottom of the page.

24. Choose **I'm bored already, just install the wiki**. and click **Continue ->**.

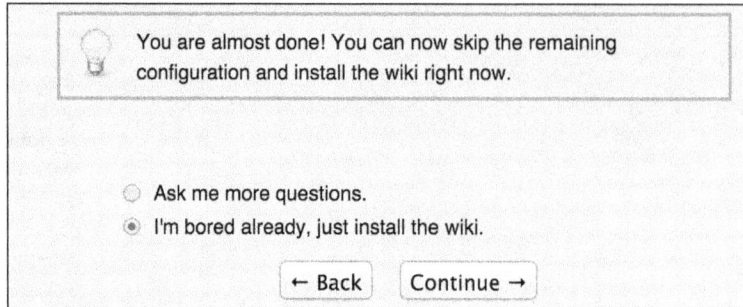

> You are almost done! You can now skip the remaining configuration and install the wiki right now.
>
> ○ Ask me more questions.
> ◉ I'm bored already, just install the wiki.
>
> [← Back] [Continue →]

The screenshot shows how to skip the optional configuration settings.

25. MediaWiki uses the supplied configuration parameters to set up the database displaying a web page listing the completed installation steps.

26. Click **Continue ->**. This step requires time to set up the database.

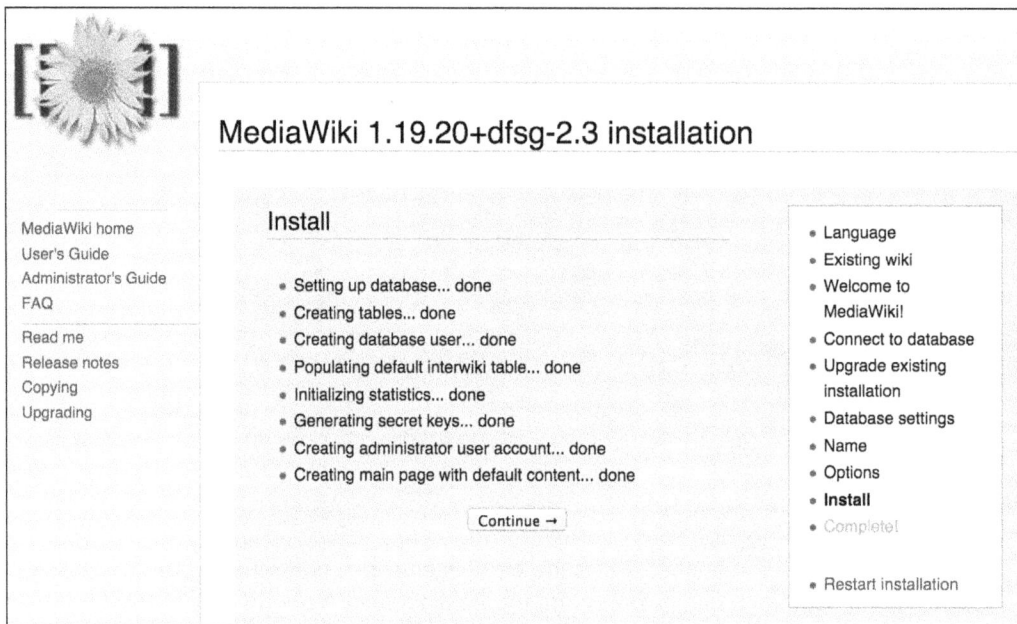

[❀]

MediaWiki 1.19.20+dfsg-2.3 installation

MediaWiki home
User's Guide
Administrator's Guide
FAQ

Read me
Release notes
Copying
Upgrading

Install

- Setting up database... done
- Creating tables... done
- Creating database user... done
- Populating default interwiki table... done
- Initializing statistics... done
- Generating secret keys... done
- Creating administrator user account... done
- Creating main page with default content... done

[Continue →]

- Language
- Existing wiki
- Welcome to MediaWiki!
- Connect to database
- Upgrade existing installation
- Database settings
- Name
- Options
- **Install**
- Complete!

- Restart installation

This screenshot shows the list of completed installation steps.

27. After the displayed installation list has been accepted, a congratulation page is displayed saying that the installation is complete. However, the `LocalSettings.php` file still needs to be downloaded and installed.

   ❑ Download the `LocalSettings.php` file.

```
Complete!                                              • Language
                                                       • Existing wiki
   ✓  Congratulations! You have successfully installed  • Welcome to
       MediaWiki.                                          MediaWiki!
                                                       • Connect to database
       The installer has generated a
       LocalSettings.php file. It contains all your    • Upgrade existing
       configuration.                                      installation
                                                       • Database settings
       You will need to download it and put it in the base of
       your wiki installation (the same directory as   • Name
       index.php). The download should have started    • Options
       automatically.                                  • Install
       If the download was not offered, or if you cancelled  • Complete!
       it, you can restart the download by clicking the link
       below:                                          • Restart installation

              📥 Download
           LocalSettings.php
       Note: If you do not do this now, this generated
       configuration file will not be available to you later if
       you exit the installation without downloading it.

       When that has been done, you can enter your
       wiki 🔗.
```

The screenshot shows the configuration file, **LocalSettings.php**, is complete.

28. Once the `LocalSettings.php` file has been downloaded, it needs to be moved to the root of the MediaWiki installation.

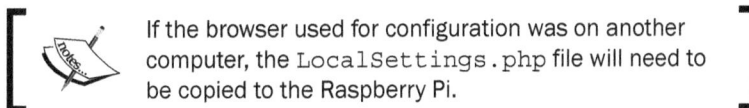

> If the browser used for configuration was on another computer, the `LocalSettings.php` file will need to be copied to the Raspberry Pi.

```
golden-macbook:~ user$ scp ~/Downloads/LocalSettings.php pi@192.168.2.13:.
pi@192.168.2.13's password:
```

```
LocalSettings.php                      100% 4689      4.6KB/s
00:00
```

```
golden-macbook:~ user$ ssh pi@192.168.2.13
pi@192.168.2.13's password:
Linux raspberrypi 3.18.11-v7+ #781 SMP PREEMPT Tue Apr 21 18:07:59 BST
2015 armv7l
Last login: Wed Aug 12 19:29:52 2015 from golden-macbook.local

pi@raspberrypi ~ $ sudo mv LocalSettings.php /var/lib/mediawiki/

pi@raspberrypi ~ $ sudo chmod a+r /var/lib/mediawiki/LocalSettings.php
```

In the preceding example, the `LocalSettings.php` file is copied from another computer (`golden-macbook`) to the MediaWiki directory (`/var/lib/mediawiki/`) on the Raspberry Pi and the file permissions are changed (`chmod a+r`) so that the MediaWiki can read the settings file.

29. After the `LocalSettings.php` file has been moved to the root of the MediaWiki installation, the MediaWiki is ready to use!

30. Browse to the MediaWiki URL on the Raspberry Pi: (`http://192.168.2.2/mediawiki/`)

31. The MediaWiki is set up and running; however, it still needs to be customized for your team (by adding a custom team logo, fonts, and styles). Follow the `User's Guide` link for more information on customizing your installation and detailed instructions on how to use the MediaWiki.

How it works...

At the beginning of this recipe, the MediaWiki software distribution package (`mediawiki`) is downloaded and installed using `apt-get install`. The MediaWiki installation includes the installation of Apache2, MySQL, and PHP5. Each of these packages can also be installed separately to provide a web server (Apache2), a database (MySQL), or a web scripting language (PHP5).

The MediaWiki installation begins by installing Apache2, MySQL, and PHP5. Neither the Apache2 installation nor the PHP5 installation requires any user input to complete successfully. However, the MySQL installation requires a password for the `root` user of the database.

The MySQL administrative `root` password is for the setup and configuration of the MySQL database management server. It is not the same password used by the user `pi`. The security of the Raspberry Pi is improved, if the password for the user pi and the password for the database are different.

After the MySQL `root` password has been entered, the installation continues. The MySQL database is installed. The MediaWiki application files are installed. The Apache2 web server is installed and started. However, the Apache2 web server is not yet configured to host the MediaWiki.

The `vi` editor is used to edit the `apache.conf` configuration file and assign the MediaWiki a website. The configuration file is located in the MediaWiki configuration directory, `/etc/mediawiki/`, and is also linked to the web server configuration directory, `/etc/apache2/conf.d/`.

The only line that needs to be changed in the Apache2 configuration file is the line that begins `#Alias`. The `#` at the beginning of the line turns the line into a comment. Comment lines are ignored when the Apache web server reads the configuration file. Removing the `#` from the beginning of the line will activate the MediaWiki the next time the web server is started.

The Alias statement has two parameters: the website's URL prefix (`/mediawiki`) and the location of the website's application files (`/var/lib/mediawiki`). The URL prefix becomes part of the wiki's URL (`http://192.168.2.13/mediawiki/`). Changing the URL prefix would also change the URL used to access the wiki. Changing the prefix to `/TeamWiki` would change the wiki's URL to `http://192.168.2.2/TeamWiki/`.

After the web server configuration file has been edited and the Alias line has been uncommented, the Apache web server is restarted with the `apachectl restart` command. This privileged command is used to restart the Apache web server.

Restarting the web server forces it to reload its configuration files, including the MediaWiki's web server configuration file. Now that MediaWiki's alias has been uncommented, the MediaWiki website is available; however, the wiki's database still needs to be set up.

Once the MediaWiki website is running, a web browser (possibly on another computer) can be used to complete the wiki's database setup. The example URL is `http://192.168.2.13/mediawiki/`. The IP address of your Raspberry Pi will most likely be different.

The first page displayed by the MediaWiki says the `LocalSettings.php` file cannot be found. The link labeled **setup the wiki** leads to the web pages that are used to complete the setup of the wiki.

The first setup page is used to define the language used by the wiki administrator (**Your language**) and the language used by other wiki users (**Wiki language**).

The next setup page shows the results of a system configuration examination and a license that must be accepted to complete the installation of MediaWiki.

Then, the database settings are entered on the next page. The password entered earlier for the MySQL administrative `root` user should be entered here.

Some additional database settings appear on the next page. Accept the defaults.

Finally, there is a setup page that asks for the wiki name and a username and password for the MediaWiki administrator. This new password is only used for configuring the wiki and is neither the MySQL administrative `root` password nor the password of the user `pi`.

At the bottom of the page is an opportunity to enter more configuration data. The example in the recipe chose **I'm bored already, just install the wiki.** and clicked **Continue ->** to complete the database installation.

After a status page is displayed, the last page of the setup triggers the download of the `LocalSettings.php` file, which is used to complete the installation of the wiki. If the file was downloaded on another computer, the `scp` command can be used to copy the file to the Raspberry Pi as shown in the example.

The `LocalSettings.php` file is a summary of the configuration parameters that were entered into the MediaWiki's setup pages. This file needs to be moved to the MediaWiki installation directory (`/var/lib/mediawiki/`) to complete the setup of the wiki.

After the `LocalSettings.php` file has been moved to the MediaWiki installation directory, setup is complete and the MediaWiki **Main Page** is now displayed at the configured URL (`http://192.168.2.13/mediawiki/`). The wiki is up and running!

Click the **[edit]** link to change the content of the **Main Page**.

Some customization could still be done to personalize the wiki (for example, change the wiki logo); however, the general setup is complete and the wiki can now be used for collaboration.

More information on using and customizing MediaWiki can be found by following the **User's Guide** link on the **Main Page** of the wiki.

See also

- ▶ **MediaWiki** (http://en.wikipedia.org/wiki/Mediawiki): This Wikipedia article is about the MediaWiki wiki server.

- ▶ **apachectl – Apache HTTP server control interface** (http://manpages. debian.net/cgi-bin/man.cgi?query=apachectl): The Debian manpage for apachectl has more about the command and its options.

- ▶ **scp – secure copy (remote file copy program)** (http://manpages.debian.net/ cgi-bin/man.cgi?query=scp): The Debian manpage for scp has more details about the command and its options.

- ▶ **mv – move (rename) files** (http://manpages.debian.net/cgi-bin/man. cgi?query=mv): The Debian manpage for mv has more details about the command and its options.

- ▶ **chmod – change file mode bits** (http://manpages.debian.net/cgi-bin/ man.cgi?query=chmod): The Debian manpage for chmod has more details about the command and its options.

Creating a wireless access point with hostapd

This recipe sets up the Raspberry Pi as a wireless access point – as a hub that other wireless devices can use to connect to the local network – or to services that are running on the Raspberry Pi.

Out of the box, the Raspbian Linux distribution supports connecting the Raspberry Pi to an existing wireless network using a wireless USB adapter. This recipe goes beyond using the Raspberry Pi as a network client and instead configures the Raspberry Pi as a network hub for other wireless devices. If the Raspberry Pi is also connected to a local network via a TCP cable, the Raspberry Pi acts as wireless network router enabling other devices to connect to the local network through the Raspberry Pi.

> Not all wireless USB adapters support Access Point (AP) mode.
>
> The recipe will test the wireless adapter to ensure that it supports AP mode.

After completing this recipe, you will be able to create a wireless network with the Raspberry Pi acting as a network hub.

Getting ready

Ingredients:

An Initial Setup or Basic Networking setup for the Raspberry Pi that has been powered on. You have also logged in as the user `pi` (see the recipes in *Chapter 1, Installation and Setup* for how to boot and log in and the recipes in *Chapter 2, Administration* for how to log in remotely).

 ▸ A supported wireless USB adapter.

This recipe does not require the desktop GUI and could either be run from the text-based console or from within an `LXTerminal`.

If the Raspberry Pi's Secure Shell server is running and the Raspberry Pi is connected to the local network via a wired network connection, this recipe can be completed remotely using a Secure Shell client.

The wireless connection will be reset during this recipe, so it is not recommended to log in remotely over a wireless connection during setup.

How to do it...

The steps for configuring the Raspberry Pi as a wireless access point are:

1. Log in to the Raspberry Pi either directly or remotely.

2. Use the `apt-get install` command to install the software packages `hostapd`, `udhcpd`, and `iw`.

    ```
    pi@raspberrypi ~ $ sudo apt-get install -y hostapd udhcpd iw
    Reading package lists... Done
    Building dependency tree
    Reading state information... Done

    The following extra packages will be installed:
      crda wireless-regdb
    ```

```
The following NEW packages will be installed:
  crda hostapd iw udhcpd wireless-regdb
0 upgraded, 5 newly installed, 0 to remove and 0 not upgraded.
Need to get 0 B/509 kB of archives.
After this operation, 1,188 kB of additional disk space will be used.
Selecting previously unselected package wireless-regdb.
(Reading database ... 88434 files and directories currently installed.)
Unpacking wireless-regdb (from .../wireless-regdb_2014.10.07-1~deb7u1_all.
deb) ...
Selecting previously unselected package crda.
Unpacking crda (from .../crda_1.1.2-1_armhf.deb) ...
Selecting previously unselected package hostapd.
Unpacking hostapd (from .../hostapd_1%3a1.0-3+deb7u2_armhf.deb) ...
Selecting previously unselected package iw.
Unpacking iw (from .../archives/iw_3.4-1_armhf.deb) ...
Selecting previously unselected package udhcpd.
Unpacking udhcpd (from .../udhcpd_1%3a1.20.0-7_armhf.deb) ...
Processing triggers for man-db ...
Setting up wireless-regdb (2014.10.07-1~deb7u1) ...
Setting up crda (1.1.2-1) ...
Setting up hostapd (1:1.0-3+deb7u2) ...
Setting up iw (3.4-1) ...
Setting up udhcpd (1:1.20.0-7) ...
udhcpd: Disabled. Edit /etc/default/udhcpd to enable it.

pi@raspberrypi ~ $
```

3. The `apt-get install` command downloads and installs the software packages `hostapd`, `udhcpd`, and `iw`.

4. Check the wireless USB adapter.

> Check your wireless USB adapter for AP mode with this command:
>
> `sudo iw list | grep '* AP'`
>
> If no lines are returned, the wireless adapter does not have AP mode.

5. Use the `iw list` command (filtered with `grep`) to see if the wireless adapter supports Access Point (AP) mode.

```
pi@raspberrypi ~ $ sudo iw list | grep '^[[:blank:]]*\* A'
                    * AP
                    * AP/VLAN
                    * AP/VLAN
                    * AP: 0x00 0x10 0x20 0x30 0x40 0x50 0x60 0x70 0x80 0x90
0xa0 0xb0
                    * AP/VLAN: 0x00 0x10 0x20 0x30 0x40 0x50 0x60 0x70 0x80
0x90 0xa0
                  * AP: 0x00 0x20 0x40 0xa0 0xb0 0xc0 0xd0
                  * AP/VLAN: 0x00 0x20 0x40 0xa0 0xb0 0xc0 0xd0
pi@raspberrypi ~ $
```

6. Display the nameserver address.

7. Use the `cat` command to display the nameserver address stored in `/etc/resolve.conf`.

```
pi@raspberrypi ~ $ cat /etc/resolv.conf
# Generated by resolvconf
nameserver 192.168.2.1

pi@raspberrypi ~ $
```

The DNS `nameserver` used by the Raspberry Pi is **192.168.2.1**.

8. Configure the `udhcpd` server.

9. Use the `vi` editor to edit the `udhcpd` configuration file `/etc/udhcpd.conf`.

```
pi@raspberrypi ~ $ sudo vi /etc/udhcpd.conf
```

10. The `vi` editor displays the contents of the configuration file. Instructions for using the editor can be found in the `vi` manpages (see the recipe *Reading the built-in documentation* in *Chapter 2,Administration*).

```
# Sample udhcpd configuration file (/etc/udhcpd.conf)

# The start and end of the IP lease block

start           192.168.0.20    #default: 192.168.0.20
end             192.168.0.254   #default: 192.168.0.254


# The interface that udhcpd will use

interface       eth0            #default: eth0

"/etc/udhcpd.conf" 123 lines, 3054 characters
```

11. Change the network interface used by udhcpd by changing the line beginning with interface to read interface wlan0.

    ```
    # The interface that udhcpd will use
    ```

    ```
    interface       wlan0
    ```

12. Change the example configuration of udhcpd by changing the section beginning with #Examples at the bottom of the file. Replace the example DNS address with the nameserver address used by your Raspberry Pi (192.168.2.1, from Step 5).

    ```
    #Examples
    opt     dns     192.168.2.1
    option  subnet  255.255.255.0
    opt     router  192.168.0.1
    option  domain  local
    option  lease   864000
    ```

13. Save the file and exit the editor (:wq).

14. Enable the udhcpd server.

    ```
    pi@raspberrypi ~ $ sudo vi /etc/default/udhcpd
    ```

15. Use the vi editor to edit the udhcpd configuration file, /etc/default/udhcpd.

16. The vi editor displays the contents of the configuration file.

    ```
    # Comment the following line to enable
    DHCPD_ENABLED="no"

    # Options to pass to busybox' udhcpd.
    #
    # -S     Log to syslog
    # -f     run in foreground

    DHCPD_OPTS="-S"
    ~
    ~
    "/etc/default/udhcpd" 9 lines, 164 characters
    ```

17. Enable the udhcpd server by commenting out the line DHCP_ENABLED="no". To comment out the line, place a # at the beginning of the line.

    ```
    # Comment the following line to enable
    #DHCPD_ENABLED="no"
    ```

18. Save the file and exit the editor (:wq).

19. Configure the hostapd server. Use the `vi` editor to create a new `hostapd` configuration file, `/etc/hostapd/hostapd.conf`.

    pi@raspberrypi ~ $ **sudo vi /etc/hostapd/hostapd.conf**

20. The `vi` editor displays the empty configuration file.

21. Add the following parameters to the hostapd configuration file:

    ```
    interface=wlan0
    ssid=Raspi_AP
    wpa_passphrase=Pr0t3ct3d
    driver=nl80211
    hw_mode=g
    channel=6
    macaddr_acl=0
    auth_algs=1
    ignore_broadcast_ssid=0
    wpa=2
    wpa_key_mgmt=WPA-PSK
    wpa_pairwise=TKIP
    rsn_pairwise=CCMP
    ```

22. Save the file and exit the editor (`:wq`).

23. Enable the hostapd server. Use the `vi` editor to enable the `hostapd` service by editing the service default file (`/etc/default/hostapd`).

    pi@raspberrypi ~ $ **sudo vi /etc/default/hostapd**

24. The `vi` editor displays the contents of the configuration file.

    ```
    # Defaults for hostapd initscript
    #
    # See /usr/share/doc/hostapd/README.Debian for information about alternative
    # methods of managing hostapd.
    #
    # Uncomment and set DAEMON_CONF to the absolute path of a hostapd configuration
    # file and hostapd will be started during system boot. An example configuration
    # file can be found at /usr/share/doc/hostapd/examples/hostapd.conf.gz
    #
    #DAEMON_CONF=""

    # Additional daemon options to be appended to hostapd command:-
    #       -d    show more debug messages (-dd for even more)
    ```

```
#        -K    include key data in debug messages
#        -t    include timestamps in some debug messages
#
# Note that -B (daemon mode) and -P (pidfile) options are automatically
# configured by the init.d script and must not be added to DAEMON_OPTS.
#
#DAEMON_OPTS=""
~
"/etc/default/hostapd" 20 lines, 770 characters
```

25. Replace the line beginning with #DAEMON_CONF with the line DAEMON_CONF="/etc/hostapd/hostapd.conf".

    DAEMON_CONF="/etc/hostapd/hostapd.conf"

26. Save the file and exit the editor (:wq).

27. Configure IP forwarding. Use the vi editor to enable IP forwarding by editing the kernel parameters file, /etc/sysctl.conf.

    pi@raspberrypi ~ $ **sudo vi /etc/sysctl.conf**

28. The vi editor displays the contents of the configuration file.

```
#
# /etc/sysctl.conf - Configuration file for setting system variables
# See /etc/sysctl.d/ for additonal system variables
# See sysctl.conf (5) for information.
#

"/etc/sysctl.conf" 64 lines, 2137 characters
```

29. The vi editor opens the kernel parameters file (/etc/sysctl.conf).

30. Uncomment the line beginning with net.ipv4.ip_forward by removing the # from the beginning of the line.

```
# Uncomment the next line to enable packet forwarding for IPv4
net.ipv4.ip_forward=1
```

31. Save the file and exit the editor (:wq).

32. Enable IP forwarding. Enable post forwarding by using the echo command to set the kernel parameter /proc/sys/net/ipv4/ip_forward to the value "1".

    pi@raspberrypi ~ $ **sudo bash -c 'echo "1" > /proc/sys/net/ipv4/ip_forward'**
    pi@raspberrypi ~ $

33. Use the `iptables` command to set up IP forwarding rules for network address translation and port forwarding.

```
pi@raspberrypi ~ $ sudo iptables -t nat -A POSTROUTING -o eth0 -j
MASQUERADE

pi@raspberrypi ~ $ sudo iptables -A FORWARD -i eth0 -o wlan0 -m state
--state RELATED,ESTABLISHED -j ACCEPT

pi@raspberrypi ~ $ sudo iptables -A FORWARD -i wlan0 -o eth0 -j ACCEPT
```

34. Save the iptables configuration (`iptables-save`) and move the output file (`iptables.ipv4.net`) to the `/etc` configuration directory for use during system boot.

```
pi@raspberrypi ~ $ sudo iptables-save > iptables.ipv4.nat
pi@raspberrypi ~ $ sudo mv iptables.ipv4.nat /etc

pi@raspberrypi ~ $ sudo chown root:root /etc/iptables.ipv4.nat

pi@raspberrypi ~ $ ls -l /etc/iptables.ipv4.nat
-rw-r--r-- 1 root root 566 Aug 13 19:30 /etc/iptables.ipv4.nat

pi@raspberrypi ~ $
```

35. Give the wireless interface a static IP address. Use the `ifconfig` command to give the wireless network interface (`wlan0`) a static IP address (`192.169.0.1`).

```
pi@raspberrypi ~ $ sudo ifconfig wlan0 192.168.0.1

pi@raspberrypi ~ $
```

36. Configure the network interface boot parameters. Use the vi editor to edit the network interface configuration file (`/etc/network/interfaces`).

```
pi@raspberrypi ~ $ sudo vi /etc/network/interfaces
```

37. The `vi` editor opens the network interface configuration file (`/etc/network/interfaces`).

38. Change the file so that it only contains the following:

```
auto lo
iface lo inet loopback

auto eth0
allow-hotplug eth0
```

```
iface eth0 inet manual

auto wlan0
iface wlan0 inet static
    address 192.68.0.1
    netmask 255.255.255.0

up iptables-restore < /etc/iptables.ipv4.nat
```

39. Save the file and exit the editor (:wq).

40. Enable the wireless access point. Use the `update-rc.d` command to enable the `hostapd` and `udhcpd` services.

    ```
    pi@raspberrypi ~ $ sudo update-rc.d hostapd enable
    update-rc.d: using dependency based boot sequencing

    pi@raspberrypi ~ $ sudo update-rc.d udhcpd enable
    update-rc.d: using dependency based boot sequencing

    pi@raspberrypi ~ $
    ```

41. The Raspberry Pi is now configured to start the `hostapd` and `udhcpd` services during system boot.

42. Disable wpa_supplicant. Use the `mv` command to move the service definition file for WPA Supplicant (`fi.epitest.hostap.WPASupplicant.service`) out of the services directory (`/usr/share/dbus-1/system-services`).

    ```
    pi@raspberrypi ~ $ mv /usr/share/dbus-1/system-services/ fi.epitest.hostap.
    WPASupplicant.service ~/

    pi@raspberrypi ~ $
    ```

43. Reboot: Reboot the system and the Raspberry Pi is a wireless access point! Look for the `Raspi_AP` network SSID and connect using the password (`Pr0t3ct3d`) that was defined in the hostapd configuration file (`/etc/hostapd/hostapd.conf`).

How it works...

The recipe starts by downloading and installing a wireless interface toolkit (`iw`), as well as two servers: a Wireless Access Point server (`hostapd`) and a DHCP server (`udhcpd`).

Before configuration begins, the wireless USB adapter is tested for compatibility.

Check the wireless USB adapter

Not all wireless USB adapters support Access Point (AP) mode. The `iw list` command is used to list the wireless capabilities of any attached wireless devices. If AP mode is supported, it will be listed in the section `Supported interface modes`.

The output of the `iw list` command is quite long. The `grep` command is used to filter the output of the `iw list` command. A pipe (`|`) is used to connect the output of the `iw list` command to the input of the `grep` command. The `grep` command limits the output of other commands using a regular expression filter ('**^[[:blank:]]** A**' – from the beginning of the line **^** any number of blanks **[[:blank:]]*** followed by an asterisk ***** followed by a space and the capital letter **A**).

If the wireless adapter is not compatible with `hostapd`, the `iw list` command will display the message "`n180211 not found.`" There may still be a chance for the adapter to work with `hostapd`; however, it requires recompiling `hostapd` with another driver (see references at the end of the chapter).

Once the wireless adapter has been tested and shown to support AP mode, configuration of the Raspberry Pi continues.

Configure the DHCP server by using udhcpd

The Dynamic Host Configuration Protocol (DHCP) server (udhcpd) assigns client computers network configuration information; such as the address of a DNS nameserver, an IP address, and a default route (or gateway). When this recipe is complete, the Raspberry Pi will configure its wireless clients using DCHP.

Three changes are made to the DHCP configuration file (`/etc/udhcpd.conf`):

- ▸ The wireless interface is selected (**wlan0**)
- ▸ The remaining flag is set to support embedded devices (for example, Raspberry Pi)
- ▸ The default network parameters are defined for wireless clients

The default network parameters are:

dns – the DNS nameserver to use. The system DNS nameserver is defined in **/etc/resolv. conf** and is displayed in Step 5.

- ▸ **subnet** – how many IP addresses are part of the same network subnet. The value **255.255.255.0** is a net mask that matches computers with the same numbers in the first three bytes of the IP address.
- ▸ **router** – the static IP address of the Raspberry Pi's wireless interface (**192.168.0.1**).
- ▸ **domain** – the name of the network (**local**).
- ▸ `lease` – how long a network address will be assigned to a specific computer (**864000** seconds or 10 days).

The **start** and **end** parameters at the top of the configuration file by default are set to the range of IP values from **192.168.0.20** to **192.168.0.254**.

If the Raspberry Pi will always be attached to a wired network that has a network timeserver, the remaining time flag does not need to be set.

After udhcpd has been configured, its boot script parameter file (`/etc/default/udhcpd`) also needs to be changed. The parameter **DHCP_ENABLED="no"** needs to be commented out (by placing a # at the beginning of the line), so that the DHCP server (`udhcpd`) is enabled.

Configure the Wireless Access Point server by using hostapd

The Wireless Access Point server (`hostapd`) manages the wireless connection between other wireless devices and the Raspberry Pi. This includes establishing a secure connection using an encryption protocol like Wi-Fi Protect Access (WPA); and setting the Service Set ID (SSID) and the pre-shared key (PSK).

The created **hostapd** configuration parameter file includes:

- **interface** – the wireless interface (**wlan0**)
- **ssid** – the network ID (**Raspi_AP**)
- **wpa_passphrase** – the passphrase or pre-shared key (`Pr0t3ct3d`)
- **driver** – the wireless device driver (**nl80211**)
- **hw_mode** – the hardware mode (**g**)
- **channel** – the radio frequency channel (**6**)
- **macaddr_acl** – access control list (**0**)
- **auth_algs** – the authorization algorithm to use (**1** – open auth)
- **ignore_broadcast_ssid** – enable broadcasting the network ID (**0** – don't ignore broadcasting)
- **wpa** – which version of WPA (**2**)
- **wpa_key_mgmt** – which key manages algorithm (**WPA-PSK**)
- **wpa_pairwise** – WPA v1 data encryption (**TKIP**)
- **rsn_pairwise** – WPA v2 data encryption (**CCMP**)

After **hostapd** has been configured, its boot script parameter file (`/etc/default/hostapd`) also needs to be changed. The parameter **DAEMON_CONF** needs to be set to the location of the hostapd configuration file (`/etc/hostapd/hostapd.conf`), so that the Wireless Access Point server is enabled.

Set up IP Forwarding

IP Forwarding is used to pass (forward) network traffic between network interfaces. In this recipe, IP Forwarding is used to pass network traffic between the wireless network and the wired network. Using IP Forwarding, the Raspberry Pi connects the clients of the wireless network to the wired network.

The first configuration step is to enable IP Forwarding in the Raspberry Pi's Linux kernel. The kernel parameters file (`/etc/sysctl.conf`) has an IP Forwarding entry (**net.ipv4. ip_forward=1**) that is by default commented out. Uncommenting this entry, by removing the **#** at the beginning of the line, enables IP Forwarding in the Linux kernel.

After IP Forwarding is enabled, the `iptables` command is used to define the net filter rules that determine which network packets are allowed to cross the Linux kernel's internal firewall. The Linux kernel's firewall organizes its rules into tables that define how network packets pass through the kernel. The `iptables` command is used to manage the rules stored in these tables.

The first Linux kernel firewall rule define in this step is appended to the postprocessing rules (**-A POSTROUTING**) of the network address translation table (**-t nat**). This rule masquerades network packets (**MASQUERADE**) as they are passed to the wired network (**-o eth0**). The IP addresses of wireless network clients are translated into the IP address of the Raspberry Pi's wired network connection as they are passed to the wired network. This is how the network packets from multiple wireless network clients are translated so they can pass through the Raspberry Pi's single wired network connection.

The second rule is appended to the packet forwarding rules (**-A FORWARD**) of the filter table (the default table). This rule allows (**-j ACCEPT**) network packets to be forwarded (**-A FORWARDED**) from the wired network (**-i eth0**) to the wireless network (**-o wlan0**) when they are related to an established connection (**-m state –state RELATED,ESTABLISHED**).

The last `iptables` command rule in this step is appended to the forwarding rules of the filter table (**-A FORWARD**). This rule allows packets to pass from the wireless network (**-i wlan0**) to the wired network (**-o eth0**).

The next command, `ifconfig wlan0`, sets the IP address of the Raspberry Pi's wireless network connection to **192.168.0.1**.

Finally, the `iptables-save` command is used to save a copy of these rules in a configuration file (`/etc/iptables.ipv4.nat`) that can be used during boot.

After this step is complete, the IP Forwarding rules have been defined and saved in a configuration file. The IP Forwarding rules are also active.

Configure the boot parameters

The network interfaces definitions used during boot are stored in a configuration file (`/etc/network/interfaces`). The file defines the network address, network mask, and the default route for each network interface.

The configuration file used in this recipe defines three network interfaces:

- ► **lo** – the loopback network
- ► **eth0** – the wired network
- ► **wlan0** – the wireless network
- ► The loopback interface (**lo**) is loaded automatically (**auto**).
- ► The wired interface interface's (**eth0**) is configured dynamically using the DHCP protocol.

The wireless interface (**wlan0**) has a static definition (**static**) – it is in this file. The wireless interface's IP **address** is defined to be **192.168.0.1**. The interface's defined network mask (**255.255.255.0**) is big enough to support 256 unique addresses on the same subnet.

After the network interfaces are brought up (**up**), the IP Forwarding definitions (`/etc/iptables.ipv4.nat`) are restored (**iptables-restore**) that were saved earlier in this recipe (using **iptables-save**).

Once the network interface definitions have been saved, the network can be started.

Start the wireless access point

Now that the configuration files have been updated:

- ► wireless access point (`/etc/hostapd/hostapd.conf`)
- ► dynamic host configuration protocol (`/etc/udhcpd.conf`)
- ► network interfaces (`/etc/network/interfaces`)
- ► IP Forwarding definitions (`/etc/iptables.ipv4.nat`)

The boot scripts for the wireless access point daemon (**hostapd**) and the dynamic host configuration protocol daemon (udhcp) can be enabled (`update-rc.d enable`).

The Raspberry Pi will now become a wireless access point every time it boots!

After the Raspberry Pi reboots, the wireless access point is ready to use! Wireless devices can now connect to the Raspberry Pi using your chosen SSID (`Raspi_AP`) and passphrase (`Pr0t3ct3d`).

There's more...

Not all USB wireless adapters support AP mode

There are a limited number of wireless USB adapters that can work with the Raspberry Pi and can also be configured as wireless access points. The links at the end of this chapter can be used to find current wireless USB adapters that can be used together with the Raspberry Pi to create a wireless access point (see *Other Resources*).

Some wireless USB adapters consume more power than the Raspberry Pi can support consistently on a continual basis. Connecting the wireless USB adapter to the Raspberry Pi indirectly via a USB hub will lead to better performance and reduce the likelihood that other USB devices (like the onboard network card!) will be starved for power.

Wireless firewall, file server, or web server

This recipe works well when combined with other recipes in this book.

Together with the file-sharing recipes in *Chapter 4, File Sharing*, the Raspberry Pi could become a file server for both wired and wireless devices connected to the local network – for exchanging document and media files; or for backup and storage.

When combined with other advanced networking recipes in this chapter, the Raspberry Pi could become a network firewall, protecting wireless access to a wired network; a teaching or support tool with remote access to desktop devices; a communication tool that serves web pages; or a collaboration tool that hosts wiki pages.

Within the Raspberry Pi and open source GNU Linux community, there are numerous other tools and applications that could be combined with this recipe to turn the Raspberry Pi into a dynamic network hub for wireless devices.

See also

- ▶ **hostapd** (http://en.wikipedia.org/wiki/Hostapd): This Wikipedia article about hostapd describes the service in more detail.

- ▶ **hostapd: IEEE 802.11 AP, IEEE 802.1X/WPA/WPA2/EAP/RADIUS Authenticator** (http://w1.fi/hostapd/): The hostapd website is a complete reference for the server.

- ▶ **Debian Linux Kernel Handbook** (http://kernel-handbook.alioth.debian.org/): The Debian Linux Kernel Handbook has more information about how iptables work.

- ▶ **Linux wireless** (http://linuxwireless.org/): The Linux Wireless website has more information on using wireless devices with Linux.

- ▶ **RPI-Wireless-Hotspot** (`http://elinux.org/RPI-Wireless-Hotspot`): This is an article about wireless hotspots on the Embedded Linux website.

- ▶ **USB Wi-Fi Adapters** (`http://elinux.org/RPi_VerifiedPeripherals#USB_ Wi-Fi_Adapters`): This is an article about Wi-Fi adapters on the Embedded Linux Wiki.

- ▶ **Raspberry Pi Wi-Fi adapter testing** (`http://www.element14.com/community/ docs/DOC-44703/1/raspberry-pi-wifi-adapter-testing`): This is an article about tested wireless adapters on the Element14 Community website.

Installing a network trace utility

This recipe installs the network trace utility My traceroute (`mtr`).

The `mtr` utility is often used for network troubleshooting. The utility displays the route that network packets take between the Raspberry Pi and another computer. The display is refreshed continuously displaying the time it takes network packets to travel between each device along the route between the two computers. By use `mrt`, you can see which devices along the network route are the slowest.

After completing this recipe, you will be able to trace network packets with `mrt`.

Getting ready

Ingredients:

An Initial Setup or Basic Networking setup for the Raspberry Pi that has been powered on. You have also logged in as the user `pi` (see the recipes in *Chapter 1*, *Installation and Setup* for how to boot and log in and the recipes in *Chapter 2*, *Administration* for how to log in remotely).

This recipe does not require the desktop GUI and could either be run from the text-based console or from within an `LXTerminal`.

If the Raspberry Pi's Secure Shell server is running, this recipe can be completed remotely using a Secure Shell client.

How to do it...

The steps to installing a network trace utility are:

1. Log in to the Raspberry Pi either directly or remotely.

2. Use the `apt-get install` command to install the `mtr` package.

   ```
   pi@raspberrypi ~ $ sudo apt-get install mtr
   Reading package lists... Done
   ```

```
Building dependency tree
Reading state information... Done
The following NEW packages will be installed:
  mtr
0 upgraded, 1 newly installed, 0 to remove and 0 not upgraded.
Need to get 59.2 kB of archives.
After this operation, 142 kB of additional disk space will be used.
Get:1 http://mirrordirector.raspbian.org/raspbian/ wheezy/main mtr armhf
0.82-3 [59.2 kB]
Fetched 59.2 kB in 0s (66.3 kB/s)
Selecting previously unselected package mtr.
(Reading database ... 88583 files and directories currently installed.)
Unpacking mtr (from .../archives/mtr_0.82-3_armhf.deb) ...
Processing triggers for menu ...
Processing triggers for man-db ...
Setting up mtr (0.82-3) ...
Processing triggers for menu ...

pi@raspberrypi ~ $
```

3. The `apt-get install` command installs the software package `mrt`.

4. Use the `mrt` command to trace the network route between your Raspberry Pi and the Raspberry Pi Foundation website.

   pi@raspberrypi ~ $ **sudo mtr raspberrypi.org**

5. The `mrt` command displays the route.

```
                        My traceroute  [v0.82]
raspberrypi (0.0.0.0)                           Sat Aug 29 16:44:37 2015
Keys:  Help   Display mode   Restart statistics   Order of fields   quit
                          Packets                  Pings
 Host                      Loss%   Snt   Last   Avg  Best  Wrst StDev
 1. 192.168.2.1            0.0%    29    2.6   0.9   0.5   3.1   0.8
 2. 10.0.0.1               3.4%    29    3.8   4.2   2.7   6.8   1.1
 3. c-24-5-176-1.hsd1.ca.comcast.net  0.0%  29  20.0  18.3  13.1  49.7  6.9
 4. te-0-6-0-14-sur03.sanmateo.ca.sf  0.0%  29  16.1  18.0  12.5  26.9  4.2
 5. he-0-13-0-0-ar01.santaclara.ca.s  0.0%  29  32.5  21.4  12.6  36.9  6.3
    he-0-13-0-1-ar01.santaclara.ca.sfba.comcast.net
 6. ???
 7. he-0-11-0-1-pe02.529bryant.ca.ib  0.0%  28  12.7  23.0  12.7  97.3  15.5
 8. 50.248.118.238         0.0%    28   22.6  20.8  14.8  44.7   5.4
 9. be2016.ccr22.sfo01.atlas.cogentc  0.0%  28  23.7  21.6  13.7  29.0   3.2
10. be2133.ccr22.mci01.atlas.cogentc  0.0%  28  59.7  64.6  57.5 120.8  11.7
11. be2157.ccr42.ord01.atlas.cogentc  0.0%  28  69.2  72.7  64.3 126.5  11.8
12. be2185.ccr22.cle04.atlas.cogentc  0.0%  28  75.2  78.4  71.1 108.7   8.8
13. be2483.ccr42.jfk02.atlas.cogentc  0.0%  28  90.6  90.8  82.7 106.7   4.5
14. be2490.ccr42.lon13.atlas.cogentc  0.0%  28 155.8 159.9 153.5 171.7   4.0
15. be2494.ccr22.lon01.atlas.cogentc  0.0%  28 160.9 161.8 157.4 178.6   4.6
16. be2352.rcr21.b015534-1.lon01.atl  0.0%  28 176.2 163.5 156.9 222.6  12.6
17. 149.11.4.86            0.0%    28  163.9 161.9 153.9 188.4   6.6
18. mythic10g-private.orochi.mythic-  0.0%  28 157.6 160.4 155.9 169.7   3.4

19. 93.93.128.230          0.0%    28  172.9 182.7 172.9 252.8  14.9
```

The display continuously refreshes until you press **q**.

How it works...

After logging in to the Raspberry Pi, this recipe installs the My traceroute software package (`mtr`).

Then the newly installed `mtr` command is used to trace the network route between the author's Raspberry Pi located in San Mateo, California and the Raspberry Pi Foundation website that is hosted by Mythic-Beasts located in London, England.

The *q* key is pressed to exit the command.

There's more...

The `mtr` dynamically updates network statistics collected from devices along the route between a remote machine and the Raspberry Pi. In addition to displaying a list of devices along the route (**Host**), `mtr` also displays stats for **Packets** and **Pings**.

The **Packets** stats show how many packets were sent (**Snt**) and how many packets were lost along the way (**Loss%**).

The **Pings** stats show how long it takes a network packet to travel from the Raspberry Pi to each device along the route. The average (**Avg**), best (**Best**), and worst (**Wrst**) time are also shown along with the standard deviation (**StDev**).

See also

- **MTR (My traceroute)** (`https://en.wikipedia.org/wiki/MTR_(software)`): This Wikipedia article has more information about `mtr`, its history, and how it works.

- **MTR** (`https://www.bitwizard.nl/mtr/`): The homepage for MTR – My traceroute.

- **mtr – a network diagnostic tool** (`http://manpages.debian.net/cgi-bin/man.cgi?query=mtr`): The Debian manpage for `mtr` describes the command and its options.

- **mythic beasts – infrastructure** (`https://www.mythic-beasts.com/article/infrastructure`): This web page describes the hosing infrastructure used by the Raspberry Pi Foundation, including the location of its data centers.

Installing a network protocol analyzer

This recipe installs the network protocol analyzer Wireshark.

The Wireshark network protocol analyzer lets you examine the traffic on your network at a microscopic level. This network tool can be used for live capture or offline analysis. Wireshark has a Graphical User Interface (GUI) and a TTY-mode utility (tshark).

Live data can be read from Ethernet, IEEE 802.11 (Wi-Fi), PPP/HDLC, ATM, Bluetooth, USB, Token Ring, Frame Relay, FDDI, and other low-level protocols. Decryption is supported for a number of higher-level protocols including IPsec, ISAKMP, Kerberos, SNMPv3, SSL/TLS, WEP, and WPA/WPA2. Data can be read/written in many forms including tcpdump, Microsoft Network Monitor, Network General Sniffer, Sniffer Pro, NetXray, and many others.

After completing this recipe, you will be able to analyze your network with wireshark.

> This recipe is only a starting point for exploring network protocol analysis. Links to more detailed information can be found at the end of the recipe.

Getting ready

Ingredients:

An Initial Setup or Basic Networking setup for the Raspberry Pi that has been powered on. You have also logged in as the user pi.

This recipe requires the desktop GUI.

If the Raspberry Pi's VNC server is running, this recipe can be completed remotely using a VNC client (see the *Remote access to the monitor* recipe earlier in this chapter).

How to do it...

The steps to installing a network protocol analyzer are:

1. Log in to the Raspberry Pi desktop GUI.

2. Use the apt-get install command to install the wireshark package.
   ```
   pi@raspberrypi ~ $ sudo apt-get install -y wireshark
   Reading package lists... Done
   Building dependency tree
   Reading state information... Done
   ```

The following extra packages will be installed:
    libc-ares2 libcap2-bin liblua5.1-0 libpam-cap libpcap0.8 libsmi2ldbl
libwireshark-data
    libwireshark2 libwiretap2 libwsutil2 wireshark-common
Suggested packages:
    libcap-dev snmp-mibs-downloader wireshark-doc
The following NEW packages will be installed:
    libc-ares2 libcap2-bin liblua5.1-0 libpam-cap libpcap0.8 libsmi2ldbl
libwireshark-data
    libwireshark2 libwiretap2 libwsutil2 wireshark wireshark-common
0 upgraded, 12 newly installed, 0 to remove and 0 not upgraded.
Need to get 14.0 MB of archives.
After this operation, 48.6 MB of additional disk space will be used.

...

3. The `apt-get install` command downloads and installs the `wireshark`
    software package.

4. Use the `dpkg-reconfigure` command to modify the default configuration for
    `wireshark`.

    pi@raspberrypi ~ $ **sudo dpkg-reconfigure wireshark-common**

    The dpkg-reconfigure command asks if non-superusers should be able to capture packets.

    ```
    ┤ Configuring wireshark-common ├──────────────

    │ Dumpcap can be installed in a way that allows members of the "wireshark" │
    │ system group to capture packets. This is recommended over the             │
    │ alternative of running Wireshark/Tshark directly as root, because less    │
    │ of the code will run with elevated privileges.                            │
    │                                                                           │
    │ For more detailed information please see                                  │
    │ /usr/share/doc/wireshark-common/README.Debian.                           │
    │                                                                           │
    │ Enabling this feature may be a security risk, so it is disabled by        │
    │ default. If in doubt, it is suggested to leave it disabled.               │
    │                                                                           │
    │ Should non-superusers be able to capture packets?                         │
    │                                                                           │
    │            <Yes>                        <No>                              │
    │                                                                           │
    ```

5. Use the **<tab>** key to select the answer **<Yes>** and then press the **<enter>** key to
    update the package configuration.

6. Use the `usermod` command to add (`-a`) the user `pi` to the `wireshark` system group
    (`-G wireshark`).

    pi@raspberrypi ~ $ **sudo usermod -a -G wireshark pi**

    pi@raspberrypi ~ $

7. Use the Desktop GUI menu to start the Wireshark application.

8. The Wireshark application is started.

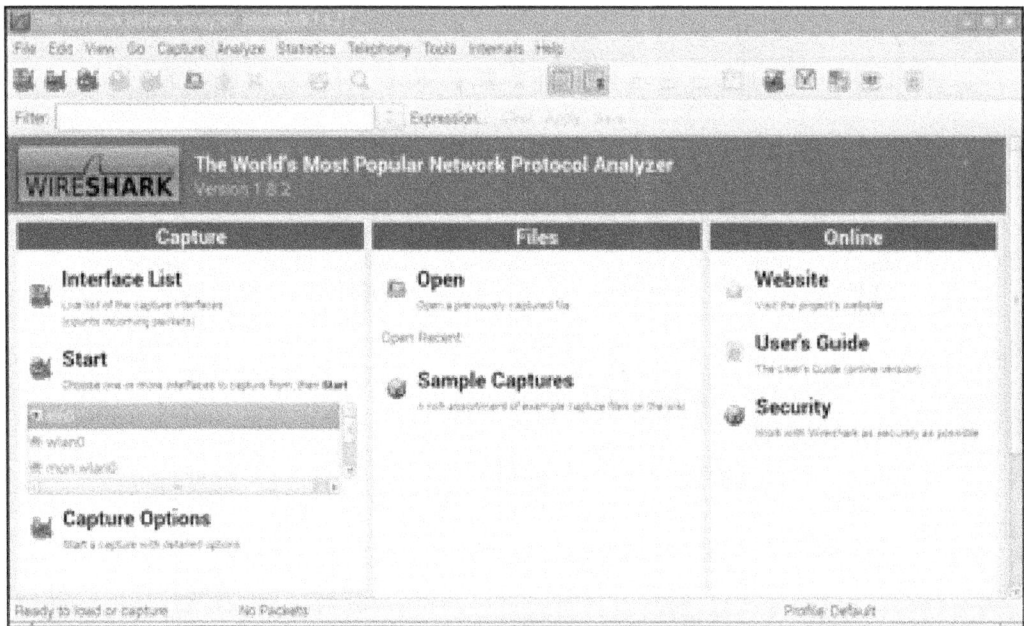

9. Choose an interface from the menu and click **Start** to begin sniffing network packets.

10. The Wireshark application displays detailed information about each network packet as they are captured (sniffed).

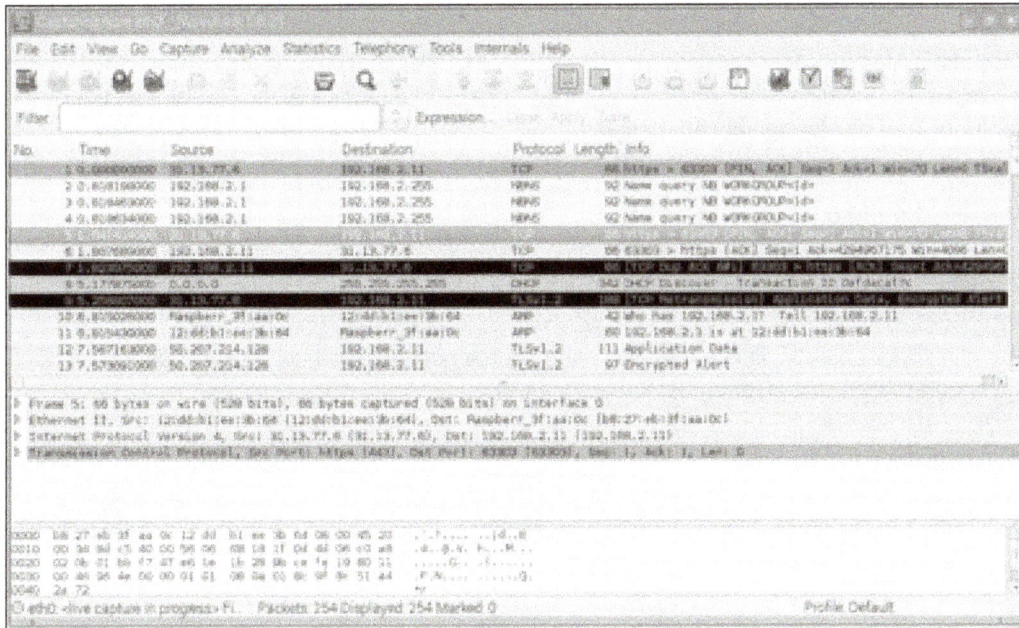

11. Use the **File** menu or *Ctrl+Q* to quit.

How it works...

After logging in to the Raspberry Pi, this recipe uses the `apt-get install` command to install the Wireshark network protocol analyzer (network packet sniffer).

After the Wireshark application is installed, the `dpkg-reconfigure` command is used to change the default application configuration (**wireshark-common**) to allow non-superusers to capture network packets. By default, only superusers are allowed to capture network packets.

After the configuration change is accepted (**<Yes>**), members of the **wireshark** system group may also capture network packets.

Before the application is started, the user **pi** is added (**-a**) to the **wireshark** user group using the **usermod** command.

The Wireshark command is started by selecting **Menu > Internet > Wireshark** from the Raspberry Pi desktop.

When the application is started, the Wireshark application main page is displayed.

From the main page, it is possible to select which network interfaces will be sniffed (monitored for incoming/outgoing network packets). After the **Start** command is clicked, Wireshark starts capturing and displaying network packets.

The Wireshark application can be exited by selecting **File > Quit** from the menu bar, or by pressing **Control-Q**.

There's more...

The Wireshark application is a free and open source network protocol analyzer popular for network troubleshooting, analysis, and education.

Promiscuous mode

Wireshark puts the selected network interface(s) into promiscuous mode. In promiscuous mode, the interface listens for all network packets, including packets that are not destined for the Raspberry Pi. Wireshark can see all the network traffic on the network interface.

Terminal-based user interface

Wireshark also has a command-line utility, `tshark`, that outputs the packets it sniffs directly to the console. The `tshark` command is installed separately from Wireshark.

```
pi@raspberrypi ~ $ sudo apt-get install -y tshark
Reading package lists... Done
Building dependency tree
Reading state information... Done
The following NEW packages will be installed:
  tshark
0 upgraded, 1 newly installed, 0 to remove and 0 not upgraded.
Need to get 173 kB of archives.
After this operation, 314 kB of additional disk space will be used.
Get:1 http://mirrordirector.raspbian.org/raspbian/ wheezy/main tshark armhf
1.8.2-5wheezy16 [173 kB]
Fetched 173 kB in 1s (149 kB/s)
Selecting previously unselected package tshark.
(Reading database ... 88953 files and directories currently installed.)
Unpacking tshark (from .../tshark_1.8.2-5wheezy16_armhf.deb) ...
Processing triggers for man-db ...
Setting up tshark (1.8.2-5wheezy16) ...

pi@raspberrypi ~ $
```

When entered on the command line without options, tshark starts capturing the packets it can sniff on the default network interface (eth0).

```
pi@raspberrypi ~ $ tshark
Capturing on eth0
7.169256 93.93.130.39 -> 192.168.2.11 TCP 74 http > 47593 [SYN, ACK] Seq=0 Ack=1
win=14480 Len=0 MSS=1460 SACK_PERM=1 TSval=3829221233 TSecr=2254282 WS=128
  7.169418 192.168.2.11 -> 93.93.130.39 TCP 66 47593 > http [ACK] Seq=1 Ack=1 win=29312
Len=0 TSval=2254310 TSecr=3829221233
  7.170328 192.168.2.11 -> 93.93.130.39 HTTP 399 GET / HTTP/1.1
  7.332273 93.93.130.39 -> 192.168.2.11 TCP 66 http > 47593 [ACK] Seq=1 Ack=334 win=15616
Len=0 TSval=3829221302 TSecr=2254310
  7.333431 93.93.130.39 -> 192.168.2.11 HTTP 324 HTTP/1.0 302 Found  (text/html)
  7.333558 192.168.2.11 -> 93.93.130.39 TCP 66 47593 > http [ACK] Seq=334 Ack=259
win=30336 Len=0 TSval=2254326 TSecr=3829221302
  7.339590 192.168.2.11 -> 93.93.130.39 TCP 66 47593 > http [FIN, ACK] Seq=334 Ack=259
win=30336 Len=0 TSval=2254327 TSecr=3829221302
  7.342519 192.168.2.11 -> 192.168.2.1  DNS 64 Standard query 0x32c4  A wpad
  7.343102  192.168.2.1 -> 192.168.2.11 DNS 139 Standard query response 0x32c4 No such
name
  7.344034 192.168.2.11 -> 192.168.2.1  DNS 79 Standard query 0x5959  A www.raspberrypi.
org
  7.371312  192.168.2.1 -> 192.168.2.11 DNS 160 Standard query response 0x5959  CNAME
lb.raspberrypi.org A 93.93.128.211 A 93.93.128.230 A 93.93.130.39 A 93.93.130.214
```

The preceding example output from tshark shows some of the network packets captured when browsing the website https://www.reaspberrypi.org.

Capture filters

Not all of the network packets passing across the Raspberry Pi's network interface are interesting. Both Wireshark and tshark can use capture filters to limit the number of packets that are captured and displayed.

In this example, the capture filter limits the display to SSL traffic.

```
pi@raspberrypi ~ $ tshark -R 'ssl'
Capturing on eth0
  1.080068 192.168.2.11 -> 216.58.209.227 TLSv1.2 135 Encrypted Alert
  1.081229 192.168.2.11 -> 74.125.224.145 TLSv1.2 135 Encrypted Alert
  1.082105 192.168.2.11 -> 74.125.224.145 TLSv1.2 135 Encrypted Alert
  1.082913 192.168.2.11 -> 216.58.192.35 TLSv1.2 135 Encrypted Alert
  1.083782 192.168.2.11 -> 74.125.20.95 TLSv1.2 135 Encrypted Alert
  1.084541 192.168.2.11 -> 74.125.224.9 TLSv1.2 135 Encrypted Alert
  1.085294 192.168.2.11 -> 74.125.20.95 TLSv1.2 135 Encrypted Alert
  1.239064 192.168.2.11 -> 173.194.202.105 SSL 206 Client Hello
  1.345864 173.194.202.105 -> 192.168.2.11 SSL 1484 [TCP Previous segment not captured]
Continuation Data
  1.345865 173.194.202.105 -> 192.168.2.11 SSL 405 Continuation Data

...
```

The following example captures data from the wireless network (wlan0) and limits the display to HTTP traffic.

```
pi@raspberrypi ~ $ tshark -i wlan0 -R http
Capturing on wlan0
  7.721824 192.168.0.75 -> 199.27.79.133 HTTP 452 GET / HTTP/1.1
  7.818987 199.27.79.133 -> 192.168.0.75 HTTP 781 [TCP Previous segment not
captured] Continuation or non-HTTP traffic
  7.831542 192.168.0.75 -> 199.27.79.133 HTTP 511 GET /css/main.css HTTP/1.1
```

More examples of the use of capture filters, as well as more detail on the use of Wireshark and `tshark`, can be found in the following references.

See also

Wireshark (`https://www.wireshark.org`): The home page for the Wireshark application has detailed documentation on how Wireshark can be used effectively.

Wireshark (`https://en.wikipedia.org/wiki/Wireshark`): This Wikipedia article has more information about Wireshark, its history, and how it works.

  ► **wireshark - interactively dump and analyze network traffic** (`http://manpages.debian.net/cgi-bin/man.cgi?query=wireshark`): The Debian manpage for wireshark describes the command, its configuration, and its options.

  ► **tshark - dump and analyze network traffic** (`http://manpages.debian.net/cgi-bin/man.cgi?query=tshark`): The Debian manpage for `tshark` describes the command, its configuration, and options.

wireshark-filter - Wireshark filter syntax and reference (`http://manpages.debian.org/cgi-bin/man.cgi?query=wireshark-filter`): This Debian manpage describes Wireshark's capture filters in detail.

  ► **CaptureFilters** (`https://wiki.wireshark.org/CaptureFilters`): This website has a number of useful capture filter examples.

Introduction to Wireshark (`https://www.wireshark.org/video/wireshark/introduction-to-wireshark/`): This video is an excellent introduction to packet sniffing with Wireshark.

Enabling the IPv6 network protocol

This recipe configures your Raspberry Pi to support IPv6.

The Internet Protocol's sixth version, IPv6, is intended to replace the current IPv4 protocol. IPv6 provides $8x10^{28}$ more IP address than IPv4. It is also a more stable, efficient, and secure protocol.

The majority of modern home network routers support both IPv4 and IPv6; however, not all of the older routers still in service support IPv6. So, IPv6 is not enabled by default on the Raspberry Pi, which saves a bit of memory and processing power. To take full advantage of modern networking services, you can enable IPv6 on your Raspberry Pi.

After completing this recipe, your Raspberry Pi will have IPv6 enabled.

Getting ready

Ingredients:

An Initial Setup or Basic Networking setup for the Raspberry Pi that has been powered on. You have also logged in as the user pi (see the recipes in *Chapter 1, Installation and Setup* for how to boot and log in and the recipes in *Chapter 2, Administration* for how to log in remotely).

This recipe does not require the desktop GUI and could either be run from the text-based console or from within an LXTerminal.

If the Raspberry Pi's Secure Shell server is running, this recipe can be completed remotely using a Secure Shell client.

How to do it...

The steps to installing a mesh network are:

1. Log in to the Raspberry Pi either directly or remotely.

2. Use the modprobe command to enable the ipv6 protocol.

    pi@raspberrypi ~ $ **sudo modprobe ipv6**

3. Use the ifconfig command to validate that all of the network interfaces now have IPv6 enabled (look for the inet6 addr).

    ```
    pi@raspberrypi ~ $ ifconfig
    eth0      Link encap:Ethernet  HWaddr b8:27:eb:3f:aa:0c
              inet addr:192.168.2.11  Bcast:192.168.2.255  Mask:255.255.255.0
              inet6 addr: fe80::ba27:ebff:fe3f:aa0c/64 Scope:Link
              UP BROADCAST RUNNING MULTICAST  MTU:1500  Metric:1
              RX packets:978305 errors:0 dropped:0 overruns:0 frame:0
              TX packets:1786420 errors:0 dropped:0 overruns:0 carrier:0
              collisions:0 txqueuelen:1000
              RX bytes:100780981 (96.1 MiB)  TX bytes:2430911170 (2.2 GiB)

    lo        Link encap:Local Loopback
              inet addr:127.0.0.1  Mask:255.0.0.0
              inet6 addr: ::1/128 Scope:Host
              UP LOOPBACK RUNNING  MTU:65536  Metric:1
              RX packets:45 errors:0 dropped:0 overruns:0 frame:0
              TX packets:45 errors:0 dropped:0 overruns:0 carrier:0
    ```

```
          collisions:0 txqueuelen:0
          RX bytes:3420 (3.3 KiB)  TX bytes:3420 (3.3 KiB)

wlan0     Link encap:Ethernet  HWaddr 00:0f:55:bb:aa:b5
          inet addr:192.168.0.1  Bcast:192.168.0.255  Mask:255.255.255.0
          inet6 addr: fe80::20f:55ff:febb:aab5/64 Scope:Link
          UP BROADCAST RUNNING MULTICAST  MTU:1500  Metric:1
          RX packets:1628703 errors:0 dropped:50 overruns:0 frame:0
          TX packets:803167 errors:0 dropped:0 overruns:0 carrier:0
          collisions:0 txqueuelen:1000
          RX bytes:2395688238 (2.2 GiB)  TX bytes:94274367 (89.9 MiB)

pi@raspberrypi ~ $
```

4. The Raspberry Pi is now using IPv6! However, the `ipv6` module will not be automatically loaded at the next boot. Use the following steps to configure the module to load automatically.

5. Add the `ipv6` module to the bottom of the kernel's module configuration file, `/etc/modules`.

   ```
   pi@raspberrypi ~ $ sudo sh -c 'echo ipv6 >>/etc/modules'
   ```

6. Use the `vi` command to edit the kernel module configuration file `/etc/modprobe.d/ipv6.conf`.

   ```
   pi@raspberrypi ~ $ sudo vi /etc/modprobe.d/ipv6.conf
   ```

7. The `vi` editor displays the contents of the configuration file. Instructions for using the editor can be found in the `vi` manpages (see the recipe *Reading the built-in documentation* in *Chapter 2, Administration*).

   ```
   # Don't load ipv6 by default
   alias net-pf-10 off
   #alias ipv6 off
   ~
   ~
   "/etc/modprobe.d/ipv6.conf" 3 lines, 65 characters
   ```

8. Change the word **off** at the end of the **alias net-pf-10** line to **on**, and delete the **alias ipv6** line as it is no longer true.

   ```
   # ipv6 is loaded by default
   alias net-pf-10 ipv6
   ~
   ~
   "/etc/modprobe.d/ipv6.conf" 3 lines, 59 characters
   ```

9. Save the file and exit the editor (`:wq`).

10. Finally, reboot the Raspberry Pi to use the new IPv6 configuration!

```
pi@raspberrypi ~ $ sudo reboot

Broadcast message from root@raspberrypi (pts/0) (Sun Aug 30 13:01:44
2015):
The system is going down for reboot NOW!
pi@raspberrypi ~ $ Connection to 192.168.2.13 closed by remote host.
Connection to 192.168.2.13 closed.
```

How it works...

After logging in to the Raspberry Pi, this recipe uses the modprobe command to load the `ipv6` module. Simply loading the module enables IPv6 networking; however, the `ipv6` module will not be automatically loaded on the next reboot. The kernel's module configuration needs to be updated to enable an automatic load at boot.

The recipe uses the `echo` command running in a subshell (`sh -c`) to append (`>>`) the module name, `ipv6`, to the bottom of the `/etc/modules` configuration file. Adding the module name to the module configuration ensures that the module will be loaded at boot.

The recipe also uses the `vi` command to update the `/etc/modprobe/ipv6.conf` file, explicitly enabling (**on**) the complete IPv6 network protocol family (`net-pf-10`).

After the configuration is updated, the Raspberry Pi is rebooted.

There's more...

Internet Protocol version 6 not only has a larger address space but also more features.

Privacy extensions

IPv6 has two interesting privacy extensions: one that creates a new random address each time it's rebooted, and another that continuously randomizes the address.

To enable the generation of a temporary random IPv6 address with each new boot, add the `net.ipv6.conf.iface.use_tempadd` Linux kernel parameter to the bottom of the `/etc/sysctl.conf` kernel configuration file.

To enable a continual refresh of the random IP address, add the kernel parameter `net.ipv6.conf.iface.temp_prefered_lft` to the bottom of the same file.

The following example uses the echo command to append (>>) the two kernel configuration parameters to the bottom of the kernel configuration file, /etc/sysctl.conf. The IPv6 kernel parameter (net.ipv6.conf) for generating a temporary address (use_tempadd) is enabled (**2**) and the parameter for refreshing it (temp_prefered_lft) every two hours (**7200** seconds) is set for all interfaces. First, the sudo sh command is use to create a subshell with superuser privileges. After the kernel parameters are added, the subshell is exited (**exit**) and the superuser privileges are discarded.

```
pi@raspberrypi ~ $ sudo sh

# echo "net.ipv6.conf.all.use_tempaddr = 2" >> /etc/sysctl.conf

# echo "net.ipv6.conf.default.use_tempaddr = 2" >> /etc/sysctl.conf

# echo "net.ipv6.conf.all.temp_prefered_lft = 7200" >> /etc/sysctl.conf

# echo "net.ipv6.conf.default.temp_prefered_lft = 7200" >> /etc/sysctl.conf

# exit

pi@raspberrypi ~ $
```

Reboot the Raspberry Pi and the changes will be applied.

Use sysctl to change kernel parameters at runtime

The following example uses the systctl command to configure the extensions at runtime specifically for the interface eth0. However, the /etc/sysctl.conf will still need to be updated to automatically use them at boot.

```
pi@raspberrypi ~ $ sudo sh

# sysctl -a --pattern 'net.ipv6.conf.eth0.use_tempaddr'
net.ipv6.conf.eth0.use_tempaddr = 0

# sysctl net.ipv6.conf.eth0.use_tempaddr=2
net.ipv6.conf.eth0.use_tempaddr = 2

# sysctl -a --pattern 'net.ipv6.conf.eth0.temp_prefered_lft'
net.ipv6.conf.eth0.temp_prefered_lft = 86400

# sysctl net.ipv6.conf.eth0.temp_prefered_lft=7200
net.ipv6.conf.eth0.temp_prefered_lft = 7200

# exit

pi@raspberrypi ~ $
```

See also

- **IPv6** (`https://en.wikipedia.org/wiki/IPv6`): This Wikipedia article has more information about Internet Protocol version 6.

- **sysctl.conf – configure kernel parameters at runtime** (`http://manpages.debian.net/cgi-bin/man.cgi?query=sysctl`): The Debian manpage for `sysctl` has limited information on the command.

- **sysctl.conf – sysctl preload/configuration file** (`http://manpages.debian.net/cgi-bin/man.cgi?query=sysctl.conf`): The Debian manpage for `sysctl.conf` has limited information on the file format.

6

IoT – Internet of Things

In this chapter, we will cover:

- ▶ Easy access to hardware
- ▶ Installing the GrovePi
- ▶ Controlling devices from a web page
- ▶ Connecting to an IoT platform
- ▶ Creating an IoT gateway

Introduction

The recipes in this chapter show how devices and sensors – things – attached to the Raspberry Pi can be connected to the **Internet of Things** (**IoT**).

The (**IoT**) describes the Internet when it is being used to enable physical objects – Things – to exchange data. When connected to the Internet, the Raspberry Pi can participate in the IoT, exchanging real-time data using its **general-purpose input/output** (**GPIO**) and other hardware interfaces. This chapter has a collection of recipes that show how the Raspberry Pi can participate in the Internet of Things.

The recipes in this chapter are specific to the Raspberry Pi. They utilize the hardware interfaces of the Raspberry Pi – the GPIO pins. The concepts can be used with other Linux computers; however, the instructions are specific to the Raspberry Pi.

After completing the recipes in this chapter, you will have configured and controlled devices and sensors attached directly to the Raspberry Pi and via the GrovePi hardware system. You will also have controlled devices attached to the Raspberry Pi from a web page hosted on the Raspberry and through the IoT service providers SmartLiving.io and ThingBox.io.

Easy access to hardware

This recipe demonstrates how simple it is to access hardware from a Raspberry Pi.

In this recipe, an LED connected to one of the Raspberry Pi's GPIO pins is made to blink using simple Bash commands (`ls`, `cat`, and `echo`).

After completing this recipe, you will be able to control the GPIO ports attached to your Raspberry Pi from the Bash command line.

Getting ready

Ingredients:

- An Initial Setup or Basic Networking setup for the Raspberry Pi that is not powered on
- An LED
- A pushbutton switch
- Three 330 Ohm resisters
- A breadboard
- A few breadboarding wires

This recipe does not require the desktop GUI and could either be run from the text-based console or from within an `LXTerminal`.

If the Raspberry Pi's Secure Shell server is running, this recipe can be completed remotely using a Secure Shell client.

How to do it...

The steps to easily accessing hardware from the command line are:

1. Before powering on the Raspberry Pi, use the following two diagrams to connect a pushbutton switch to GPIO port 23 (pin 16) and an LED to GPIO port 24 (pin 18).

The following diagram shows the component layout for this recipe:

2. The pushbutton switch should be connected to pin 2 (5V) on one side. The other side of the pushbutton switch should have two 330 Ohm resisters connected – one resister leading to pin 6 (GND) and one resistor leading to pin 16 (GPIO 23).

3. The LED should be connected to pin 18 (GPIO port 24) on one side. The other side of the LED should have a 330 Ohm resistor connected leading to pin 20 (GND).

> Turn the LED around if the first try does not work.
>
> An LED is a light emitting diode. Diodes only allow current to flow in one direction. A reversed diode is a common electronic circuit bug.

4. After you have validated that the pushbutton switch, the LED, and the two 330 Ohm resistors are connected correctly, power on the Raspberry Pi.

The following diagram shows the pin layout of the Raspberry Pi's GPIO interface:

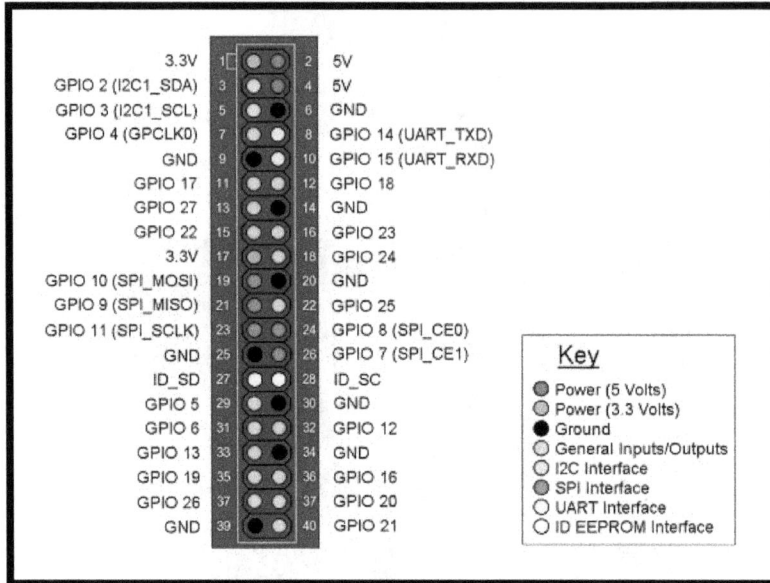

5. Log in to the Raspberry Pi either directly or remotely.

6. Use the `cd` command to navigate through the Raspberry Pi's kernel parameters to the `/sys/class/gpio` directory.

```
pi@raspberrypi ~ $ cd /sys/class/gpio

pi@raspberrypi ~ $
```

7. Use the `ls` command to list the contents of the kernel parameter directory containing GPIO parameters and interfaces.

```
pi@raspberrypi /sys/class/gpio $ ls
export  gpiochip0  unexport

pi@raspberrypi /sys/class/gpio $
```

8. Use the `echo` command to tell the Raspberry Pi's kernel to `export` the interfaces to GPIO ports `23` and `24` into user space.

   ```
   pi@raspberrypi /sys/class/gpio $ echo 23 >export

   pi@raspberrypi /sys/class/gpio $ echo 24 >export

   pi@raspberrypi /sys/class/gpio $
   ```

9. Use the `ls` command to once again display the contents of the kernel parameters and interfaces directory, `/sys/class/gpio`.

   ```
   pi@raspberrypi /sys/class/gpio $ ls
   export  gpio23  gpio24  gpiochip0  unexport

   pi@raspberrypi /sys/class/gpio $
   ```

10. Notice the two new user space accessible kernel interfaces to GPIO port 23 (`gpio23`) and GPIO port 24 (`gpio24`).

11. Use the `echo` command to configure GPIO port 23 (`gpio23`) to receive input signals (`in`) and GPIO port 24 (`gpio24`) to send output signals (`out`).

    ```
    pi@raspberrypi /sys/class/gpio $ echo in >gpio23/direction

    pi@raspberrypi /sys/class/gpio $ echo out >gpio24/direction

    pi@raspberrypi /sys/class/gpio $
    ```

12. Use the `cat` command to see the current state of the pushbutton switch when it's not being pressed (`0`) and when it is pressed (`1`).

    ```
    pi@raspberrypi /sys/class/gpio $ cat gpio23/value
    0

    pi@raspberrypi /sys/class/gpio $ # WHILE PRESSING THE BUTTON...

    pi@raspberrypi /sys/class/gpio $ cat gpio23/value
    1

    pi@raspberrypi /sys/class/gpio $
    ```

13. The pushbutton switch works!

14. Use the `echo` command to turn the LED on (`1`) and then off (`0`).
```
pi@raspberrypi /sys/class/gpio $ echo 1 >gpio24/value

pi@raspberrypi /sys/class/gpio $ echo 0 >gpio24/value
pi@raspberrypi /sys/class/gpio $
```

15. The LED works!

16. Use the following `while` loop to control the LED with the pushbutton. Use *Ctrl-C* (`^c`) to stop the `while` loop.
```
pi@raspberrypi /sys/class/gpio $ in=gpio23/value

pi@raspberrypi /sys/class/gpio $ out=gpio24/value

pi@raspberrypi /sys/class/gpio $ while true; do echo $(cat $in) >$out;
done

^C

pi@raspberrypi /sys/class/gpio $
```

17. The pushbutton switch controls the LED!

18. Use the `echo` command to `unexport` GPIO ports `23` and `24` from user space, and use the `ls` command to see that the Raspberry Pi kernel has removed the `gpio23` and `gpio24` interfaces.
```
pi@raspberrypi /sys/class/gpio $ ls
export  gpio23  gpio24  gpiochip0  unexport

pi@raspberrypi /sys/class/gpio $ echo 23 >unexport

pi@raspberrypi /sys/class/gpio $ echo 24 >unexport

pi@raspberrypi /sys/class/gpio $ ls
export  gpiochip0  unexport
```

How it works...

This recipe uses a connected input device (pushbutton switch) to activate an output device (LED). The recipe begins by connecting the input and output devices to the Raspberry Pi. Once the devices are connected, each of the devices is tested individually. Finally, a Bash script activates the output device whenever the input device signals.

Before the Raspberry Pi is powered on two devices, a pushbutton switch and an **LED**, are connected to the Raspberry Pi.

Connect the pushbutton switch to GPIO port 23

The pushbutton switch acts as an input device. It is connected to +5v on one side via pin 2 and to GPIO port 23 on the other side via pin 16. When the pushbutton switch is pressed, GPIO port 23 (pin 16) detects a high signal coming from +5v (pin 2) through the closed pushbutton switch.

In addition to the pushbutton switch, two 330 Ohm resistors are necessary to safely complete this part of the circuit. One 330 Ohm resistor is used to limit the current flow when the pushbutton switch is pressed (closed) and the signal is high. The other 330 Ohm resistor is used to pull the signal down to low when the pushbutton switch is not pressed (open).

The current-limiting resistor connects the pushbutton switch to GPIO port 23 (pin 16). The pull-down resistor connects GPIO port 23 (pin 16) to GND (pin 6).

When the pushbutton switch is open, GPIO port 23 (pin 16) detects a low signal coming through the pull-down resistor connected to GND (pin 6). When the pushbutton switch is closed, GPIO port 23 (pin 16) detects a high signal coming from +5v (pin 2) through the current-limiting resistor.

Connect the LED to GPIO port 24

The LED acts as an output device. It is connected to GPIO port 24 (pin 18) on one side. On the other side, the LED is connected to a current-limiting 330 Ohm resistor leading to GND (pin 20).

When GPIO port 24 (pin 18) emits a high signal, enough current passes through the circuit to light the LED. When the signal is low, the LED remains unlit.

Power on and log in

Once you have validated that the LED, the pushbutton switch, and the three protective 330 Ohm resistors are connected correctly, turn on the Raspberry Pi and log in.

Navigating the Linux kernel with sysfs

After you have logged in, the recipe uses the `cd` command to navigate to the `/sys/class/gpio` directory within the `sysfs` virtual file system. The `sysfs` virtual file system is a user space mapping of Linux kernel parameters and interfaces. The kernel parameters for the GPIO interface are accessible from `/sys/class/gpio`.

The `ls` command is used to see which GPIO port interfaces are currently exported from kernel space to user space. So far, no interfaces have been exported.

The gpio directory only contains three entries: two pseudo-parameters, `export` and `unexport`; and one interface, `gpiochip0`. The interface to `gpiochip0` is not used in this recipe. The two pseudo-parameters are used to `export` and `unexport` GPIO port interfaces from kernel space to user space.

Export GPIO ports 23 and 24

The recipe uses the `echo` command to write the numbers 23 and 24 to the `export` pseudo-parameter. This tells the Raspberry Pi's Linux kernel to export the interfaces to GPIO ports 23 and 24 into user space (at `/sys/class/gpio`).

The command line for exporting the GPIO port 23 interface, `echo 23 >export`, works because it writes (**>**) the number 23 (echo 23) to the Linux kernel pseudo-parameter `/sys/class/gpio/export` telling the kernel to create an interface subdirectory (gpio23) for GPIO port 23.

After the kernel has been told to export the two GPIO ports, the `ls` command is used once again to show that the Linux kernel has created two new GPIO port interface subdirectories, one for GPIO port 23, `/sys/class/gpio/gpio23`, and one for GPIO port 24, `/sys/class/gpio/gpio24`.

Configure each interface direction as input or output

The recipe then uses the `echo` command to write (**>**) either `in` (for input) or `out` (for output) to the `direction` parameter within each of the GPIO ports' interface subdirectories (gpio23 and gpio24).

The input device (pushbutton switch) is connected to GPIO port 23, so the direction parameter for GPIO port 23 (gpio23) is set to input (`echo in > gpio23/direction`).

The output device (LED) is connected to GPIO port 24, so the direction for GPIO port 24 (gpio24) is set to output (`echo out > gpio24/direction`).

Once the input/output direction for each GPIO port has been configured, the interface to each port can be tested.

Testing the input device

The input device is tested using the `cat` command to display the value of GPIO port 23 (`gpio23/value`).

The value of GPIO port 23 (`gpio23/value`) is displayed when the pushbutton switch is released and when it is being pressed. When the pushbutton switch is released (the switch is open), the value of GPIO port 23 (`gpio23/value`) is low (0). When the pushbutton switch is pressed (closed), the value is high (1).

Testing the output device

The output device is tested using the `echo` command.

When the value high is sent to GPIO port 24 (echo 1 >gpio24/value), the LED glows. When the value low is sent (echo 0 >gpio24/value), the LED stops glowing.

Using the input device to activate the output device

After successfully testing the input (pushbutton switch) and output (LED) devices, the recipe connects the two devices with a simple `while` loop.

First, the shell variable `in` is defined to be an alias for the value of GPIO port 23 (`gpio23/value`) and the variable `out` is defined to be an alias for the value of GPIO port 24 (`gpio24/value`).

Then, the two variables are used in an infinite loop (`while true; do`) that reads the input signal from GPIO port 23 (`$(cat in)`) and uses the `echo` command to write the signal to GPIO port 24 (`>$out`).

While the loop is running, the LED lights whenever the pushbutton switch is pressed.

Pressing *Ctrl+C* stops the loop.

Cleanup

After running the loop, the `cat` command is used to unexport the Linux kernel interfaces from user space to GPIO port 23 (`/sys/class/gpio/gpio23`) and GPIO port 24 (`/sys/class/gpio/gpio24`).

After the GPIO port interfaces have been unexported, the `ls` command is used to validate that the two GPIO port interfaces (`gpio23` and `gpio24`) have been removed from the `/sys/class/gpio` user space directory.

See also

▸ **General-purpose input/output** (`https://en.wikipedia.org/wiki/General-purpose_input/output`): This Wikipedia article describes how General-purpose input/output interfaces work.

▸ **sysfs** (`https://en.wikipedia.org/wiki/Sysfs`): This Wikipedia article describes the `sysfs` filesystem, its history, and how it works.

▸ **Pull-up resistor** (`https://en.wikipedia.org/wiki/Pull-up_resistor`): This Wikipedia article describes how pull-up resistors are used to ensure a circuit has valid logic levels.

▸ **Diode** (`https://en.wikipedia.org/wiki/Diode`): This Wikipedia article explains diodes in great detail.

▸ **Bash Guide for Beginners** (`http://tldp.org/LDP/Bash-Beginners-Guide/html/index.html`): This book is a practical guide for using Bash and the Bash scripting language.

Installing the GrovePi

This recipe configures access to the Grove Pi extension board for the Raspberry Pi.

The Grove hardware system by Seeed is a Lego-like system for plugging together electronic components without the need for soldering.

The GrovePi by Dexter Industries turns the Raspberry Pi into a central control hub for Grove components.

The following image shows the GrovePi+ installed on a Raspberry Pi 2:

After completing this recipe, you will be able to control Grove components attached to the GrovePi from your Raspberry Pi using the Python scripting language.

Getting ready

Ingredients:

- ▸ An Initial Setup or Basic Networking setup for the Raspberry Pi that has been powered on, but the GrovePi has not yet been installed. You have also logged in as the user `pi` (see the recipes in *Chapter 1, Installation and Setup* for how to boot and log in, and the recipes in *Chapter 2, Administration* for how to log in remotely).
- ▸ A GrovePi GPIO expansion board.
- ▸ A Grove LED.
- ▸ A Grove pushbutton switch.
- ▸ Two Grove connector wires.

If the Raspberry Pi's Secure Shell server is running, this recipe can be completed remotely using a Secure Shell client.

How to do it...

The steps to installing the GrovePi are:

1. Before attaching the GrovePi to the Raspberry Pi, use the `git` command to download the GrovePi installation files from the `DexterInd/GrovePi` repository on `github.com`.

```
pi@raspberrypi ~ $ git clone https://github.com/DexterInd/GrovePi

Cloning into 'GrovePi'...
remote: Counting objects: 2206, done.
remote: Total 2206 (delta 0), reused 0 (delta 0), pack-reused 2206
Receiving objects: 100% (2206/2206), 1.22 MiB | 1.37 MiB/s, done.
Resolving deltas: 100% (1134/1134), done.

pi@raspberrypi ~/ $
```

2. Use the `cd` command to navigate to the directory containing the installation script, `GrovePi/Scripts`.

```
pi@raspberrypi ~ $ cd GrovePi/Script/

pi@raspberrypi ~/GrovePi/Script $
```

3. Use the `sh` command to execute the installation script. The command requires super user privileges (use `sudo`).

```
pi@raspberrypi ~/GrovePi/Script $ sudo sh ./install.sh
```

```
   ____            _
  |  _ \          | |
  | | | | _____  _| |_ ___ _ __
  | | | |/ _ \ \/ / __/ _ \ '__|
  | |_| |  __/>  <| ||  __/ |
  |____/ \___/_/_____|_|  _
  |_   _|         | |        | |      (_)
    | |  _ __   __| |_   _ ___| |_ _ __ _  ___  ___
    | | | '_ \ / _` | | | / __| __| '__| |/ _ \/ __|
   _| |_| | | | (_| | |_| \__ \ |_| |  | |  __/\__ \
  |_____|_| |_|\__,_|\__,_|___/\__|_|  |_|\___||___/
```

Welcome to GrovePi Installer.

Requirements:

1) Must be connected to the internet

2) This script must be run as root user

Steps:

1) Installs package dependencies:
     - python-pip   alternative Python package installer
     - git   fast, scalable, distributed revision control system
     - libi2c-dev   userspace I2C programming library development files
     - python-serial   pyserial - module encapsulating access for the
                           serial port
     - python-rpi.gpio   Python GPIO module for Raspberry Pi
     - i2c-tools   This Python module allows SMBus access through the
                           I2C /dev
     - python-smbus   Python bindings for Linux SMBus access through
                           i2c-dev
     - arduino   AVR development board IDE and built-in libraries
     - minicom   friendly menu driven serial communication program

2) Installs wiringPi in GrovePi/Script

3) Removes I2C and SPI from modprobe blacklist /etc/modprobe.d/
   raspi-blacklist.conf

4) Adds I2C-dev, i2c-bcm2708 and spi-dev to /etc/modules

5) Installs gertboard avrdude_5.10-4_armhf.deb package

6) Runs gertboard setup
     - configures avrdude
     - downloads gertboard known boards and programmers
     - replaces avrsetup with gertboards version
     - in /etc/inittab comments out lines containing AMA0
     - in /boot/cmdline.txt removes: console=ttyAMA0,115200
       kgdboc=ttyAMA0,115200 console=tty1
     - in /usr/share/arduino/hardware/arduino creates backup of boards.txt
     - in /usr/share/arduino/hardware/arduino creates backup of
       programmers.txt

Special thanks to Joe Sanford at Tufts University. This script was derived
from his work. Thank you Joe!

Raspberry Pi will reboot after completion.

4. As the installation continues, it will prompt for permission to install new software packages. Press the *Enter* key to accept the default answer to the prompts (Y).

5. When the installation script completes, you will be prompted to restart the Raspberry Pi. Instead, use the `poweroff` command to shut down the Raspberry Pi.

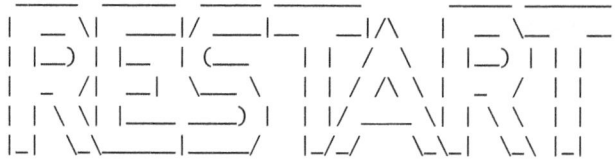

```
|   _ \|   _|/ __|_    _|/\   |   _ \_    _|
| |_) | |_  | (__     | | / \  | |_) | | |
|  _ /|  _| \___ \    | |/ /\ \ |  _ /  | |
| | \ \| |___ ___) |  | |/ ___ \| | \ \  | |
|_|  _____|____/   |_/_/    \_\_|  \_\ |_|

Please restart to implement changes!
To Restart type sudo reboot

pi@raspberrypi ~ $ sudo poweroff

Broadcast message from root@raspberrypi (pts/0) (Sun Sep 27 21:42:34
2015):
The system is going down for system halt NOW!
```

6. While the Raspberry Pi is shut down and the power has been disconnected, attach the GrovePi to the Raspberry Pi.

   The following image shows how to attach the GrovePi+ to the Raspberry Pi 2:

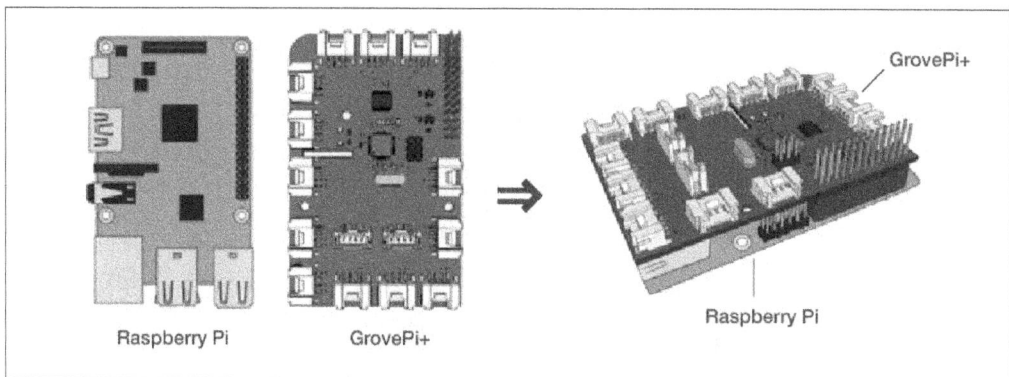

Raspberry Pi   GrovePi+   GrovePi+

Raspberry Pi

7. After the GrovePi has been attached to the Raspberry Pi, reconnect the power and log in once the Raspberry Pi finishes booting.

8. After logging in, use the `i2cdetect` command to validate that the GrovePi has been installed correctly. Note: if you are using an original Raspberry Pi, use the option `-y 0` instead of `-y 1`.

```
pi@raspberrypi ~ $ sudo i2cdetect -y 1
     0  1  2  3  4  5  6  7  8  9  a  b  c  d  e  f
00:          -- 04 -- -- -- -- -- -- -- -- -- -- --
10: -- -- -- -- -- -- -- -- -- -- -- -- -- -- -- --
20: -- -- -- -- -- -- -- -- -- -- -- -- -- -- -- --
30: -- -- -- -- -- -- -- -- -- -- -- -- -- -- -- --
40: -- -- -- -- -- -- -- -- -- -- -- -- -- -- -- --
50: -- -- -- -- -- -- -- -- -- -- -- -- -- -- -- --
60: -- -- -- -- -- -- -- -- -- -- -- -- -- -- -- --
70: -- -- -- -- -- -- -- --
```

9. Now, use the `apt-get install` command to install the Python setup tools (`python-setuptools`).

```
pi@raspberrypi ~ $ sudo apt-get install -y python-setuptools
Reading package lists... Done
Building dependency tree
Reading state information... Done
The following extra packages will be installed:
  python-pkg-resources
Suggested packages:
  python-distribute python-distribute-doc
The following NEW packages will be installed:
  python-pkg-resources python-setuptools
0 upgraded, 2 newly installed, 0 to remove and 39 not upgraded.
Need to get 0 B/513 kB of archives.
After this operation, 1,308 kB of additional disk space will be used.
Selecting previously unselected package python-pkg-resources.
(Reading database ... 82496 files and directories currently installed.)
Unpacking python-pkg-resources (from .../python-pkg-resources_0.6.24-1_
all.deb) ...
Selecting previously unselected package python-setuptools.
Unpacking python-setuptools (from .../python-setuptools_0.6.24-1_all.deb)
...
Setting up python-pkg-resources (0.6.24-1) ...
Setting up python-setuptools (0.6.24-1) ...

pi@raspberrypi ~ $
```

10. Use the `cd` command to navigate to the GrovePi Python software library (`~/GrovePi/Software/Python`).

```
pi@raspberrypi ~ $ cd GrovePi/Software/Python

pi@raspberrypi ~/GrovePi/Software/Python $
```

11. Use the `python setup.py` command to `build` and `install` the `grovepi` module.

```
pi@raspberrypi ~/GrovePi/Software/Python $ python setup.py build
running build
running build_py
creating build
creating build/lib.linux-armv7l-2.7
copying grovepi.py -> build/lib.linux-armv7l-2.7


pi@raspberrypi ~/GrovePi/Software/Python $ sudo python setup.py install
running install
Checking .pth file support in /usr/local/lib/python2.7/dist-packages/
/usr/bin/python -E -c pass
TEST PASSED: /usr/local/lib/python2.7/dist-packages/ appears to support
.pth files
running bdist_egg
running egg_info
creating grovepi.egg-info
writing grovepi.egg-info/PKG-INFO
writing top-level names to grovepi.egg-info/top_level.txt
writing dependency_links to grovepi.egg-info/dependency_links.txt
writing manifest file 'grovepi.egg-info/SOURCES.txt'
reading manifest file 'grovepi.egg-info/SOURCES.txt'
writing manifest file 'grovepi.egg-info/SOURCES.txt'
installing library code to build/bdist.linux-armv7l/egg
running install_lib
running build_py
creating build/bdist.linux-armv7l
creating build/bdist.linux-armv7l/egg
copying build/lib.linux-armv7l-2.7/grovepi.py -> build/bdist.linux-armv7l/
egg
byte-compiling build/bdist.linux-armv7l/egg/grovepi.py to grovepi.pyc
creating build/bdist.linux-armv7l/egg/EGG-INFO
copying grovepi.egg-info/PKG-INFO -> build/bdist.linux-armv7l/egg/EGG-INFO
copying grovepi.egg-info/SOURCES.txt -> build/bdist.linux-armv7l/egg/EGG-
INFO
copying grovepi.egg-info/dependency_links.txt -> build/bdist.linux-armv7l/
egg/EGG-INFO
copying grovepi.egg-info/top_level.txt -> build/bdist.linux-armv7l/egg/
EGG-INFO
zip_safe flag not set; analyzing archive contents...
creating dist
creating 'dist/grovepi-0.0.0-py2.7.egg' and adding 'build/bdist.linux-
armv7l/egg' to it
removing 'build/bdist.linux-armv7l/egg' (and everything under it)
Processing grovepi-0.0.0-py2.7.egg
creating /usr/local/lib/python2.7/dist-packages/grovepi-0.0.0-py2.7.egg
Extracting grovepi-0.0.0-py2.7.egg to /usr/local/lib/python2.7/dist-
packages
```

```
Adding grovepi 0.0.0 to easy-install.pth file

Installed /usr/local/lib/python2.7/dist-packages/grovepi-0.0.0-py2.7.egg
Processing dependencies for grovepi==0.0.0
Finished processing dependencies for grovepi==0.0.0

pi@raspberrypi ~/GrovePi/Software/Python $
```

12. Attach a `Grove LED` device to port `D2` and a `Grove pushbutton switch` to port `D4` of the `GrovePi`.

13. A `Grove pushbutton switch` and a `Grove LED` are attached to the `GrovePi+`, as depicted in the following image:

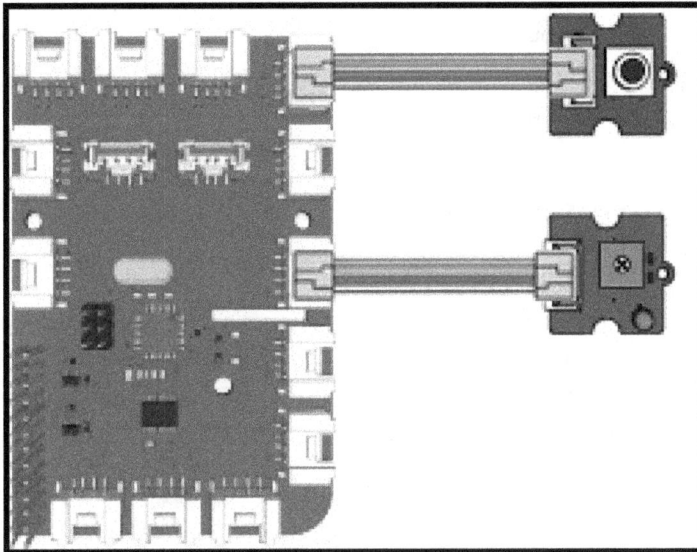

14. Now, use the following Python script (`button.py`), to test the `Grove pushbutton switch`. Run the test script (`button.py`) twice - once without pressing the pushbutton switch (`0`) and once while pressing the pushbutton switch (`1`). Notice the different results.

```
pi@raspberrypi:~$ cat <<EOD >button.py
from grovepi import *
button = 4
pinMode( button, "input" )
print digitalRead( button )
EOD

pi@raspberrypi:~$ # without pressing the pushbutton switch
pi@raspberrypi:~$ python button.py
```

```
0

pi@raspberrypi:~$ # while pressing the pushbutton switch
pi@raspberrypi:~$ python button.py
1

pi@raspberrypi:~$
```

15. Next, use the following Python script (`led.py`) to test the LED. When the script (`led.py`) is run, the LED should glow for one second.

```
pi@raspberrypi:~$ cat <<EOD >led.py
from grovepi import *
from time import sleep
led = 2
pinMode( led, "output" )
digitalWrite( led, 1 )
sleep( 1 )
digitalWrite( led, 0 )
EOD

pi@raspberrypi:~$ python led.py

pi@raspberrypi:~$
```

16. Finally, use the following Python script to light the LED whenever the Grove pushbutton switch is pressed. Press *Ctrl+C* to stop the script.

```
pi@raspberrypi:~$ cat <<EOD >loop.py
from grovepi import *
from time import sleep
led = 2
pinMode( led, "output" )
button = 4
pinMode( button, "input" )
while True:
  try:
    state = digitalRead( button )
    digitalWrite( led, state )
    sleep( 0.01 )
  except KeyboardInterrupt:
    digitalWrite( led, 0 )
    break
  except IOError:
    print "IOError"
EOD

pi@raspberrypi:~$ python loop.py

^C
```

How it works...

This recipe uses the GrovePi attached to the Raspberry Pi to activate an output device (`Grove LED`) when the state of an attached input device (`Grove pushbutton switch`) changes. The recipe begins by connecting the GrovePi and the input and output devices to the Raspberry Pi. Once the devices are connected, each of the devices is tested individually. Finally, a Python script is used to activate the output device whenever the input device changes state.

Before the GrovePi is attached to the Raspberry Pi, the GrovePi drivers are installed.

Installing the GrovePi drivers and interfaces

The GrovePi drivers and interfaces are downloaded directly from their source repository on GitHub (`https://github.com/`). The `git clone` command uses a secure Internet connection (`https://`) to download the GrovePi interfaces and drivers from their repository, `DexterInd/GrovePi`. The downloaded files include the installation scripts.

The installation script, `install.sh`, is located in the `GrovePi/Scripts` directory. The `cd` command is used to navigate to the `GrovePi/Scipts` directory.

In the `GrovePi/Scipts` directory, the `sh` command is used to run the `install.sh` script. The script requires super user privileges, so `sudo` is used as a command prefix.

Before starting the installation, the `install.sh` script displays a complete list of the changes it will make to your Raspberry Pi. The installation script prompts you to continue with the install. Press the *Enter* key to accept the defaults to all questions during the installation process.

After the GrovePi interfaces and drivers are installed, you are prompted to restart the Raspberry Pi. Shut down the Raspberry Pi instead, so that you can remove the power from the Raspberry Pi and attach the GrovePi to it.

Attach the GrovePi to the Raspberry Pi

Follow the manufacturer's instructions on `http://www.dexterindustries.com/grovepi/` to attach the GrovePi to the Raspberry Pi.

If you are attaching the original 26 pin GrovePi to one of the 40 pin models of the Raspberry Pi, make sure that pin 1 is lined up correctly. Even though the GrovePi does not cover all of the pins, it will still work perfectly.

You may need to put a protective layer between the GrovePi and the Raspberry Pi to prevent the bottom of the GrovePi from touching the Raspberry Pi's USB connectors. A snippet of the electrostatic bag in which the GrovePi was shipped is a perfect protective layer.

Power on and log in

Once you have validated that the GrovePi is attached to the Raspberry Pi correctly, attach the power cable to the Raspberry Pi and log in after it reboots.

The `i2cdetect` command is used to validate that the GrovePi has been connected correctly. The `-y` option is used to bypass interactive mode. Only the original Raspberry Pi uses bus 0, whereas all of the newer Raspberry Pis use bus 1.

If the GrovePi is connected correctly, its chip ID 04 will be displayed at address 00 4.

Now that the GrovePi has been attached and detected, it is time to install the GrovePi's Python language **Application Programming Interface (API)**.

Install the Python API

Before the GrovePi API can be installed, the Python setup tools need to be installed. The `apt-get install` command is used to install the `python-setuptools` software package. After Python's setup tools are installed, the GrovePi API can be installed.

The sources for the GrovePi API are located in the `GrovePi/Software/Python` directory. The `cd` command is used to navigate to that directory.

The `python` command is used to run the `setup.py` script, first to build the API and then to install the API. Installation requires super user privileges, so `sudo` command is used as a command prefix during `install`.

Once the GrovePi Python API is installed, the hardware devices can be tested.

Test the Grove pushbutton switch

The `cat` command is used to create a new script, `button.py`, which tests the state of the Grove pushbutton switch. The lines immediately following the `cat` command up to the end of the data marker (`<<EOD`) are copied to the new script (`>button.py`).

The `python` command is used to run the `button.py` test script twice.

The first time the `button.py` script is run, it is run without pressing the pushbutton switch. The result is 0 because the switch is open (not pressed).

The second time the script is run, it is run while pressing the pushbutton switch. The result is 1 because the switch is closed (pressed).

Test the Grove LED

The `cat` command is also used to create another test script, `led.py`, which tests the Grove LED. The lines immediately following the `cat` command up to the end of data marker (`<<EOD`) are copied to the new script (`>led.py`).

The python command is used to run the led.py test script. When the script (led.py) is run, the Grove LED should glow for one second.

Pressing the pushbutton switch lights the LED

The cat command is used once more to create the loop.py Python script. This short program will loop forever sending signal values from the input device (pushbutton switch) to the output device (LED).

The loop.py script imports the complete (*) grovepi API. It also imports the sleep function from the time API.

A variable, led, is used to represent digital port 2, the port that connects the LED to the GrovePi. The pinMode function from the grovepi API is used to set the signal direction for the LED port to output.

Another variable, button, is used to represent digital port 4, the port that connects the pushbutton switch to the GrovePi. The pinMode function is used to set the signal direction for the button port to input.

The main body of the script is an infinite loop (while True:) that only breaks when a KeyboardInterrupt exception occurs.

The loop first uses the digitalRead function to receive the current value of the button port. The value received is stored in the variable state.

The value of the state variable is then sent to the led port using the digitalWrite function.

Before the while loop continues, the program sleeps for 0.01 seconds. This gives the Raspberry Pi a chance to do something else in between setting the state of the led port and reading the next state from the button port.

The while loop listens for two exceptions: KeyboardInterrupt and IOError. When a KeyboardInterrupt occurs, the script uses the digitalWrite function to send the LED port the signal for off (0) and the script breaks the while loop ending the program. When an IOError occurs, the message IOError is printed.

The python command is used to run the loop.py script. While the script is running, the LED glows whenever the pushbutton switch is pressed. The LED stops glowing whenever the pushbutton switch is released. Use *Ctrl+C* to send a KeyboardInterrupt exception and end the program.

There's more...

The GrovePi expansion board from Dexter Industries can connect the Raspberry PI to more than 100 components from the Grove hardware platform developed by Seeed Studio. The official website is `http://www.seeedstudio.com/depot/`. These components can be manipulated with simple Python scripts as well as integrated into larger applications programmed in C, Go, or Java.

In addition to the digital ports used in this recipe, The GrovePi also has analog ports that can receive signal levels ranging from 0 to 1023 and can end signal levels from 0 to 255. The GrovePi also has 3 I2C ports and a **Universal Asynchronous Receiver/Transmitter (UART)** serial port that can be used to communicate with more complex devices.

Complete GrovePi documentation, including the Python API, can be found on Dexter Industries' website. More information about the Grove System can be found on Seeed Studio's wiki.

See also

> ▸ **GrovePi**: at `http://www.dexterindustries.com/grovepi/`. The GrovePi home page has a complete list of compatible sensors and devices.

> ▸ **The Grove System**: `http://www.seeedstudio.com/wiki/Category:Grove`. This wiki page describes the Lego-like Grove hardware system in more detail.

> ▸ **The Grove System – Python Library Documentation**: `http://www.dexterindustries.com/GrovePi/programming/python-library-documentation/`. This website documents the Python programming language library for the GrovePi.

> ▸ **Python**: `https://www.python.org/`. The Python website has complete reference documentation for the Python language.

> ▸ **GrovePi Windows IoT: LED Blink**: `https://www.hackster.io/9381/grove-pi-windows-iot-getting-started-94bf38`. A blinking LED example for Windows 10 and the GrovePi.

> ▸ **Dexter Industries**: `https://en.wikipedia.org/wiki/Dexter_Industries`. Dexter Industries is best known for their robotic sensors for the Raspberry Pi.

> ▸ **Seeed Studio**: `http://www.seeedstudio.com/depot/`. Seeed is a hardware innovation platform developed in Shenzhen, China.

> ▸ **GitHub**: `http://github.com`. GitHub is a collaborative repository for open source software.

> ▸ **i2cdetect**: `http://manpages.debian.org/cgi-bin/man.cgi?query=i2cdetect`. The Debian man page for i2cdetect documents the command and its options.

Controlling devices from a web page

This recipe uses a simple Python script to show how devices attached to the Raspberry Pi can be controlled from a web page.

The web.py programming framework for Python can be used to serve web pages from scripts that are written in the Python programming language. This recipe features a Python script that serves a web page displaying the current state of a GrovePi LED and enables a button on the web page to turn a GrovePi LED on and off. It is a simple example, but is an excellent foundation for simple Internet of Things projects.

After completing this recipe, you will have installed and applied the web.py Python framework to serve a web page that can be used to turn an LED on and off.

Getting ready

The following are the ingredients for controlling devices from a web page:

▶ An initial setup or basic networking setup for the Raspberry Pi that already has the GrovePi interfaces and drivers installed (see the previous recipe, *Installing the GrovePi*, for instructions). You have also logged in as the user pi (see the recipes in *Chapter 1, Installation and Setup*, for how to boot and log in and the recipes in *Chapter 2, Administration*, for how to log in remotely).

▶ A GrovePi should already be attached to the Raspberry Pi.

▶ A Grove LED should be attached to port D2 of the GrovePi.

This recipe does not require the desktop GUI and could either be run from the text-based console or from within an LXTerminal application.

If the Raspberry Pi's secure shell server is running, this recipe can be completed remotely using a secure shell client.

How to do it...

The steps to controlling devices from a web page are:

1. Log in to the Raspberry Pi either directly or remotely.

2. Use the apt-get install command to install the web.py web framework for Python.

   ```
   pi@raspberrypi ~ $ apt-get install -y python-webpy
   Reading package lists... Done
   Building dependency tree
   Reading state information... Done
   ```

```
The following extra packages will be installed:
  libpq5 python-cheetah python-egenix-mxdatetime python-egenix-mxtools
  python-flup python-psycopg2 python2.6
  python2.6-minimal
Suggested packages:
  python-markdown python-pygments python-memcache python-egenix-
mxdatetime-dbg python-egenix-mxdatetime-doc
  python-egenix-mxtools-dbg python-egenix-mxtools-doc python-psycopg2-doc
python2.6-doc binfmt-support
The following NEW packages will be installed:
  libpq5 python-cheetah python-egenix-mxdatetime python-egenix-mxtools
  python-flup python-psycopg2 python-webpy
  python2.6 python2.6-minimal
0 upgraded, 9 newly installed, 0 to remove and 39 not upgraded.
Need to get 923 kB/4,773 kB of archives.
After this operation, 16.5 MB of additional disk space will be used.

...
```

3. After `web.py` is installed, use the `cat` command to create a Python script that serves a web page used to turn the Grove LED on and off.

```
pi@raspberrypi ~ $ cat <<EOD >ledpage.py

import grovepi
import web

LED  = 2
URLS = ( '/(.*)', 'request_handler' )


class request_handler:

  def GET( self, url_match ):

    web.header( 'Content-Type', 'text/html; charset=utf-8' )

    if url_match == 'on':
      grovepi.digitalWrite( LED, 1 )
      return html_page( 'off' )

    if url_match == 'off':
      grovepi.digitalWrite( LED, 0 )
      return html_page( 'on' )

    return html_page( 'on' )


  def html_page( state ):
    form  = '<form action="/' + state + '">'
```

```
        form +=    '<input type="submit" value="' + state + '">'
        form += '</form>'
        return '<html><body>' + form + '</body></html>'


if __name__ == '__main__':
    grovepi.pinMode( LED, 'output' )
    app = web.application( URLS, globals() )
    app.run()
```

EOD

```
pi@raspberrypi ~ $
```

4. Use the `python` command to start serving the web page.

```
pi@raspberrypi ~ $ python ledpage.py
http://0.0.0.0:8080/
```

5. From a web browser, you will be able to see the web page. Use the IP address of your Raspberry Pi plus the port `8080` to access the web page (for example, `http://192.168.2.19:8080`).

6. The web page displays one button. If the LED is off, the button is labeled `on`. If the LED is on, the button is labeled `off`. Clicking the button sets the LED as stated by the button's label.

7. Use *Ctrl+C* to stop serving the web page.

How it works...

After logging in to the Raspberry Pi, the recipe first uses the `apt-get install` command to install the `python-webpy` software package. This software package contains the `web.py` web framework for Python.

The `web.py` web framework is a toolkit for creating web servers that use the Python programming language to create web pages. The Python script in this recipe also uses the GrovePi API introduced in the previous recipe, *Installing the GrovePi*.

Create and run the ledpage website

The `cat` command is used to create a new script, `ledpage.py`. The lines immediately following the `cat` command up to the end of the data marker (`<<EOD`) are copied to the new script (`>ledpage.py`).

This new script will serve a web page that can be used to control a GrovePi LED. In the example script, the LED is attached to port D2 of the GrovePi.

The `ledpage.py` script is run using the `python` command. When the script is run, a web server is started listening on port `8080` of every network interface attached to the Raspberry Pi (`http://0.0.0.0`).

The output of the web server can be viewed in a web browser. Open a browser and browse to `http://ipaddress:8080`, the URL of the running `ledpage.py` script. Replace the `ipaddress` in the URL with the IP address of your Raspberry Pi (instructions for determining the IP address can be found in *Chapter 2, Administration*).

Action URLs

The default view (`http://ipaddress:8080/`) shows a single button that can be used to change the current state of the LED. The button is labeled `on` when the LED is off and it's labeled `off` when the LED is on. When clicked, the button turns the LED to the labeled state.

When the button is labeled `on`, clicking the button sends the browser to the URL `http://ipaddress:8080/on`; and when the button is labeled `off`, clicking the button sends the browser to the URL `http://ipaddress:8080/off`.

Browsing to the `/on` URL turns the light on and displays an `off` button. Browsing to the `/off` URL turns the light off and displays an `on` button. The action URLs, `/on` and `/off`, are defined in `ledpage.py`.

Use Ctrl+C to quit

The Python web server continues to run until *Ctrl+C* is pressed.

There's more...

The `ledpage.py` script is a simple yet complete example of a web service that controls a device attached to the Raspberry Pi. The script can be broken into four parts: initialization, the `request handler` class, the `html_page` function, and the `main` loop.

Initialization

The script begins with two `import` statements: one for the `grovepi` API and one for the `web` API. The `web` API is used to set up the web server and the `grovepi` API is used to connect to the Grove LED.

After the `import` statements, two constants are defined: `LED` and `URLS`. The `LED` constant defines which digital output port will be used on the GrovePi (2), and the `URLS` constant defines a mapping between a regular expression (`/(.*)`) and a request handler (`request_handler`).

The defined regular expression (`/(.*)`) matches all URLs. The matched part of the URL, anything after the slash (`(.*)`), will be passed to the `request_handler` (as `url_match`).

The request_handler class

The request_handler class defines how HTTP requests are handled by the web server. In this script, only the GET method of the **HyperText Transfer Protocol** (**HTTP**) is implemented.

When you browse to the Python web server's URL (http://ipaddress:8080), a GET method is received by the web server and the GET method (GET (self, url_match)) of the request_handler class is called.

The GET method uses the web API function header to set the Content-type of the HTTP response to be text/html and the character set encoding to be UTF-8 (charset=utf-8). The Content-type response header tells the browser what type of web content (web page, plain text, image, audio, video, and so on) is located at this URL. The response for this URL is a web page (text/html) that uses the UTF-8 character set.

Then, the GET method checks the value of the url_match parameter.

When the url_match is on (http://ipaddress:8080/on), the grovepi API function digitalWrite is used to first turn the LED on (1) and then return an html_page to the browser with an off button.

When the url_match is off (http://ipaddress:8080/off), the digitalWrite function is used to turn the LED off (0) and an html_page is returned to the browser with an on button.

If the matched URL (url_match) is neither on nor off, an html_page with an on button is returned to the browser. The state of the LED is not changed.

The html_page function

The html_page function (html_page (state)) renders the HTML that will be sent to the browser to display the web page.

The function has one parameter, state, which is used to specify the label (value) for the button (<input type="submit">) and the action for the HTML <form> tag.

A string variable, form, is created to build the HTML <form> part of the web page.

The action attribute of the HTML <form> tag is set either to /on or /off depending on the value of the state parameter. The action attribute defines the URL where the browser will be sent when the HTML <form> is submitted (that is, when the button is pressed).

The value attribute (the label) of the <input type="submit"> tag (the button) is set either to on or to off depending on the value of the state parameter. When clicked, the tag (the button) will submit the HTML <form>.

Once the HTML <form> tag is completely defined including its end tag </form>, it is wrapped in a <body> tag and an <html> tag to complete the minimal HTML web page.

The complete web page is returned to the `request_handler`, which sends the web page to the browser.

The main loop

The main loop begins `if __name__ == '__main__':` and is called once after the `html_page` function and the `request_handler` have been defined.

The main loop first uses the `grovepi` API to initialize the `LED` to the `output pinMode`. The GrovePi digital ports can either be used to listen for signals or to trigger them. For this script, the `LED` port is configured for `output`.

After the `LED` port is configured, the `web` API's `application` function is used to create a web application that listens for the specified `URLS` using Python's default global variables (`globals()`) as the application context.

The first parameter to the `web.application` function, `URLS`, defines the mapping between URL request patterns (regular expressions) and their request handlers (Python classes). The second parameter defines the application context (in this case, it is the `global` context). The `web.application` function returns a web application object (`app`) that encapsulates the HTTP protocol and manages the web server.

Finally, the web server is started using the `run` function of the newly created web application object (`app`).

The web application listens by default on port `8080` of all the network interfaces attached to the Raspberry Pi (`0.0.0.0`). The `app.run` function continues until it is interrupted (by *Ctrl+C*).

More information on using `web.py` to create web applications using the Python scripting language can be found on the `web.py` website (`http://webpy.org/`).

See also

▸ **web.py** (`http://webpy.org/`): This web framework was originally developed at reddit.com where it grew to serve millions of page views per day.

▸ **web.py – Tutorial** (`http://webpy.org/docs/0.3/tutorial`): This is the root of the `web.py` tutorial.

▸ **Regular Expression HOWTO** (`https://docs.python.org/2/howto/regex.html`): This is an introductory tutorial to using regular expressions in Python.

- ▸ **Hypertext Transfer Protocol (**`https://en.wikipedia.org/wiki/Hypertext_Transfer_Protocol`**):** This Wikipedia article is about the HTTP protocol.

- ▸ **HTML (**`https://en.wikipedia.org/wiki/HTML`**):** This Wikipedia article describes the Hypertext Markup Language (HML) and its history.

Connecting to an IoT platform

This recipe connects your Raspberry Pi to the SmartLiving (`http://smartliving.io`) Internet of Things (IoT) platform.

The SmartLiving IoT platform uses a web browser to configure rules that respond to sensors and/or activate IoT devices attached to your Raspberry Pi. The SmartLiving API includes drivers for the GrovePi from Dexter Industries. This recipe integrates your Raspberry Pi with the SmartLiving platform and uses it to control a GrovePi device attached to your Raspberry Pi.

After completing this recipe, you will be able to control Grove devices attached to your Raspberry Pi using the SmartLiving Internet of Things platform.

Getting ready

Ingredients:

- ▸ A Basic Networking setup for the Raspberry Pi that already has the GrovePi interfaces and drivers installed (see the previous recipe, *Installing the GrovePi*, for instructions). You have also logged in as the user `pi` (see the recipes in *Chapter 1*, *Installation and Setup* for how to boot and log in and the recipes in *Chapter 2*, *Administration* for how to log in remotely).

- ▸ The Raspberry Pi should be connected to the Internet.

- ▸ A GrovePi should already be attached to the Raspberry Pi.

- ▸ A Grove LED should be attached to port D2 of the GrovePi.

This recipe does not require the desktop GUI and could either be run from the text-based console or from within an `LXTerminal`.

If the Raspberry Pi's Secure Shell server is running, this recipe can be completed remotely using a Secure Shell client.

How to do it...

The steps to controlling IoT devices from the SmartLiving platform are:

1. First, create a free account and log in to the SmartLiving platform at
    `http://beta.smnartliving.io`.

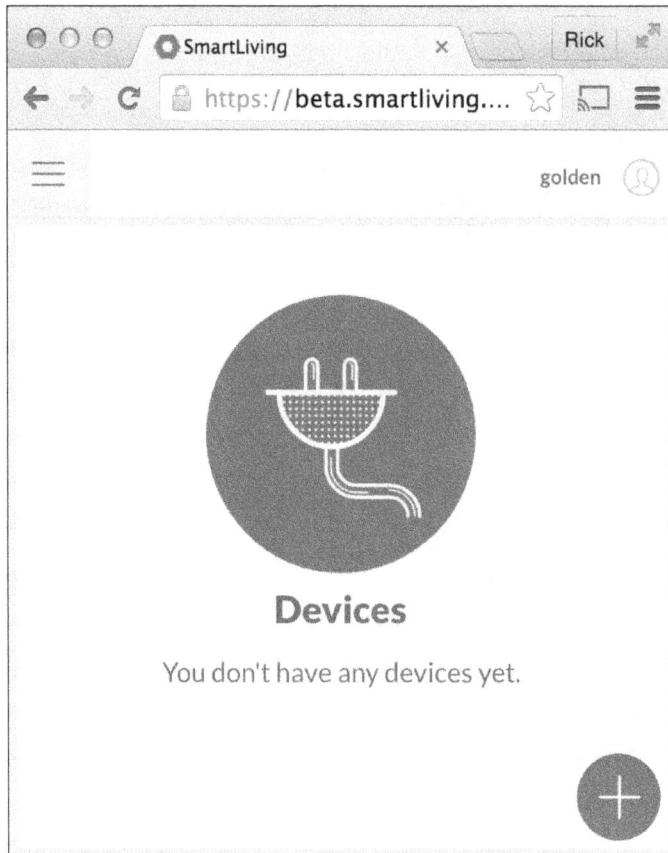

2. Click on the plus icon to create a new device.

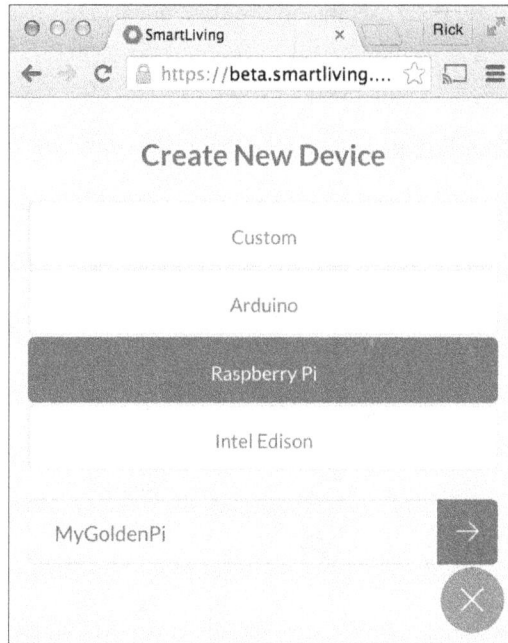

3. Select the device type Raspberry Pi and name the device (**MyGoldenPi**). Click the **right arrow icon** to continue.

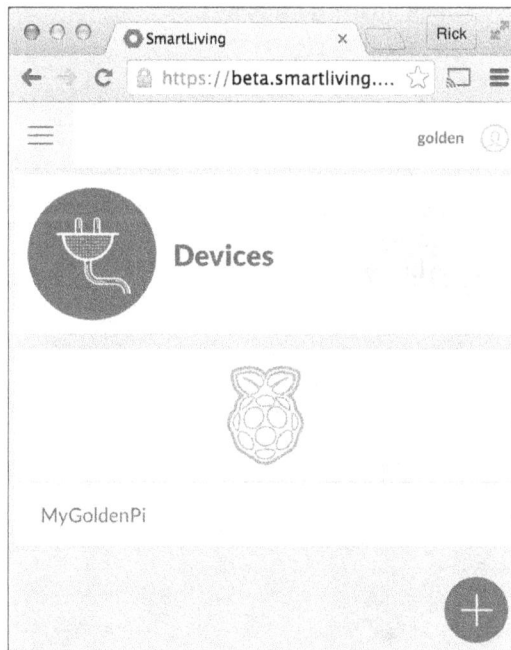

4. Select the Raspberry Pi by clicking on the Raspberry Pi logo.

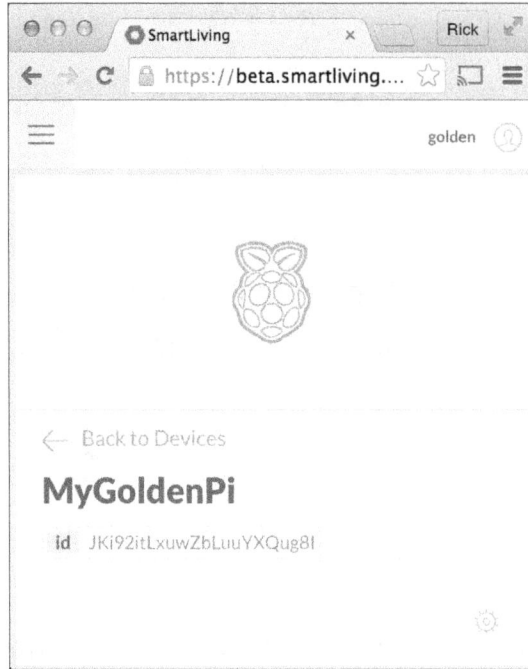

5. Select settings by clicking on the **gear icon**.

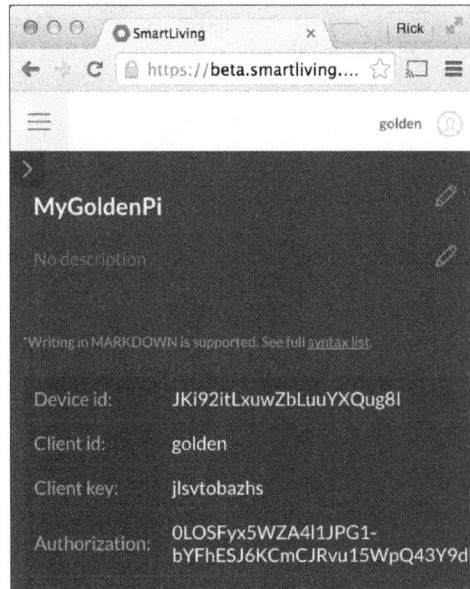

6. Now that your Raspberry Pi is registered and you can see the device ID, client ID, and client key, it's time to switch back to the Raspberry Pi.

7. Log in to the Raspberry Pi (locally or remotely).

8. Use the `git clone` command to download the All Things Talk (`allthingstalk`) client for Python (`raspberrypi-python-client`).

    ```
    pi@raspberrypi ~ $ git clone https://github.com/allthingstalk/raspberrypi-
    python-client

    Cloning into 'raspberrypi-python-client'...
    remote: Counting objects: 369, done.
    Receiving objects: 100% (369/369), 85.93 KiB, done.
    remote: Total 369 (delta 0), reused 0 (delta 0), pack-reused 369
    Resolving deltas: 100% (240/240), done.

    pi@raspberrypi ~ $
    ```

9. Use the `cd` command to enter the client install directory, and then use the Bash script `setupGrovePi.sh` to install the client.

    ```
    pi@raspberrypi ~ $ cd raspberrypi-python-client

    pi@raspberrypi ~/raspberyypi-python-client $ sudo bash setupGrovePi.sh

    Reading package lists... Done
    Building dependency tree
    Reading state information... Done
    The following extra packages will be installed:
      python2.7-dev
    The following NEW packages will be installed:
      python-dev python2.7-dev
    0 upgraded, 2 newly installed, 0 to remove and 0 not upgraded.
    Need to get 0 B/28.7 MB of archives.

    ...
    ```

10. Press the *Enter* key in response to any and all installation prompts to accept the defaults.

11. When the installation script is complete, use the `reboot` command to restart the Raspberry Pi.

    ```
    ...

    Please restart to implement changes!
     ____  _____   ____  ____   _____   _    ____  _____
    |  _ \|  ___| / ___||_  _| |_   _| | |  |  _ \|_   _|
    | |_) | |_   | |     | |   / _ \   | |  | |_) | | |
    |  _ /|  _|  | |___  | |  / /\ \   | |  |  _ <  | |
    | | \ \| |___ |____| | | / ____ \  | |  | | \ \ | |
    |_|  _____||____/  |_|/_/    \_\ |_|  |_|  \_\|_|
    ```

```
Please restart to implement changes!
To Restart type sudo reboot

pi@raspberrypi ~/raspberrypi-python-client $ sudo reboot
Broadcast message from root@raspberrypi (pts/0) (Mon Oct 12 17:07:11
2015):
The system is going down for reboot NOW!
```

12. Now that the All Things Talk (Smart Living) client has been installed, it's time to test the Internet of Things.

13. Log back in to the Raspberry Pi (locally or remotely).

14. Use the cd command to change to the directory with the Smart Living Python client, `raspberrypi-python-client`.

```
pi@raspberrypi ~ $ cd raspberrypi-python-client

pi@raspberrypi ~/ raspberrypi-python-client $
```

15. Use the `cat` command to create a Python script (`ledserver.py`) that connects a Grove LED on port D2 to the Smart Living platform. Make sure you replace the values of the three configuration parameters (`IOT.DeviceId`, `IOT.ClientId`, and `IO.ClientKey`) with the values from your Smart Living account (from step 6).

```
pi@raspberrypi ~/ raspberrypi-python-client $ cat <<EOD >ledserver.py

import grovepi
import ATT_IOT as IOT
import time

LED = 2

def on_message( id, value ):

    if id.endswith( str( LED ) ):

        value = value.lower()

        if value == "true":
            grovepi.digitalWrite( LED, 1 )

        if value == "false":
            grovepi.digitalWrite( LED, 0 )

    # ignore unkown ids and values


if __name__ == '__main__':
```

```
grovepi.pinMode( LED, 'output' )

IOT.DeviceId  = "JKi92itLxuwZbLuuYXQug8I"
IOT.ClientId  = "golden"
IOT.ClientKey = "jlsvtobazhs"

IOT.on_message = on_message

IOT.connect()
IOT.addAsset( LED, "LED", "Light Emitting Diode", True, "boolean" )
IOT.subscribe()

while True:
    time.sleep( .1 )

EOD

pi@raspberrypi ~ $
```

16. Use the `python` command to run the newly created script.

```
pi@raspberrypi ~/ raspberrypi-python-client $ python ledserver.py
connected with http server
HTTP PUT: /asset/JKi92itLxuwZbLuuYXQug8I2
HTTP HEADER: {'Auth-ClientId': 'golden', 'Content-type': 'application/
json', 'Auth-ClientKey': 'jlsvtobazhs'}
HTTP BODY:{"name":"LED","description":"Light Emitting Diode", "style": "Un
defined","is":"actuator","profile": {"type":"boolean" },"deviceId":"JKi92itL
xuwZbLuuYXQug8I" }
(200, 'OK')
{"deviceId":"JKi92itLxuwZbLuuYXQug8I","id":"JKi92itLxuwZbLuuYXQu
g8I2","name":"LED","is":"actuator","description":"Light Emitting
Diode","createdOn":"2015-10-13T00:36:01.742Z","createdBy":"555a3d487ae2530
b385b2173","updatedOn":"2015-10-13T01:07:44.074Z","updatedBy":"555a3d487ae
2530b385b2173","profile":{"type":"boolean"},"state":null,"style":"undefined"
,"control":{"name":null,"widgetUrl":null}}
Connected to mqtt broker with result code 0
subscribing to: client/golden/in/device/JKi92itLxuwZbLuuYXQug8I/asset/+/
command
(0, 1)
Subscribed to topic, receiving data from the cloud: qos=(0,)
```

17. In the browser, refresh the Smart Living device page. The Raspberry Pi device (**MyGoldenPi**) now has a new device (**LED**).

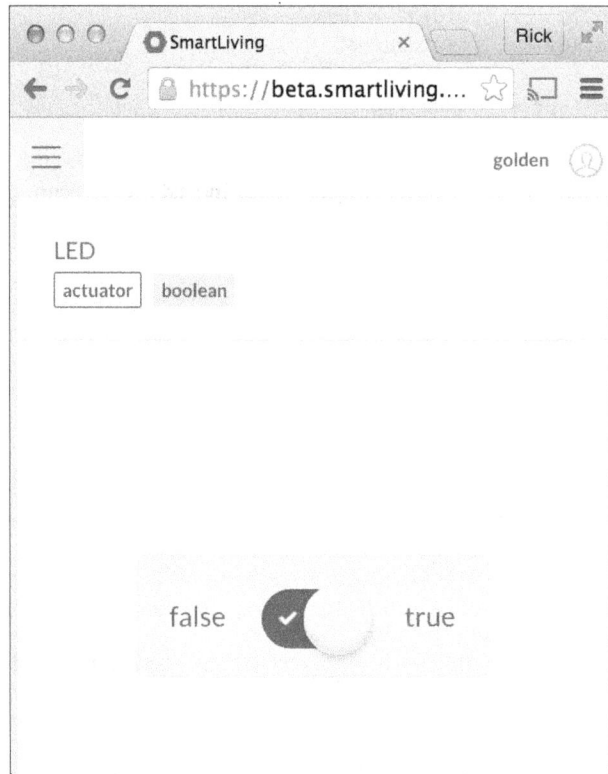

18. Toggle the **boolean** switch on the Smart Living web page and the Grove LED turns on and off while the running `ledserver.py` script prints additional status messages.

```
Incoming message - topic: client/golden/in/device/JKi92itLxuwZbLuuYXQug8I/
asset/JKi92itLxuwZbLuuYXQug8I2/command, payload: true
Incoming message - topic: client/golden/in/device/JKi92itLxuwZbLuuYXQug8I/
asset/JKi92itLxuwZbLuuYXQug8I2/command, payload: false
```

19. Press *Ctrl+C* to stop the `ledserver.py` script.

How it works...

This recipe has three parts: registering a Raspberry Pi device with the Smart Living IoT platform, installing the Smart Living client API, and finally running a script that exchanges signals between the Smart Living platform and the Raspberry Pi.

Register your Raspberry Pi with the IoT platform

The recipe begins by registering for a free account at `http://beta.smartliving.io`.

After registering for an account, a new Raspberry Pi device interface (**MyGoldenPi**) is created and the **Device id**, **Client id**, and **Client key** for this device are displayed. These three configuration values are used later in this recipe to connect the Raspberry Pi to the Smart Living IoT platform.

Install the IoT platform API

The recipe continues by logging in to the Raspberry Pi.

The `git clone` command is used to download the All Things Talk client API for the Raspberry Pi (`allthingstalk/raspberrypi-python-client`) – the Python API that is used to communicate with the Smart Living IoT platform.

After the client API is downloaded, the `bash` command is used to run the `setGrovePi.sh` script from the client API directory (`raspberrypi-python-client`). The `setupGrovePi.sh` installation script installs additional software packages and Python libraries.

Exchange signals with the IoT platform

Once the Smart Living client API is installed, the `cat` command is used to create a short Python script (`ledserver.py`) that listens for signals from the Smart Living IoT platform.

The script is run from the `raspberrypi-python-client` directory using the `python` command. While the script is running, the Raspberry Pi is connected to the Smart Living IoT platform and receives signals from the IoT platform that turn the LED on and off.

The IoT signals are sent using the Raspberry Pi device page on the Smart Living website. The device page has an **actuator** labeled **LED**. By toggling the **false** – **true** switch under the **LED** label, a signal is sent from Smart Living platform through the Internet of Things to the Raspberry Pi. A **false** signal turns the LED off. A **true** signal turns the LED on.

A local keyboard interrupt signal (pressing *Ctrl+C* on the keyboard) stops the script.

There's more...

The Python script, `ledserver.py`, is a simple demonstration of how a Raspberry Pi can be connected to an Internet of Things platform. The script listens for and responds to a binary signal sent from the Smart Living IoT platform. The signal sent from the IoT platform controls a device attached to the Raspberry Pi (an LED).

The script has three parts: initialization, the signal handler, and the main loop.

Initialization

The script begins with three `import` statements: one for the GrovePi API (`grovepi`), one for the All Things Talk API (`ATT_IOT`), and one for the `time` API. The `time` API provides the `sleep` function; the ATT_IOT API is used to connect with the Smart Living IoT platform, and the `grovepi` API is used to connect to the Grove LED.

After the `import` statements, a single constant is defined, **LED**, to represent the digital port that will be used on the GrovePi (2).

The signal handler

The signal handler function `on_message( ID, value )` defines the actions that are taken when signals (messages) are received from the IoT platform.

When the last character (`endswith`) of the message **id** is equal to the registered asset ID of the LED (`str( LED )`), then the message applies to the **LED** asset.

If the value of the message (converted to lowercase, **lower**) is "**true**", the LED will be turned on using the grovepi API (`digitalWrite( LED, 1 )`). When the value is "**false**", the LED will be turned off (`digitalWrite( LED, 0 )`).

The main loop

The main loop (`if __name__ == '__main__':`) begins by using the GrovePi API to set the pinmode of the LED to output.

The Smart Living client API (IOT) is configured using the **DeviceId**, **ClientId**, and **ClientKey** configuration parameters. They are set to the values displayed earlier, during the Smart Living registration. The IOT signal handler parameter, `on_message`, is set to the signal handling function, `on_message`.

Now that the client API (IOT) is configured, the Raspberry Pi is ready to `connect` to the Smart Living IoT platform, register a new device asset (`addAsset`), and subscribe to messages coming from the IoT platform.

The `IOT.connect` method establishes a connection to the Smart Living IoT platform using the previously specified **DeviceId**, **ClientId**, and **ClientKey**.

With the connection established, the Raspberry Pi lets the IoT platform know (`addAsset`) that there is a binary (**"boolean"**) output (**True**) device attached to port D2 (**LED**). The output device is labeled **"LED"** and has a short description, **"Light Emitting Diode"**.

The `IOT.subscribe` method lets the Smart Living IoT platform know that the Raspberry Pi is ready to receive signals (messages) from the platform.

The `on_message` function was previously defined as the signal handler. So, when a new signal (message) arrives for the Raspberry Pi, the `on_message` function receives the signal and acts upon its **id** and **value**.

When a **"true"** signal is received, the LED is turned on. When a **"false"** signal is received, the LED is turned off.

IoT Rules

Although this recipe does show how the Raspberry Pi can connect to and exchange signals with the Smart Living IoT platform, it does not show how to create new IoT Rules.

The Smart Living website (`http://smartliving.io`) has a number of examples of how IoT Rules can be used to react to and control the Raspberry Pi:

- ▶ Detect movement – light an LED when a sensor detects movement
- ▶ Unplugged smartphone – vibrate when a phone is removed from its charger
- ▶ Smart doorbell – the doorbell rings your smartphone
- ▶ Light sensor – display light levels in a remote room on your smartphone
- ▶ Smart shop window – use a QR code to control the light in a window
- ▶ Visit the Smart Living website for detailed instructions and a complete reference to using the Smart Living IoT platform with the Raspberry Pi and other devices.

See also

- ▶ **SmartLiving** (`http://www.smartliving.io/`): Use the Maker link to sign up for a Smart Living account.
- ▶ **All Things Talk** (`http://allthingstalk.com/`): The All Things Talk website has more details about the home and business versions of their Internet of Things platform.
- ▶ **Raspberry Pi kit** (`http://docs.smartliving.io/kits/linux-raspberry-pi/stepbystep/`): This tutorial is a guide for connecting your Raspberry Pi to Smart Living.
- ▶ **Raspberry Pi kit Experiments Guide** (`http://docs.smartliving.io/kits/linux-raspberry-pi/experiments/`): There are five experiments on this website to get you started with the IoT.

Creating an IoT gateway

This recipe turns your Raspberry Pi into an IoT gateway using The ThingBox (`http://thethingbox.io/`) powered by Node-RED (`http://nodered.org/`).

The ThingBox is a Raspbian-based operating system distribution for wiring together hardware devices, APIs, and online services in new and interesting ways. It comes preinstalled with the Node-RED visual tool for wiring the Internet of Things.

In this recipe, The ThingBox is deployed and a new flow is created that lights an LED attached to the Raspberry Pi while a pushbutton is pressed. This is a very simple example, but completely demonstrates how The ThingBox is used. At the end of the recipe, there is a list of additional nodes that could be used in your next project.

After completing this recipe, your Raspberry Pi will be an IoT gateway.

Getting ready

Ingredients:

▶ An Internet connection for downloading The ThingBox distribution

▶ An SD card – 4 GB or greater (class 10 has the best performance)

▶ A Raspberry Pi connected to the local network

This recipe only requires the desktop GUI to set up a wireless network.

Once the Raspberry Pi is running and connected to the network, this recipe is completed from another computer using a web browser.

How to do it...

The steps to creating an IoT gateway from your Raspberry Pi are:

1. Download the latest image file from The ThingBox website, `http://thethingbox.io/#packagestable` (see the recipe *Downloading new SD cards* in *Chapter 1, Installation and Setup*).

2. Write the image file to the SD card (see the appropriate disk utility recipe for your computer in *Chapter 1, Installation and Setup*).

3. Boot your Raspberry Pi using the updated SD card.

4. If your Raspberry Pi uses a Wi-Fi adapter to connect to the local network, you will need to log in to the Raspberry Pi GUI once (username: `root`, password: `raspberry`) and use the Wi-Fi config utility to configure the wireless network adapter.

5. After the Raspberry Pi has successfully booted and connected to the network (this might take a few seconds longer during the first boot), The ThingBox server running on your Raspberry Pi will be available at the local network address, `http://thethingbox.local/`.

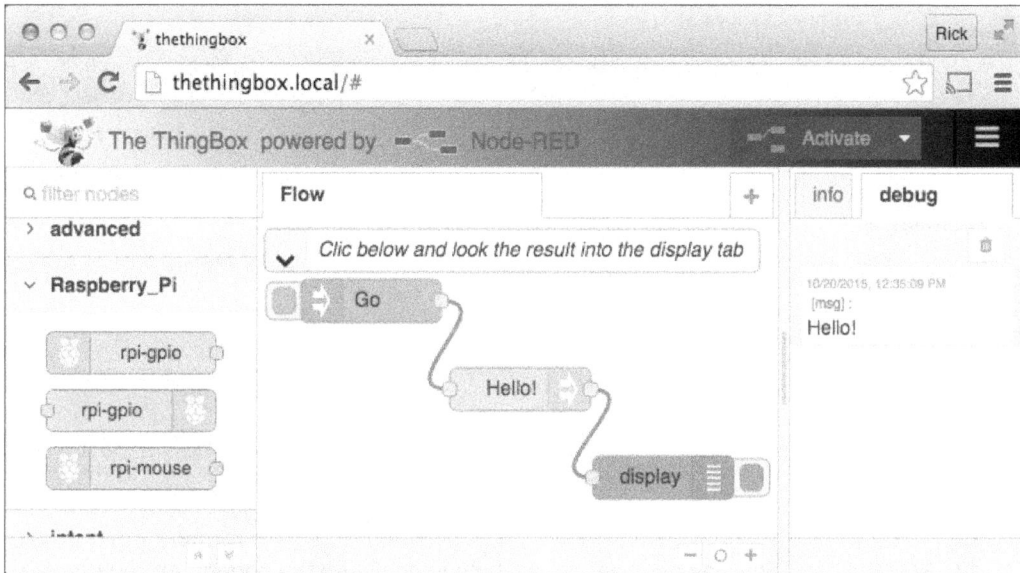

6. If you click the colored square on the left side of the **Go** node at the beginning of the default **Flow**, the message **Hello!** is displayed in the **debug** tab.

7. Click the **+** tab on the far right side of the center panel (opposite the **Flow** tab) to create a new flow.

8. Add an `rpi-gpio` in node to the flow by dragging an in node from the toolbox on the left and dropping it on the flow diagram in the center.

9. Add an `rpi-gpio` out node to the flow by dragging and dropping the out node from the toolbox.

10. Connect the two nodes by dragging the output connector of the **rpi-gpio** in node to the input connector of the **rpi-gpio** out node.

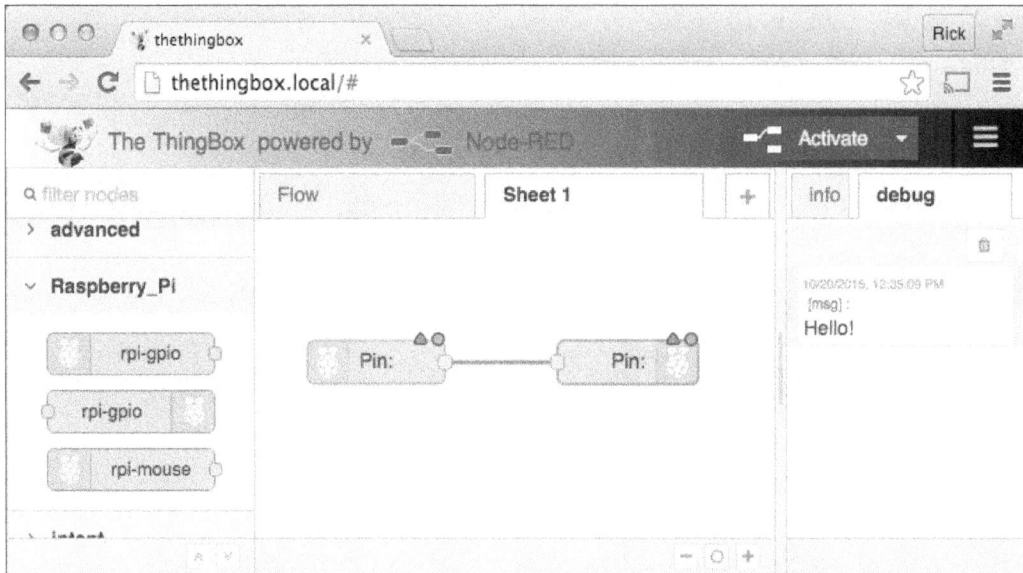

11. Now the basic flow has been set up, it's time to configure the nodes. The red triangle and blue circle badges on the input and output nodes indicate the configuration is not yet complete.

12. Configure the `Pushbutton` node. Double-click on the `rpi-gpio` in node. Change the **GPIO Pin** to **16 – GPIO4 – BCM23**. Change the **Resistor** to **pullup**. Change the **Name** parameter to `Pushbutton`. Click on the **Ok** button.

13. Configure the LED node. Double-click on the rpi-gpio out node. Change the **GPIO Pin** to **18 – GPIO5 – BCM24**. Change the **Type** to **Digital output**. Change the **Name** to **LED**. Click on the **Ok** button.

Edit rpi-gpio out node

- GPIO Pin   [18 - GPIO5 - BCM24 ▲▼]   Model B+

  Type   [Digital output ▲▼]

  ☐ Initialise pin state?

- Name   LED

  Pins in Use: 16,18

  Tip: For digital output - input must be 0 or 1.

[Ok] [Cancel]

14. Rename the flow diagram. Double-click on the name, **Sheet 1**. Change the **Name** of the flow diagram to **Pushbutton LED**. Click on the Ok button.

Rename sheet ✕

- Name   Pushbutton LED

[Delete]   [Ok] [Cancel]

15. Start the flow by clicking on the red **Activate** button. Wait until the **Successfully Deployed** message appears.

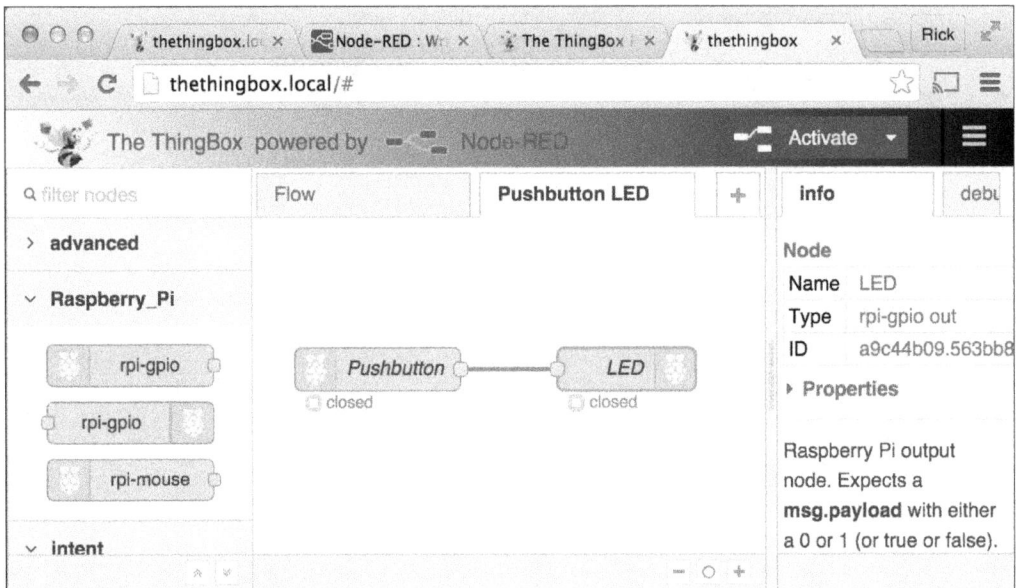

16. The **Pushbutton LED** flow has started!

17. Press and hold the **Pushbutton**. The LED glows. Release the **Pushbutton** and the **LED** stops glowing.

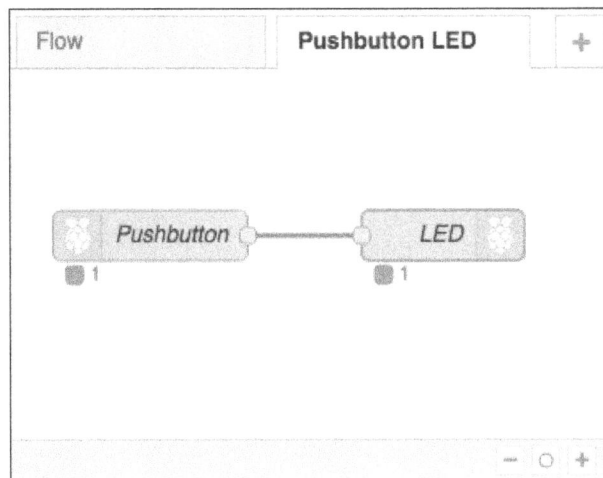

18. Notice that the values next to the green status indicators under the input and output nodes change from **0** to **1** whenever the pushbutton is pressed.

19. The ThingBox IoT gateway is responding to a hardware signal by sending a hardware signal. Your IoT gateway works!

How it works

This recipe has two main parts:

▸ Creating the bootable SD card for The ThingBox IoT gateway

▸ Creating the **Pushbutton LED** flow in the running IoT gateway

You may also need to configure your Raspberry Pi's wireless networking.

And you may want to run the example flow when The ThingBox is ready.

Creating the bootable SD card

The current ThingBox bootable disk image is available from The ThingBox website (`http://thethingbox.io/#packagestable`). After the image is downloaded, it needs to be written to an SD card that has at least 4 GB of disk space. Class 10 SD cards have the best performance. Instructions for creating a bootable SD card can be found in *Chapter 1, Installation and Setup*.

Once the ThingBox image is written to the SD card, use it to boot the Raspberry Pi. The initial boot takes longer as the filesystem is expanded to fill the whole SD card. After the initial boot, subsequent boots will be much faster.

Configuring wireless networking

If your Raspberry Pi depends on a Wi-Fi adapter for networking, you will need to log in to the Raspberry Pi desktop after the initial boot and configure wireless networking. Use the username `root` and the default password `raspberry`.

The wireless networking configuration application is available from the **Raspberry Pi Menu > Preferences > WiFi Configuration** menu.

Once the WiFi Configuration application is running, click **Scan** to display the available networks. Double-click on your network's **SSID** to enter your network's **Private Security Key** (**PSK**) and then click **Add** to add this device to the list of known Wi-Fi interfaces.

Close the **Scan Results** window and you can observe connection status changes in the **WiFi Configuration** window. After adding the **SSID** and **PSK** for your network, the Raspberry Pi will continue to use that configuration by default at each boot.

The Wi-Fi configuration can also be set from the ThingBox user interface. Choose **Settings** from the configuration menu at the top-right of the user interface (the three bars next to the **Activate** button).

The ThingBox is ready

After the Raspberry Pi boots, it broadcasts its name, `thethingbox`, to the local multicast DNS server. In a few seconds, after the mDNS server updates, the ThingBox user interface is accessible at the URL `http://thethingbox.local/`.

There is no need for additional network configuration. However, the device name and other network parameters can be changed from the configuration menu at the top-right of the user interface.

Running the example flow

When the ThingBox is first accessed, it displays a default **Flow** made up of three nodes: **Go**, **Hello!**, and **display**.

Each node has configuration parameters that are set by double-clicking on the node. Nodes can also have multiple inputs and outputs, and can process more than one message.

The default **Flow** is activated by clicking the colored square that is on the left side of the **Go** node. Clicking the square sends a message (`msg`) to the **Hello!** node.

The **Hello!** node receives the message (`msg`) and sets the `payload` parameter of the message to "`Hello!`" and then sends the message on to the **display** node.

The **display** node outputs the value of the `msg.payload` parameter in the **debug** tab of the right sidebar.

This completes the default **Flow**.

Go with the flow

All flows follow the same basic pattern.

A message (`msg`) is sent from node to node along the paths that connect each node.

Each node can read and update the `msg` as it passes through the node adding, updating, or removing `msg` parameters until the `msg` is passed on to the next node.

After reaching the end of a flow, the message (`msg`) is discarded.

Creating the pushbutton LED flow

The Pushbutton LED flow is created by clicking on the **+** tab at the top-right of the center panel. This creates a new flow sheet with the default name of **Sheet 1**.

From the Raspberry Pi section of the toolbox on the left, drag an `rpi-gpio` in node onto the blank flow sheet. Also drag an `rpi-gpio` out node onto the flow sheet.

Connect the two nodes by first clicking on the output connector of the **rpio-gpio** in node and dragging until a path forms and connects to the input connector of the **rpio-cpio** out node.

Now, double-click on each node and enter the appropriate configuration information. The **rpi-gpio** in node is named **Pushbutton**, connected to **GPIO4**, and has a **pullup Resistor**. The **rpi-gpio** out node is named **LED**, has the **Type Digital output**, and connects to **GPIO5**. The flow sheet is renamed **Pushbutton LED** by double-clicking the sheet name, **Sheet 1**.

Once the nodes are configured, clicking on the red **Activate** button deploys the flow. The **Activate** button is red whenever there are changes to the flow. When the flow has been deployed, the button turns gray.

While the Pushbutton LED flow is active, the LED glows while the pushbutton is pressed and the LED stops glowing when the pushbutton is released.

Notice that the green status indicators under the two nodes also change from **0** to **1** while the pushbutton is pressed. The Node-RED platform is processing each button press.

Your Raspberry Pi is now a gateway for the Internet of Things!

There's more...

This recipe is a very simple example of The ThingBox powered by Node-RED.

There is a large library of available nodes

There are dozens of additional APIs and services in the Node-RED platform.

- Raspberry Pi
  - GPIO – the hardware GPIO pins
  - Mouse – pressing the mouse buttons
- General I/O
  - HTTP – ReSTful services and web pages
  - MQTT – message queues
  - Web Sockets – JSON messages
  - TCP/UDP – data streams
  - Serial Port – character streams

- ▸ Data Parsing
    - ❑ CSV – comma-separated values
    - ❑ JSON – JavaScript object notation
    - ❑ XML – extensible markup language
    - ❑ HTML – hypertext markup language

- ▸ Social
    - ❑ Email – send/receive e-mail messages
    - ❑ Twitter – send/receive tweets
    - ❑ Esendx – send SMS messages
    - ❑ Google Calendar – add, update, and react to events
    - ❑ RSS – monitor RSS/Atom feeds

- ▸ Storage
    - ❑ File – read/write files on disk
    - ❑ Carriots – data collection from connected objects
    - ❑ Emoncms – process and visualize environmental data
    - ❑ Evrythng – drive applications with real-time data
    - ❑ Exosite – operationalized cloud processing
    - ❑ Thingspeak – open IoT platform
    - ❑ Tinamous – IoT platform for privacy and collaboration
    - ❑ Xively – enterprise IoT application platform

Wait 40 seconds before powering off or rebooting

There is one particular caution that is repeated in The ThingBox documentation. It says do not shut down or reboot the Raspberry Pi for at least 40 seconds after activating (saving) any flow – even if the flow starts working earlier than that!

Saving the updated flow diagram to disk is scheduled as an independent task that runs in parallel with the other tasks (nodes) that are currently running in the Node-RED server. So, it is quite likely that changes to the flow diagrams are activated in the Node-RED server before they are persisted to disk.

See also

- **The ThingBox Project** (`http://thethingbox.io/`): Use Internet of Things technologies without any technical knowledge and for free.

- **Node-RED** (`http://nodered.org/`): Node-RED is a visual tool for wiring the Internet of Things.

- **Carriots** (`https://www.carriots.com/`): Carriots is an IoT platform that will store a year of data for 10 devices for free.

- **Emoncms** (`http://emoncms.org/`): Emoncms is a powerful open source web app for processing, logging, and visualizing energy, temperature, and other environmental data.

- **Evrythng** (`https://evrythng.com/`): Evrythng is an IoT platform that connects any consumer product to the web and manages real-time data to drive applications.

- **Thingspeak** (`https://thingspeak.com/`): Thingspeak is an open source platform for the Internet of Things.

- **Tinamous** (`https://www.tinamous.com/`): Tinamous integrates status posts, alerts, and sensor measurements using simple, open connectivity solutions easily connecting people and Internet of Things devices.

- **Xively** (`https://xively.com/`): Xively simplifies the way companies securely and robustly connect their products and users, manage IoT data at scale, and engage more closely with their customers, users, and partners.

- **Zero-configuration networking** (`https://en.wikipedia.org/wiki/Zero-configuration_networking`): This Wikipedia article describes the zero-configuration networking that The ThingBox uses to announce its location at `http://thethingbox.local/`.

7
Clustering

In this chapter, we will cover:

- ▶ Installing a high-availability load balancer
- ▶ Installing a distributed filesystem
- ▶ Creating a super computer

Introduction

The recipes in this chapter are for network clusters of Raspberry Pis.

A network cluster is more than one computer networked together as a single system. Computers are clustered for scaling and high availability. Clusters are used to scale performance by distributing the workload of the system across all of the computers in the cluster. In a highly available system, the network cluster continues to function even if one of the computers in the cluster goes down.

Clusters of Raspberry Pis can be used to keep a website up and running, even if one of the Raspberry Pis used to host the website fails. Raspberry Pi clusters can also be used to distribute processing and data storage across a number of Raspberry Pis to create a Raspberry Pi supercomputer.

The recipes in this chapter are not specific to the Raspberry Pi. They can be repeated on most (Debian-based) Linux operating systems. The recipes are included in the book to demonstrate the possibilities of clustering Raspberry Pi computers.

After completing the recipes in this chapter, you will have used load balancers to keep a website highly available, distributed files and data over the combined storage in a cluster of Raspberry Pis, and created a Raspberry Pi supercomputer.

Installing a high-availability load balancer

This recipe turns four Raspberry Pis into a highly available website cluster.

Two Raspberry Pis are used as web servers sharing the load of hosting the website. The other two Raspberry Pis are load balancers and they distribute the load of the incoming web requests across the two web servers.

Only one load balancer is required to balance the load. The second is configured to replace the first, if the first load balancer should fail.

The web servers in this recipe use the Apache HTTP server to serve simple stateless websites that demonstrate load balancing in action.

The load balancers in this recipe use HA Proxy to balance web requests between the two web servers and **Keepalived** to create a virtual IP address for the website that will be automatically redirected to the backup load balancer, if the current load balancer fails.

After completing this recipe, you will have created a highly available website.

Getting ready

These are the ingredients for this recipe:

- Four basic networking setups for the Raspberry Pi all connected to the same network switch
- Five available IP addresses on the local network

This recipe does not require the desktop GUI and could either be run from the text-based console or from within an LXTerminal.

With the Secure Shell server running on each Raspberry Pi, this recipe can be completed remotely using a Secure Shell client. Websites are typically managed remotely.

How to do it...

The steps to building a highly available Raspberry Pi website cluster are:

1. Log in to each Raspberry Pi. Set its hostname and IP address. Name the two load balancers lb1 and lb2. Name the two web servers web1 and web2. Use IP addresses from your network.

    The following hostnames and IP addresses are used in this recipe: lb1 – 192.168.2.101; lb2 – 192.168.2.102; web1 – 192.168.2.111, and web2 – 192.168.2.112.

> The `raspi-config` command can be used to change the hostname of your Raspberry Pi. *Chapter 2, Administration*, has recipes for configuring the Raspberry Pi that use the `raspi-config` command. *Chapter 5, Advanced Networking*, has a recipe for changing the static IP address.

2. Next, we'll set up the web servers. Log in to each of the web servers: `web1` and `web2`.

> Repeat the following steps on both of the web servers: `web1` and `web2`.

3. Now, we'll install Apache2 on each web server. Use the `apt-get install` command to install the Apache web server daemon (Apache2).

```
pi@web1 ~ $ sudo apt-get install -y apache2

Reading package lists... Done
Building dependency tree
Reading state information... Done
The following extra packages will be installed:
  apache2-bin apache2-data apache2-utils libapr1 libaprutil1 libaprutil1-
dbd-sqlite3 libaprutil1-ldap liblua5.1-0 ssl-cert
Suggested packages:
  apache2-doc apache2-suexec-pristine apache2-suexec-custom openssl-
blacklist
The following NEW packages will be installed:
  apache2 apache2-bin apache2-data apache2-utils libapr1 libaprutil1
libaprutil1-dbd-sqlite3 libaprutil1-ldap liblua5.1-0 ssl-cert
0 upgraded, 10 newly installed, 0 to remove and 0 not upgraded.
...
```

4. Create unique test pages for each web server.

5. Change the directories (`cd`) to the web server root (`/var/www/html`).

```
pi@web1 ~ $ cd /var/www/html

pi@web1 /var/www/html $
```

6. Use the `chown` command to give the user `pi` ownership to the directory (`.`) and all of the files in it (`*`).

    ```
    pi@web1 /var/www/html $ sudo chown pi:www-data . *

    pi@web1 /var/www/html $
    ```

7. Create a web page for the web server using the `echo` command.

    ```
    pi@web1 /var/www/html $ echo '<html><body>web1</body></html>' > index.html

    pi@web1 /var/www/html $
    ```

> During normal operation, both web servers will be serving identical content.
>
> For testing, the page contents, `<body>web1</body>`, should be unique for each web server. Use `<body>web2</body>` for web server web2.

8. Use the `touch` command to create a file (`lb-check.txt`) that can be used by the load balancers to validate that the web server is running.

    ```
    pi@web1 /var/www/html $ touch lb-check.txt

    pi@web1 /var/www/html $
    ```

9. Now, test the web servers. Use a web browser to test the web servers. Test both their hostnames: `http://web1.local/` and `http://web2.local/`, as well as their IP addresses: `http://192.168.2.111/` and `http://192.168.2.112/`.

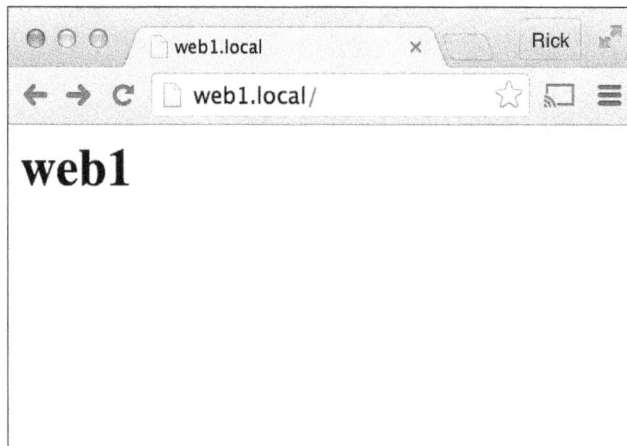

10. Set up the load balancers. Log in to each of the load balancers, `lb1` and `lb2`.

> 🖋️ Repeat the following steps on both `lb1` and `lb2`.

11. Install HAProxy and Keepalived on each load balancer. Use the `apt-get install` command to download and install the `haproxy` and `keepalived` packages.

    ```
    pi@lb1 ~ $ sudo apt-get install -y haproxy keepalived

    Reading package lists... Done
    Building dependency tree
    Reading state information... Done
    The following extra packages will be installed:
      iproute ipvsadm libpci3 libperl5.20 libsensors4 libsnmp-base libsnmp30
    Suggested packages:
      heartbeat ldirectord lm-sensors snmp-mibs-downloader vim-haproxy
    haproxy-doc
    The following NEW packages will be installed:
      iproute ipvsadm keepalived libpci3 libperl5.20 libsensors4 libsnmp-base
      libsnmp30 haproxy
    0 upgraded, 9 newly installed, 0 to remove and 0 not upgraded.

    ...
    ```

12. Configure HAProxy for each load balancer. Use the `cat` command to add the `listen stats` and `listen webfarm` sections to the bottom of the `/etc/haproxy/haproxy.cfg` configuration file.

    ```
    pi@lb1 ~ $ sudo bash

    root@lb1:/home/pi# cat <<EOD >>/etc/haproxy/haproxy.cfg

    listen stats
      bind 0.0.0.0:8880
      stats enable
      stats hide-version
      stats uri     /
      stats realm   HAProxy\ Statistics
      stats auth    pi:raspberry

    listen webfarm 192.168.2.100:80
      mode http
    ```

```
    balance roundrobin
    option httpclose
    option httpchk HEAD /lb-check.txt HTTP/1.0
    server web1 192.168.2.111:80 check
    server web2 192.168.2.112:80 check

EOD

root@lb1:/home/pi# exit

pi@lb1 ~ $
```

13. Use the `systemctl restart` command to restart `haproxy.service`.

```
pi@lb1 ~ $ sudo systemctl restart haproxy.service

pi@lb1 ~ $
```

14. Enable listening on virtual IP addresses for both load balancers. Add the configuration parameter `net.ipv4.ip_nonlocal_bind=1` to the bottom of the `sysctl.conf` configuration file.

```
pi@lb1 ~ $ sudo bash

root@lb1:/home/pi# echo "net.ipv4.ip_nonlocal_bind=1" >>/etc/sysctl.conf

root@lb1:/home/pi# exit

pi@lb1 ~ $
```

15. Use the `sysctl -p` command to load the updated configuration.

```
pi@lb1 ~ $ sudo sysctl -p

kernel.printk = 3 4 1 3
vm.swappiness = 1
vm.min_free_kbytes = 8192
net.ipv4.ip_nonlocal_bind = 1

pi@lb1 ~ $
```

16. Configure Keepalived for both load balancers.

17. Use the `cat` command to create the `keepalived.conf` configuration file that defines the following: a function to check the status of the HAProxy daemon (`chk_haproxy`); the network interface `eth0` to listen on; the load balancer's priority (the highest is the master load balancer); and the virtual IP address (192.168.2.100) that the load balancers share.

> It is important that the load balancers have different priorities. On load balancer `lb1`, use `priority 101` (as shown next). On load balancer `lb2`, use `priority 100`.

```
pi@lb2 ~ $ sudo bash

root@lb2:/home/pi# cat <<EOD >/etc/keepalived/keepalived.conf

vrrp_script chk_haproxy
{
        script "killall -0 haproxy"
        interval 2
        weight 2
}

vrrp_instance VI_1
{
        interface eth0
        state MASTER
        virtual_router_id 51

        priority 101

        virtual_ipaddress
        {
            192.168.2.100
        }

        track_script
        {
            chk_haproxy
        }
}
```

EOD

```
root@lb2:/home/pi# exit

exit

pi@lb2 ~ $
```

18. Use the `systemctl restart` command to restart `keepalived.service`.
    ```
    pi@lb1 ~ $ sudo systemctl restart keepalived.service

    pi@lb1 ~ $
    ```

19. Test the cluster. Use a web browser to test the cluster. Browse to the cluster's virtual IP address (`http://192.168.2.100`).

20. Notice that with each refresh of the browser, the web page displayed alternates between the web page from web server `web1` and the web page from `web2`. The cluster is working!

> For an actual website, the web servers `web1` and `web2` should be serving the same content, stateless copies of the same website, or the same web service.

21. Test web server failure. Log in to `web1` and use the `poweroff` command to shut it down.
    ```
    golden-macbook:~ rick$ ssh pi@web1.local

    Warning: Permanently added the RSA host key for IP address
    'fe80::ba27:ebff:fec9:7ea9%en5' to the list of known hosts.
    pi@web1.local's password:

    The programs included with the Debian GNU/Linux system are free software;
    the exact distribution terms for each program are described in the
    individual files in /usr/share/doc/*/copyright.

    Debian GNU/Linux comes with ABSOLUTELY NO WARRANTY, to the extent
    permitted by applicable law.
    Last login: Sat Oct 24 14:34:34 2015 from fe80::12dd:b1ff:feee:dfc6%eth0

    pi@web1 ~ $ sudo poweroff

    Connection to web1.local closed by remote host.
    Connection to web1.local closed.

    golden-macbook:~ rick$
    ```

22. Use a web browser to validate that the virtual IP address of the cluster (192.1682.1.00) is still working.

23. Notice that with every refresh of the browser, the web page displayed is from the only running web server, web2.

24. Use a web browser to check the status of the HA Proxy on lb1 (http://lb1.local:8880).

Statistics Report for HAP × | History × | Setting Up A High-Avail × | 192.168.2.100 × | Rick

← C lb1.local:8880

HAProxy

Statistics Report for pid 4155

> General process information

pid = 4155 (process #1, nbproc = 1)
uptime = 0d 4h21m16s
system limits: memmax = unlimited; ulimit-n = 4034
maxsock = 4034; maxconn = 2000; maxpipes = 0
current conns = 1; current pipes = 0/0; conn rate = 1/sec
Running tasks: 1/7; idle = 100 %

active UP
active UP, going down
active DOWN, going up
active or backup DOWN
active or backup DOWN for maintenance (MAINT)
active or backup SOFT STOPPED for maintenance

backup UP
backup UP, going down
backup DOWN, going up
not checked

Note: "NOLB"/"DRAIN" = UP with load-balancing disabled.

Display option:
- Scope :
- Hide 'DOWN' servers
- Refresh now
- CSV export

External resources:
- Primary site
- Updates (v1.5)
- Online manual

stats

| | Queue | | | Session rate | | | Sessions | | | | | | Bytes | | Denied | | Errors | | Warnings | | | Server | | | | | | | |
	Cur	Max	Limit	Cur	Max	Limit	Cur	Max	Limit	Total	LbTot	Last	In	Out	Req	Resp	Req	Conn	Resp	Retr	Redis	Status	LastChk	Wght	Act	Bck	Chk	Dwn	Dwntme	Thrtle
Frontend				1	1	-	1	2	2 000	3			3 978	154 419	0	0	1					OPEN								
Backend	0	0		0	0		0	0	200	0	0	0s	3 978	154 419	0	0		0	0	0	0	4h21m UP		0	0	0		0		

webfarm

| | Queue | | | Session rate | | | Sessions | | | | | | Bytes | | Denied | | Errors | | Warnings | | | Server | | | | | | | |
	Cur	Max	Limit	Cur	Max	Limit	Cur	Max	Limit	Total	LbTot	Last	In	Out	Req	Resp	Req	Conn	Resp	Retr	Redis	Status	LastChk	Wght	Act	Bck	Chk	Dwn	Dwntme	Thrtle
Frontend				0	0	-	0	0	2 000	0			0	0	0	0	0					OPEN								
web1	0	0		0	0		0	0	-	0	0	?	0	0		0		0	0	0	0	4h21m DOWN	L4TOUT in 2002ms	1	Y	-	1	1	4h21m	-
web2	0	0	-	0	0		0	0	-	0	0	?	0	0		0		0	0	0	0	4h21m UP	L7OK/200 in 2ms	1	Y	-	0	0	0s	-
Backend	0	0		0	0		0	0	200	0	0	?	0	0	0	0		0	0	0	0	4h21m UP		1	1	0		0	0s	

---

25. Notice that the status of web server web1 is displayed in red indicating that it is down. The status of web2 is green because it is still running.

26. Restart the web server, web1.

27. Refresh the HAProxy status page (http://lb1.local:8880) and notice that the status of web server web1 is once again green.

28. Continually refresh the virtual IP address of the cluster (http://192.168.2.100) and notice that the web page displayed once again alternates between the web page from web server web1 and the web page from web server web2.

29. The cluster runs even if one web server fails!

30. Test load balancer failure. Log in to the master load balancer, lb1.

31. Use the ip addr command to show the IP addresses that share the network interface eth0.

```
pi@lb1 ~ $ ip addr show eth0

2: eth0: <BROADCAST,MULTICAST,UP,LOWER_UP> mtu 1500 qdisc pfifo_fast state
UP group default qlen 1000
```

```
           link/ether b8:27:eb:57:79:6d brd ff:ff:ff:ff:ff:ff
           inet 192.168.2.101/24 brd 192.168.2.255 scope global eth0
              valid_lft forever preferred_lft forever
           inet 192.168.2.100/32 scope global eth0
              valid_lft forever preferred_lft forever
           inet6 fe80::9b32:5b03:f901:4777/64 scope link
              valid_lft forever preferred_lft forever

   pi@lb1 ~ $
```

32. Notice that there are two IPv4 (`inet`) addresses including the cluster's virtual IP address (`http://192.168.2.100`) assigned to network interface `eth0`.

33. Now, log in to the failover load balancer `lb2`.

34. Use the `ip addr` command to show the IP addresses that share the network interface `eth0` on load balancer `lb2`.

    pi@lb2 ~ $ **ip addr show eth0**

```
   2: eth0: <BROADCAST,MULTICAST,UP,LOWER_UP> mtu 1500 qdisc pfifo_fast state
   UP group default qlen 1000
           link/ether b8:27:eb:42:f6:a2 brd ff:ff:ff:ff:ff:ff
           inet 192.168.2.102/24 brd 192.168.2.255 scope global eth0
              valid_lft forever preferred_lft forever
           inet6 fe80::9284:5714:5216:6cde/64 scope link
              valid_lft forever preferred_lft forever

   pi@lb2 ~ $
```

35. Notice that there is only one IPv4 (`inet`) address assigned to the network interface `eth0` on load balancer `lb2` and it is not the cluster's virtual IP address.

36. Remove the master load balancer `lb1` from the cluster by disconnecting its network cable.

37. Use the `ip addr` command once again to show the IP addresses that are sharing the network interface `eth0` on load balancer `lb2`.

    pi@lb2 ~ $ **ip addr sh eth0**

```
   2: eth0: <BROADCAST,MULTICAST,UP,LOWER_UP> mtu 1500 qdisc pfifo_fast state
   UP group default qlen 1000
           link/ether b8:27:eb:42:f6:a2 brd ff:ff:ff:ff:ff:ff
           inet 192.168.2.102/24 brd 192.168.2.255 scope global eth0
              valid_lft forever preferred_lft forever
           inet 192.168.2.100/32 scope global eth0
```

```
        valid_lft forever preferred_lft forever
    inet6 fe80::9284:5714:5216:6cde/64 scope link
        valid_lft forever preferred_lft forever

pi@lb2 ~ $
```

38. Notice that there are now two IPv4 (inet) addresses including the cluster's virtual IP address (http://192.168.2.100) assigned to network interface eth0 on lb2.

39. Notice by continuously refreshing the cluster's virtual IP address (http://192.168.2.100) that load balancing still works—that the web page still alternates between web1 and web2.

40. The cluster runs even if one load balancer fails!

41. Now, let's restore normal operation. Add lb1 back to the cluster by connecting its network cable.

42. Use the ip addr command on load balancer lb2 to show that the cluster's virtual IP address (192.168.2.100) is no longer assigned to network interface eth0 on load balancer lb2 (see step 32).

43. Use the ip addr command on load balancer lb1 to show that load balancer lb1 once again has the cluster's virtual IP address assigned to its network interface eth0 (see step 29).

44. The highly available website cluster is up and running!

How it works...

The recipe begins by setting up four Raspberry Pis with new hostnames and IP addresses so that they can be used more effectively in a cluster.

The load balancers are named lb1 and lb2; and their IP addresses are respectively set to 192.168.2.101 and 192.168.2.102.

The web servers are named web1 and web2 with their respective IP addresses set to 192.168.2.111 and 192.168.112.

The raspi-config command can be used to change the Raspberry Pi hostname (examples of using the raspi-config command can be found in *Chapter 2, Administration*).

A recipe for *Configuring a static IP address* can be found in *Chapter 5, Advanced Networking*.

Setting up the web servers

After each Raspberry Pi is properly named and addressed, the Apache HTTP daemon is set up on each of the two web servers, web1 and web2.

Installing Apache2 on each web server

The `apt-get install` command is used to install the `apache2` package on each web server.

Installation includes starting the Apache HTTP server and restarting it with each boot.

> Chapter 5, *Advanced Networking*, has a recipe for installing a web server with more detailed instructions on setting up a web server.

Creating unique test web pages for each web server

The `cd` command is used to change the web server's root directory, `/var/www/html`, where two files will be created: the default web page, `index.html`, and a file for the load balancers to check periodically to ensure that the web server is still running, `lb-check.txt`.

The `chown` command is used to change the ownership of the root directory (`.`) and all the files in it (`*`) to the user `pi`. After changing ownership, the user `pi` can create and delete files in the web server's root directory.

Two files are created on each web server: `index.html` and `lb-check.txt`. The `lb-check.txt` file can be empty. It just needs to exist.

The `echo` command is used to write the very simple `index.html` file, and the `touch` command is used to create an empty `lb-check.txt` file.

This recipe intentionally uses unique `index.html` files on each web server to demonstrate load balancing in action. On web server `web1`, the body of the web page is `web1` and on web server `web2` the `body` is `web2`.

During the normal operation of a website cluster, clients of the website should see the same web page regardless of which web server the load balancer has selected.

During the normal operation of a website cluster, each of the cluster's web servers will be identical. They will either have identical `index.html` files or they will be configured to serve the same web application.

This recipe uses two different `index.html` files to demonstrate load balancing.

Testing the web servers

A web browser is used to test that each web server is up and running. The hostname and IP address of both web servers are tested:

```
http://web1.local/  http://192.168.2.111/
http://web2.local/  http://192.168.2.112/
```

Setting up the load balancers

After the web servers have been installed and tested, HA Proxy and Keepalived are set up on the two load balancers, **lb1** and **lb2**. HA Proxy is the load balancer service, and Keepalived is the failover service. HA Proxy distributes web requests between the two web servers and Keepalived replaces the master load balancer with another, if it fails.

Install haproxy and keepalived on each load balancer

The `apt-get install` command is used to install the HAProxy and Keepalived software distribution packages on each load balancer.

Installation includes starting and restarting both HAProxy and Keepalived with each boot. However, HAProxy and Keepalived still need to be configured.

Configuring HAProxy for each load balancer

The default HAProxy configuration file (`/etc/haproxy/haproxy.cfg`) needs two new sections: `listen stats` and `listen webfarm`.

The `listen stats` section creates a protected single-page web server on port `8880` for all network interfaces of the load balancer (0.0.0.0) including the virtual network interface for the cluster (192.168.2.100). The statistics web server is protected (`stats auth`) by a username (`pi`) and a password (`raspberry`).

The `listen webfarm` section defines the collection of web servers (server `web1`, server `web2`) that the HAProxy will load balance using the roundrobin load-balancing algorithm, as well as the method (`httpchk HEAD`) and URL (`/lb-check.txt`) that are used to test if the web servers are still running.

A secure shell (`sudo bash`) is used to update the HAProxy's configuration file (`/etc/haproxy/haproxy.cfg`).

Within the Secure Shell, the `cat` command is used to append the lines following the `cat` command up to the end of data mark (`<<EOD`) to the bottom of the file (`>>haproxy.cfg`).

The Secure Shell is released (`exit`) after the file is updated.

The `systemctl` command is used to restart the HAProxy service (`happroxy.service`) on each load balancer, so that the service on each load balancer can update its configuration.

Enable listening on virtual IP addresses for both load balancers

The Raspberry Pi's Linux kernel is not by default configured to listen on the virtual IP addresses used by Keepalived. The system kernel configuration file (`/etc/sysctl.conf`) needs to be updated to permit non-local network binding.

A secure shell (`sudo bash`) is used to update the system kernel configuration file (`sysctl.conf`).

Within the Secure Shell, the `echo` command is used to enable virtual IP addresses by appending the statement `net.ipv4.ip_nonlocal_bind=1` to the bottom of the system kernel configuration file (`systctl.conf`) (`>>`).

The Secure Shell is released (`exit`) after the file is updated.

The `sysctl -p` command is used to load the updated kernel configuration.

Configuring Keepalived for both load balancers

Although Keepalived is installed and ready, it has not been configured.

A secure shell (`sudo bash`) is used to create a Keepalived configuration file (`/etc/keepalived/keepalived.conf`).

Within the secure shell, the `cat` command is used to create the configuration file by copying the lines following the `cat` command up to the end of data mark (`<<EOD`) to the configuration file (`>keepalived.conf`).

The Secure Shell is released (`exit`) after the file is updated.

Keepalived configuration has two sections: `vrrp_script chk_haproxy` and `vrrp_instance VI_1`.

The `vrrp_script chk_haproxy` section defines a script (`killall -0 haproxy`) that will complete with an OK status so long as a process named `haproxy` is running.

The command name `killall` is misleading; the `-0` parameter tells the command to do nothing more than exit with an OK status. The `killall` command can also be used to `kill` processes; however, that is not its purpose here.

The `vrrp_instance VI_1` section defines the `virtual_ipaddress` that is shared by the two load balancers (192.168.2.100). This section also defines the network interface (`eth0`) that is used to bind the virtual IP address, the `track_script` (chk_haproxy) that is used to keep track of the `haproxy` process, and a priority that is used to determine which of the load balancers is the `MASTER`.

> The `priority` parameter should be different on the two load balancers.
>
> The master load balancer, lb1, should have a higher priority (priority 101) than the failover load balancer, lb2 (priority 100).

The priority should be different on each of the load balancers. In this recipe, load balancer lb1 has the priority 101 and load balancer lb2 has the priority 100. The load balancer with the highest priority (lb1) is used as the master and the other load balancer (lb2) is used as a failover slave.

Only the master load balancer (lb1) listens on the defined virtual network address (192.168.2.100). The failover load balancer (lb2) does not.

The HAProxy running on the master load balancer (lb1) is the service used by the cluster to balance web requests between the web servers. The HAProxy on the failover load balancer (lb2) is still running, but it is not used by the cluster because the failover load balancer (lb2) is not listening on the cluster's virtual IP address (192.168.2.100).

If the master load balancer (lb1) does fail, the load balancer with the next highest priority (lb2) becomes the master.

If the master `track_script` reports of load balancer (lb1) indicates that the master's `haproxy` process is no longer running, the master transfers control of the virtual IP address (192.168.2.100) to the failover load balancer (lb2).

If the failover load balancer (lb2) can no longer connect to the master load balancer (lb1), the failover load balancer (lb2) will attempt to take over the virtual IP address.

The `virtual_router_id` parameter defines a unique ID (51) that is used by the load balancers keeping the same virtual IP address up and running.

The Secure Shell is released (`exit`) after the file is created.

The `systemctl` command is used to restart the Keepalived service (`keepalived.service`) on both load balancers, so that the service on each load balancer can update its configuration.

Testing the cluster

A web browser is used to validate that the website cluster is up and running on the defined virtual IP address (192.168.2.100).

When the website URL (`http://192.168.2.100/`) is refreshed in the browser, the page displayed in the browser alternates between the default web page (`index.html`) from web server `web1` and the default page from web server `web2`. The master load balancer (lb1) is alternating web requests (round robin) between the two web servers.

The cluster is working!

Testing web server failure

In order to test that the website cluster's virtual IP address still responds to web requests after the failure of a single web server, web server `web1` is shut down using the `poweroff` command.

After web server `web1` has been shut down, a web browser is used to validate that the website cluster is still up and running on the defined virtual IP address (192.168.2.100).

When the website URL (http://192.168.2.100/) is refreshed in the browser, the web page displayed in the browser no longer alternates between the two web servers. Now, only the default page (index.html) from web server web2 is displayed. The master load balancer (lb1) is still running but can only serve web requests from web server web2.

Then, the web browser is used to browse the URL of the HAProxy statistics page (http://lb1.local:8880/) of the master load balancer (lb1). The statistics page shows that web server web1 is no longer available by displaying the statistics for the web server with a red background color. Web server web2 is still running, so its statistics are displayed with a green background color.

The website continues to work properly, even if one web server is down.

Next, web server web1 is restarted.

After web server web1 has restarted, the master load balancer (lb1) detects the availability of the web server's tracking file (http://lb1.local/chk_haproxy.txt) and web server web1 is added back to the load balancer's webfarm.

A refresh of the HAProxy statistics page shows that the statistics from web server web1 are once again green, and continually refreshing the website's virtual URL (http://192.168.2.100/) once again alternates between web1 and web2.

The website is protected from web server failure and web servers can be added on demand to handle more requests!

Testing load balancer failure

Removing the master load balancer (lb1) from the network by disconnecting its network cable tests the failover of the master load balancer.

Before the master load balancer (lb1) is disconnected from the network, the ip addr command is used to show that the website cluster's virtual IP address (192.168.2.100) is bound to the master load balancer's network interface (eth0). The ip addr command is also used on the failover load balancer (lb2) to show that it does not have the cluster's virtual IP address bound to its network interface (eth0).

After the master load balancer (lb1) has been disconnected from the network, the ip addr command is run again on the failover load balancer (lb2). Now that the master load balancer (lb1) is disconnected from the network, the failover load balancer (lb2) has taken over the cluster's virtual IP address (192.168.2.100).

While the master load balancer (lb1) is disconnected from the network, a web browser is used to validate that the website cluster is still up and running on the defined virtual IP address (192.168.2.100).

When the website URL (`http://192.168.2.100/`) is refreshed in the browser, the web page displayed in the browser continues to alternate between the two web servers. Load balancing still works even though the master load balancer (lb1) is offline. The failover load balancer (lb2) has taken over load balancing successfully!

The website cluster continues to work properly, even if one load balancer is down!

Restoring normal operation

Normal operation is restored to the website cluster by reconnecting the master load balancer (lb1) to the network.

After the master load balancer (lb1) has been reconnected, the `ip addr` command is again run on each load balancer. The master load balancer (lb1) once again has the cluster's virtual IP address (`192.168.2.100`) bound to its network interface (`eth0`) and the failover load balancer (lb2) no longer has the virtual IP address bound to its network interface.

The highly available website cluster is up and running!

There's more...

This recipe is a very simple example of a highly available website cluster that can be used to serve any stateless website such as a collection of static web pages or a website created with a website generator like **Jekyll** (`http://jekyllrb.com/`).

Scaling horizontally by adding more web servers

A cluster is scaled horizontally by adding more servers.

The website cluster in this recipe can be scaled horizontally by adding more Raspberry Pi web servers. Each additional web server added to the cluster should be configured exactly the same as the existing web servers (see steps 2 through 8).

Scaling a Raspberry Pi cluster vertically is limited by the amount of memory available in a Raspberry Pi. The memory allocated by the GPU can be reduced freeing more memory for use by services; however, the physical memory of a Raspberry Pi cannot be increased.

The fixed memory size of the Raspberry Pi puts limits on scaling Raspberry Pi clusters. They can be easily scaled horizontally, but not vertically.

Session cookies

Many websites are stateful, not stateless. Stateful websites use session cookies to create unique sessions that require a login. The HAProxy configuration in this recipe is for stateless websites and does not recognize session cookies.

A user session is stored in a web application server and the session cookie is a unique key that is used to identify each unique user session in the web server. In most situations, sessions cannot be shared across web servers. The load balancer needs to ensure that once a user starts a session with one web server, all requests to the website cluster are directed to that web server and not to any other.

Web application servers and frameworks like Apache Tomcat and PHP depend on session cookies. Apache Tomcat uses the session cookie `JSESSIONID`, and PHP uses the `PHPSESSID` session cookie.

For websites that depend on session cookies, the load balancer for the website cluster needs to ensure that web requests from the same unique user (as identified by the session cookie) are always sent to the same web server because only that web server has the user's session.

To enable the HAProxy servers in this recipe to recognize session cookies for Apache Tomcat (or other Java application servers), replace the two server configuration parameters in the HAProxy configuration file (`/etc/haproxy/haproxy.cfg`) with the following three lines:

```
option cookie JSESSIONID prefix
server web1 192.168.2.111:80 check cookie web1
server web2 192.168.2.112:80 check cookie web2
```

The first line turns on the cookie tracking option using the `JSESSIONID` cookie plus a unique prefix for each web server. The two server configuration parameters have been updated to set a unique `cookie` prefix for each server (`web1` and `web2`).

After restarting the HAProxy service (`systemctl restart haproxy.service`), the cluster will recognize session cookies.

See also

- ▶ **Computer cluster** (`https://en.wikipedia.org/wiki/Computer_cluster`): This Wikipedia article describes the concepts and history of computer clusters.

- ▶ **Keepalived** (`http://www.keepalived.org/`): The main goal of this project is to provide simple and robust facilities for load balancing and high availability to a Linux system and Linux-based infrastructures.

- ▶ **HAProxy** (`http://www.haproxy.org/`): HAProxy is a free, very fast, and reliable solution offering high availability, load balancing, and proxying for TCP and HTTP-based applications.

- ▶ **systemctl – control the systemd system and service manager** (`http://manpages.debian.org/cgi-bin/man.cgi?query=systemctl`): The Debian manual page for `systemctl` describes the command and its options.

- **sysctl – read/write system parameters** (`http://manpages.debian.org/cgi-bin/man.cgi?query=sysctl&sektion=8`): The Debian manual page for `sysctl` describes the command and its options.

- **killall – kill processes by name** (`http://manpages.debian.org/cgi-bin/man.cgi?query=killall`): The Debian manual page for `killall` describes the command and its options.

- **Jekyll** (`http://jekyllrb.com/`): Transform your plain text into static websites and blogs.

- **Scalability** (`https://en.wikipedia.org/wiki/Scalability`): This Wikipedia article defines scalability, both horizontal and vertical.

- **Session cookie** (`https://en.wikipedia.org/wiki/HTTP_cookie#Session_cookie`): This Wikipedia article about HTTP cookies also defines session cookies.

Installing a distributed filesystem

This recipe turns four Raspberry Pis into a highly available distributed filesystem using GlusterFS.

GlusterFS is a scalable network filesystem suitable for data-intensive tasks such as cloud storage and media streaming. GlusterFS is free and open source software and can utilize common off-the-shelf hardware like the Raspberry Pi.

After completing this recipe, you will have clustered four Raspberry Pis to create a highly available distributed filesystem.

Getting ready

Here are the ingredients for this recipe:

- Four basic networking setups for the Raspberry Pi
- Four available IP addresses on the local network

This recipe does not require the desktop GUI and could either be run from the text-based console or from within an LXTerminal.

With the Secure Shell server running on each Raspberry Pi, this recipe can be completed remotely using a Secure Shell client. A distributed filesystem is typically managed remotely.

How to do it...

The steps to building a highly available Raspberry Pi distributed filesystem are:

1. Log in to each of the four Raspberry Pis and set their hostnames. Name the Raspberry Pis `gluster1`, `gluster2`, `gluster3`, and `gluster4`.

> The `raspi-config` command can be used to change the hostname of your Raspberry Pi. *Chapter 2, Administration*, has recipes for configuring the Raspberry Pi that use the `raspi-config` command.

Installing the GlusterFS server on each Raspberry Pi

1. Log in to each of the four Raspberry Pis: `gluster1`, `gluster2`, `gluster3`, and `gluster4`.

2. Use the `apt-get install` command to install the GlusterFS server (`glusterfs-server`).

    ```
    pi@gluster1 ~ $ sudo apt-get install -y glusterfs-server

    Reading package lists... Done
    Building dependency tree
    Reading state information... Done
    The following extra packages will be installed:
      glusterfs-client glusterfs-common libaio1 libibverbs1 librdmacm1
    The following NEW packages will be installed:
      glusterfs-client glusterfs-common glusterfs-server libaio1 libibverbs1
      librdmacm1
    0 upgraded, 6 newly installed, 0 to remove and 0 not upgraded.
    Need to get 7,604 kB of archives.
    After this operation, 13.6 MB of additional disk space will be used.
    ...
    ```

> Repeat the installation of `glusterfs-server` on each of the four Raspberry Pis: `gluster1`, `gluster2`, `gluster3`, and `glsuter4`.

3. Now, let's create a trusted storage pool. After each of the Raspberry Pis has had GlusterFS installed, log in to `gluster1` and use the `gluster peer probe` command to link the other three Raspberry Pis into a single trusted storage pool.

   ```
   pi@gluster1 ~ $ sudo gluster peer probe gluster2.local

   peer probe: success.

   pi@gluster1 ~ $ sudo gluster peer probe gluster3.local

   peer probe: success.

   pi@gluster1 ~ $ sudo gluster peer probe gluster4.local
   peer probe: success.

   pi@gluster1 ~ $
   ```

4. Use the `gluster peer status` command to check that the storage pool has been created successfully.

   ```
   pi@gluster1 ~ $ sudo gluster peer status

   Number of Peers: 3

   Hostname: gluster2.local
   Uuid: 5b969ed1-01c2-406e-9710-944436c41c98
   State: Peer in Cluster (Connected)

   Hostname: gluster3.local
   Uuid: 9a00c151-af6e-44c5-9d14-5607270b4038
   State: Peer in Cluster (Connected)

   Hostname: gluster4.local
   Uuid: f036b1c4-7a51-49eb-aa63-81babb843b7e
   State: Peer in Cluster (Connected)

   pi@gluster1 ~ $
   ```

5. Also use the `gluster peer status` from another peer in the storage pool (`gluster2`) to validate the storage pool.

   ```
   pi@gluster2 ~ $ sudo gluster peer status

   Number of Peers: 3

   Hostname: 192.168.2.12
   Uuid: 4147586b-a723-4068-b8cb-d417df6766d8
   ```

```
State: Peer in Cluster (Connected)

Hostname: gluster3.local
Uuid: 9a00c151-af6e-44c5-9d14-5607270b4038
State: Peer in Cluster (Connected)

Hostname: gluster4.local
Uuid: f036b1c4-7a51-49eb-aa63-81babb843b7e
State: Peer in Cluster (Connected)

pi@gluster2 ~ $
```

6. Notice that the `Hostname` displayed for `gluster1` is an IP address (`192.168.2.12`).

7. Use the `gluster peer probe` command on any other peer (`gluster2`) to add the hostname of `gluster1` to the storage pool.

> Do not use the `gluster peer probe` command to add itself to the trusted server pool! *A storage peer cannot add itself to the pool!*
>
> Any attempt for a peer to add itself could damage the entire storage pool.

```
pi@gluster2 ~ $ sudo gluster peer probe gluster1.local

peer probe: success.

pi@gluster2 ~ $ sudo gluster peer status

Number of Peers: 3

Hostname: gluster1.local
Uuid: 4147586b-a723-4068-b8cb-d417df6766d8
State: Peer in Cluster (Connected)

Hostname: gluster3.local
Uuid: 9a00c151-af6e-44c5-9d14-5607270b4038
State: Peer in Cluster (Connected)

Hostname: gluster4.local
Uuid: f036b1c4-7a51-49eb-aa63-81babb843b7e
State: Peer in Cluster (Connected)

pi@gluster2 ~ $
```

8. It's time to create a striped replicated volume from the trusted storage pool. From any peer in the trusted storage pool (gluster1), use the gluster volume create command to create a distributed striped replicated volume (stripe 2 replica 2) using the four peers of the trusted storage pool (gluster1, gluster2, gluster3, and gluster4). On each peer, the /srv/vol0 directory is used to store the GlusterFS configuration and data for the new volume (vol0).

```
pi@gluster1 ~ $ sudo gluster volume create vol0 stripe 2 replica 2
gluster1.local:/srv/vol0 gluster2.local:/srv/vol0 gluster3.local:/srv/vol0
gluster4.local:/srv/vol0 force

volume create: vol0: success: please start the volume to access data

pi@gluster1 ~ $
```

9. Use the gluster volume start command to start the newly created volume (vol0).

```
pi@gluster1 ~ $ sudo gluster volume start vol0

volume start: vol0: success

pi@gluster1 ~ $
```

10. Now, let's mount the distributed striped replicated volume. Use the mount command to mount the glusterfs volume vol0 from the peer, gluster1.local, on the local mount point, /mnt.

```
pi@gluster1 ~ $ sudo mount -t glusterfs gluster1.local:/vol0 /mnt
pi@gluster1 ~ $
```

11. Test the striped replicated volume. Use the cp command to copy a large file (/boot/kernel.img) to the local mount point (/mnt) of the newly created distributed striped replicated volume (vol0).

```
pi@gluster1 ~ $ ls -l /boot/kernel.img

-rwxr-xr-x 1 root root 4056224 Sep 23 16:10 /boot/kernel.img

pi@gluster1 ~ $ sha1sum /boot/kernel.img

d5e64d892b308b99e9c2c55deaa39c579a2335ec   /boot/kernel.img

pi@gluster1 ~ $ sudo cp /boot/kernel.img /mnt/


pi@gluster1 ~ $ ls -l /mnt/kernel.img
```

```
-rwxr-xr-x 1 root root 4056224 Oct 31 23:37 /mnt/kernel.img

pi@gluster1 ~ $ sha1sum /mnt/kernel.img

d5e64d892b308b99e9c2c55deaa39c579a2335ec  /mnt/kernel.img

pi@gluster1 ~ $
```

12. Notice that the copied file (`/mnt/kernel.img`) has the same size (`4056224`) and checksum (`d5e64…35ec`) as the original file.

13. Use the `ls -la` command to display the entire contents of the GlusterFS storage directory for the distributed volume (`/srv/vol0`).

```
pi@gluster1 ~ $ ls -la /srv/vol0/

total 2068
drwxr-xr-x 3 root root    4096 Oct 31 23:37 .
drwxr-xr-x 3 pi   pi      4096 Oct 31 23:12 ..
drw------- 7 root root    4096 Oct 31 23:37 .glusterfs
-rwxr-xr-x 2 root root 2090144 Oct 31 23:37 kernel.img

pi@gluster1 ~ $
```

14. Notice that only part of the data from the large file (`kernel.img`) is stored on this peer (`gluster1`). The size of the file (`2090144`) in the storage directory (`/srv/vol0`) is significantly smaller than the size (`4056224`) of the original file (`/boot/kernel.img`).

15. Log in to each of the other three peers (`gluster2`, `gluster3`, and `gluster4`) and use the `ls -l` command to check the size of the files in each of the other storage directories for the volume (`/srv/vol0`).

[log in to peer `gluster2`]

```
pi@gluster2 ~ $ ls -la /srv/vol0/

total 2068
drwxr-xr-x 3 root root    4096 Oct 31 23:37 .
drwxr-xr-x 3 pi   pi      4096 Oct 31 23:12 ..
drw------- 7 root root    4096 Oct 31 23:37 .glusterfs
-rwxr-xr-x 2 root root 2090144 Oct 31 23:37 kernel.img

pi@gluster2 ~ $

[log in to peer gluster3]
pi@gluster3 ~ $ ls -la /srv/vol0/
```

```
total 1936
drwxr-xr-x 3 root root    4096 Oct 31 23:37 .
drwxr-xr-x 3 pi   pi      4096 Oct 31 23:12 ..
drw------- 7 root root    4096 Oct 31 23:37 .glusterfs
-rwxr-xr-x 2 root root 1966080 Oct 31 23:37 kernel.img
pi@gluster3 ~ $


[log in to peer gluster4]
pi@gluster4 ~ $ ls -la /srv/vol0/

total 1936
drwxr-xr-x 3 root root    4096 Oct 31 23:37 .
drwxr-xr-x 3 pi   pi      4096 Oct 31 23:12 ..
drw------- 7 root root    4096 Oct 31 23:37 .glusterfs
-rwxr-xr-x 2 root root 1966080 Oct 31 23:37 kernel.img

pi@gluster4 ~ $
```

16. Notice that there are two different file sizes (`2090144` and `1966080`) for the data storage file (`/srv/vol0/kernel.img`) on each of the peers.

17. Notice that the data storage files (`/srv/vol0/kernel.img`) on peers `gluster1` and `gluster2` have the same size; and that the data storage files on peers `gluster3` and `gluster4` also have the same size. This is an example of how a replicated volume duplicates storage across replicated peers in case one of the replicated peers goes down.

18. Notice that the sum of the two file sizes is equal to the size of the original file (`4056224`). This is an example of how a striped volume divides the data of large files across striped peers.

19. Test the high availability of the cluster. Remove one of the Raspberry Pis (`gluster4`) from the network by disconnecting its network cable.

20. Use the `gluster` peer status command on one of the remaining peers (`gluster1`) to check the status of the distributed filesystem's secure storage pool.

```
pi@gluster1 ~ $ sudo gluster peer status

Number of Peers: 3

Hostname: gluster2.local
Uuid: 5b969ed1-01c2-406e-9710-944436c41c98
State: Peer in Cluster (Connected)

Hostname: gluster3.local
Uuid: 9a00c151-af6e-44c5-9d14-5607270b4038
```

```
State: Peer in Cluster (Connected)

Hostname: gluster4.local
Uuid: f036b1c4-7a51-49eb-aa63-81babb843b7e
State: Peer in Cluster (Disconnected)

pi@gluster1 ~ $
```

21. Notice that `Hostname: gluster4.local` is shown as `Disconnected`.

22. Use the `sha1sum` command on `gluster1` to validate the large file stored in the filesystem (`/mnt/kernel.img`) has not changed.

```
pi@gluster1 ~ $ sha1sum /mnt/kernel.img

d5e64d892b308b99e9c2c55deaa39c579a2335ec   /mnt/kernel.img

pi@gluster1 ~ $
```

23. Notice that the checksum (`d5e64...35ec`) is still the same.

24. The distributed filesystem functions, even if one peer is down!

25. Test the healing of replicated peers. While `gluster4` is still disconnected from the cluster, use the `cp` command to copy another large file (`/boot/kernel7.img`) to the self-healing distributed striped replicated filesystem.

```
pi@gluster1 ~ $ sudo cp /boot/kernel7.img /mnt/

pi@gluster1 ~ $
```

26. Use the `ls` and `sha1sum` commands to check that the copied file (`/mnt/kernel7.img`) is identical to the original file (`/boot/kernel7.img`).

```
pi@gluster1 ~ $ ls -l /boot/kernel7.img

-rwxr-xr-x 1 root root 4032544 Sep 23 16:10 /boot/kernel7.img

pi@gluster1 ~ $ sha1sum /boot/kernel7.img

8a2b1f065fc9459de79ba40e7cb791216f2f501b   /boot/kernel7.img

pi@gluster1 ~ $ ls -la /mnt

total 7912
drwxr-xr-x  3 root root    4096 Nov  1 00:47 .
drwxr-xr-x 21 root root    4096 Oct 31 20:29 ..
-rwxr-xr-x  1 root root 4032544 Nov  1 00:47 kernel7.img
```

```
-rwxr-xr-x  1 root root 4056224 Oct 31 23:37 kernel.img

pi@gluster1 ~ $ sha1sum /mnt/kernel7.img

8a2b1f065fc9459de79ba40e7cb791216f2f501b  /mnt/kernel7.img

pi@gluster1 ~ $
```

27. Use the `ls -l` command to check the file sizes in the storage directory (`/srv/vol0`) of each peer to validate that the newly copied file (`kernel7.img`) is also striped and replicated.

[log in to peer `gluster1`]
```
pi@gluster1 ~ $ ls -la /srv/vol0/

total 4092
drwxr-xr-x 3 root root    4096 Nov  1 00:47 .
drwxr-xr-x 3 pi   pi      4096 Oct 31 23:12 ..
drw------- 8 root root    4096 Nov  1 00:47 .glusterfs
-rwxr-xr-x 2 root root 2066464 Nov  1 00:47 kernel7.img
-rwxr-xr-x 2 root root 2090144 Oct 31 23:37 kernel.img

pi@gluster1 ~ $
```

[log in to peer gluster2]
```
pi@gluster2 ~ $ ls -la /srv/vol0/

total 4092
drwxr-xr-x 3 root root    4096 Nov  1 00:47 .
drwxr-xr-x 3 pi   pi      4096 Oct 31 23:12 ..
drw------- 8 root root    4096 Nov  1 00:47 .glusterfs
-rwxr-xr-x 2 root root 2066464 Nov  1 00:47 kernel7.img
-rwxr-xr-x 2 root root 2090144 Oct 31 23:37 kernel.img

pi@gluster2 ~ $
```

[log in to peer `gluster3`]

```
pi@gluster3 ~ $ ls -la /srv/vol0/

total 3864
drwxr-xr-x 3 root root    4096 Nov  1 00:47 .
drwxr-xr-x 3 pi   pi      4096 Oct 31 23:12 ..
drw------- 8 root root    4096 Nov  1 00:47 .glusterfs
-rwxr-xr-x 2 root root 1966080 Nov  1 00:47 kernel7.img
```

```
-rwxr-xr-x 2 root root 1966080 Oct 31 23:37 kernel.img

pi@gluster3 ~ $
```

28. Notice that the data storage file (`/srv/vol0/kernel7.img`) on peers `gluster1` and `gluster2` has the same size and that the total size of the striped files (`2066464 + 1966080`) is equal to the size of the original file (`4032544`). The distributed filesystem continues to stripe and replicate files even if one peer is down!

29. Reconnect peer `gluster4` to the network.

30. Immediately use the `ls -l` command to check the files in the data storage directory (`/srv/vol0`) on reconnected peer `gluster4`.

    `pi@gluster4 ~ $` **`ls -la /srv/vol0/`**

```
total 1940
drwxr-xr-x 3 root root    4096 Nov  1 00:47 .
drwxr-xr-x 3 pi   pi      4096 Oct 31 23:12 ..
drw------- 8 root root    4096 Nov  1 00:50 .glusterfs
-rwxr-xr-x 2 root root       0 Nov  1 00:47 kernel7.img
-rwxr-xr-x 2 root root 1966080 Oct 31 23:37 kernel.img

pi@gluster4 ~ $
```

31. Notice that the newly copied file (`kernel7.img`) has been created in the data storage directory (`/srv/vol0`), but the file size is empty (`0`).

32. After waiting five minutes, use the `ls -l` command to once again check the data storage directory on `gluster4`.

    `pi@gluster4 ~ $` **`ls -la /srv/vol0/`**

```
total 3864
drwxr-xr-x 3 root root    4096 Nov  1 00:47 .
drwxr-xr-x 3 pi   pi      4096 Oct 31 23:12 ..
drw------- 8 root root    4096 Nov  1 00:50 .glusterfs
-rwxr-xr-x 2 root root 1966080 Nov  1 00:47 kernel7.img
-rwxr-xr-x 2 root root 1966080 Oct 31 23:37 kernel.img

pi@gluster4 ~ $
```

33. Notice that the storage file `kernel7.img` is no longer empty. The data storage file (`kernel7.img`) on `gluster4` is now the same size (`1966080`) as the storage file on peer `gluster3`.

34. The distributed filesystem has healed itself!

35. This cluster of four Raspberry Pis is now a highly available distributed filesystem!

How it works...

The recipe begins by changing the hostnames of four Raspberry Pis that are linked together on the same network. The new hostnames of the Raspberry Pis are `gluster1`, `gluster2`, `gluster3`, and `gluster4`.

Installing the GlusterFS server on each Raspberry Pi

After the Raspberry Pis are renamed, the `apt-get install` command is used on each of the Raspberry Pis to install the GlusterFS server software distribution package (`glusterfs-server`).

The installation of the `glusterfs-server` package includes starting the GlusterFS server on each of the Raspberry Pis: `gluster1`, `gluster2`, `gluster3`, and `gluster4`.

The `gluster peer probe` command is used from the `gluster1` Raspberry Pi to link the other Raspberry Pis (`gluster2`, `gluster3`, and `gluster4`) into a trusted peer relationship.

The first peer in the storage pool (`gluster1`) establishes the trusted peer relationship with the other storage pool peers (`gluster2`, `gluster3`, `gluster4`). However, once the trusted relationship is established, any peer can be used as the storage pool master—to manage storage volumes, to manage the trusted peer relationships, or to be mounted as the distributed filesystem's network attachable endpoint.

The `gluster peer status` command is used on both `gluster1` and `gluster2` to validate the trusted storage pool is up and running. On both peers, the other three storage pool peers are displayed as being part of the storage pool.

The `gluster peer status` command on `gluster2`, however, displays an IP address for the `Hostname` field of the first peer, `gluster1`. So, the `gluster peer` command is used on `gluster2` to add the hostname of `gluster1` to the metadata of the storage pool.

> Do not have a peer add itself to the trusted storage pool!
>
> A peer using the command `gluster peer probe` with its own hostname could damage the trusted storage pool!

Creating a striped replicated volume in the trusted storage pool

The `cluster volume create` command is used from `gluster1` to create a new striped replicated volume that is distributed across the four storage pool peers (`gluster1.local`, `gluster2.local`, `gluster3.local`, `gluster4.local`).

The new volume is named `vol0`. It has two stripes (`stripe 2`) and two replicas (replica 2). It uses the same storage directory (`/srv/vol0`) on each of the storage pool peers (`gluster1.local`, `gluster2.local`, `gluster3.local`, and `gluster4.local`).

Using a storage directory on a peer's root filesystem (/) is not recommended, nor is it allowed by default. The `force` keyword is used to override the default behavior.

This recipe uses the root filesystem to keep the recipe simple. For a more robust, reliable distributed filesystem with higher performance, attach a high-speed external USB disk to each Raspberry Pi and configure the storage directory for the volume to be on the external disk instead of on the root filesystem. *Chapter 4, File Sharing*, has more than one recipe for mounting an external USB disk on a Raspberry Pi.

After the volume (`vol0`) is created, the `gluster volume start` command is used to start sharing the newly created volume with GlusterFS clients. The `gluster volume start` command could be run from any peer in the cluster. In this case, it is run from `gluster1`.

Mount the distributed striped replicated volume

Now that the distributed striped replicated volume (`vol0`) has been created and started, it is time for a GlusterFS client to mount the newly created volume.

To keep this recipe simple, `gluster1` is used as the client. However, any computer on the local network with the GlusterFS client software installed should now be able to mount the distributed volume (`vol0`) from any trusted peer in the GlusterFS storage pool.

The `mount -t glusterfs` command is used from `gluster1` to mount the distributed volume (`vol0`) from the trusted storage peer `gluster1.local` on its local directory, `/mnt`. The Raspberry Pi named `gluster1` is both the client and the server of the distributed volume (`vol0`).

Testing the striped replicated volume

The `cp` command is used to copy a large file from the local filesystem (`/boot/kernel.img`) to the distributed striped replicated volume mounted at `/mnt`.

The `ls -l` command and the `sha1sum` command are used to validate that the copied file (`/mnt/kernel.img`) has been copied successfully by checking that its size (`4056224`) and checksum (`d5e64...35ec`) are the same as the original file (`/boot/kernel.img`).

The `ls -la` command is used on each peer of the storage pool (`gluster1`, `gluster2`, `gluster3`, and `gluster4`) to display the contents of the peer's storage directory (`/srv/vol0`).

None of the peer's storage directories has a file (`/srv/kernel.img`) as large as the original file (`/boot/kernel.img`).

Replication

There are two sets of storage files (`/srv/kernel.img`) with the same size. The first set of storage files with the same size (`2090144`) can be found on peers `gluster1` and `gluster2`. The second set of peers, `gluster3` and `gluster4`, also have storage files that are the same size (`1966080`). The peers `gluster1` and `gluster2` are replicas of each other; `gluster3` and `gluster4` are also replicas.

Data replication is used to keep the distributed volume highly available. If one of the trusted storage peers goes down or is disconnected from the network, a replica of the unavailable peer's stored data is still available. If `gluster1` were to go down, `gluster2` would still have a replica of the stored data. If `gluster4` were disconnected from the network, `gluster3` would still have a replica of its data.

Striping

The sum of the two different file sizes (`2090144` and `1966080`) equals the size of the original file (`4056224`). The original file has been distributed (striped) across the trusted storage peers. The trusted storage peers `gluster1` and `gluster2` are replicating one part (`2090144`) of the large file (`kernel.img`), and the trusted peers `gluster3` and `gluster4` are storing replicas of the other part (`1966080`).

Data striping is a technique for distributing large files across multiple storage peers. Parts of the file (stripes) are distributed evenly across the striped storage peers so that sequentially reading (or writing) a large amount of data from a single large file does not continuously put a load on only one of the trusted storage peers. Striping a file distributes the load to access the file across the striped storage peers by distributing the data across the peers. Striping increases the data transfer rate of the distributed volume.

Testing the high availability of the cluster

In order to test the cluster's ability to remain available when one of the trusted data storage peers goes down, the trusted data storage peer `gluster4.local` is removed from the cluster by disconnecting its network cable.

After the network cable has been removed from `gluster4`, the `gluster peer status` command is used (on any remaining peer) to show that trusted storage peer `gluster4.local` has been `Disconnected` from the cluster.

The `sha1sum` command is used to validate that the checksum (`d5e64…35ec`) of the distributed file (`/mnt/kernel.img`) still matches the checksum of the original file (`/boot/kernel.img`).

The GlusterFS distributed filesystem still functions properly when one peer is removed from the storage pool! The cluster is highly available!

Testing the healing of replicated peers

While the trusted storage peer `gluster4` is still disconnected from the cluster, the `cp` command is used to copy another large file (`/boot/kernel7.img`) to the distributed storage volume (`vol0`) mounted locally on `gluster1` at `/mnt`.

The checksum of the copied file (`/mnt/kernel7.img`) is compared to the checksum of the original file (`/boot/kernel7.img`) using the `sha1sum` command. The files are identical.

The `ls -la` command is used on each of the remaining trusted storage peers (`gluster1`, `gluster2`, and `gluster3`) to validate that the new large file (`kernel7.img`) has also been striped and replicated across the storage directories (`/srv/vol0`) of the distributed volume. The trusted storage peers `gluster1` and `gluster2` have replicas of one portion of the file while peer `gluster3` has the other portion of the file.

After the new large file has been striped and replicated across the distributed volume, the trusted peer `gluster4` is once again connected to the cluster.

Immediately after the peer `gluster4` has been reconnected to the cluster, the `ls -la` command is used to display the contents of the data storage directory (`/srv/vol0`) on `gluster4`. The file copied to the distributed volume (`vol0`) while `gluster4` was disconnected from the cluster (`kernel7.img`) has been created in the data storage directory; however, the file is empty (`0`).

After waiting a few minutes for the GlusterFS healing service to finish replicating the striped portion of the new large file (`kernel7.img`) from peer `gluster3` to peer `gluster4`, the `ls -la` command is used once again to validate that peer `gluster4` has replicated its portion of the striped file and that the distributed volume (`vol0`) has been healed.

The four Raspberry Pis are now a self-healing highly available distributed filesystem.

There's more ...

GlusterFS is a peer-based distributed filesystem. There is no master server in a GlusterFS trusted storage pool. In this recipe, `gluster1` was the first peer in the trusted storage pool and invited the other trusted peers to join the pool. Even though it was the first peer in the storage pool, `gluster1` is still an equal peer and not the master.

On the other hand, the current recipe only allows a GlusterFS client to mount a filesystem endpoint from one of the trusted storage pool peers (`gluster1`, `gluster2`, `gluster3`, or `gluster4`). In this recipe, `gluster1` was the peer providing the distributed filesystem endpoint.

Should the mounted peer (`gluster1`) go down, the client would not be able to access the distributed filesystem even if the other peers in the cluster have kept the filesystem available. In the recipe, `gluster1` was also the client, so this issue was not possible.

A GlusterFS distributed filesystem is normally accessed from outside the cluster, not from a trusted storage peer within the cluster. Mounting the distributed filesystem from one of the storage peers directly defeats the high availability of the cluster by making the client dependent on a single trusted peer instead of being dependent on the cluster as a whole.

Using Keepalived to create a virtual filesystem endpoint

The virtual IP address service Keepalived can be used to create a distributed filesystem endpoint that is kept alive by all peers of the trusted storage pool. The previous recipe, *Installing a high-availability load balancer*, shows how to install and configure Keepalived for use with the HA Proxy.

Keepalived can also be used with GlusterFS to create a virtual IP for accessing the distributed filesystem that will remain available so long as the distributed filesystem remains available.

Using Keepalived, a virtual endpoint (IP address) is created for the distributed filesystem. Clients will mount the virtual endpoint of the filesystem instead of mounting the endpoint directly from a trusted storage peer.

Even though the trusted storage peer currently serving the virtual filesystem endpoint may fail, the virtual endpoint provided by Keepalived will not fail; instead, another trusted storage peer will be selected to replace the peer that did fail. The virtual filesystem endpoint will remain alive no matter which trusted peer goes down.

To use Keepalived with this recipe, first enable (=1) the kernel parameter that permits listening for virtual IP addresses (net.ipv4.ip_nonlocal_bind) on each of the trusted storage peers in the cluster (gluster1, gluster2, gluster3, and gluster4).

```
pi@gluster1 ~ $ sudo -i bash

root@gluster1:~# echo "net.ipv4.ip_nonlocal_bind=1" >>/etc/sysctl.conf

root@gluster1:~# sysctl -p

kernel.printk = 3 4 1 3
vm.swappiness = 1
vm.min_free_kbytes = 8192
net.ipv4.ip_nonlocal_bind = 1

root@gluster1:~# exit

exit

pi@gluster1 ~ $
```

Next, install the `keepalived` software distribution package using the `apt-get install` command.

```
pi@gluster1 ~ $ sudo apt-get install -y keepalived

Reading package lists... Done
Building dependency tree
Reading state information... Done
The following extra packages will be installed:
   iproute ipvsadm libpci3 libperl5.20 libsensors4 libsnmp-base libsnmp30
Suggested packages:
   heartbeat ldirectord lm-sensors snmp-mibs-downloader
The following NEW packages will be installed:
   iproute ipvsadm keepalived libpci3 libperl5.20 libsensors4 libsnmp-base
libsnmp30
0 upgraded, 8 newly installed, 0 to remove and 0 not upgraded.
Need to get 3,902 kB of archives.
After this operation, 7,093 kB of additional disk space will be used.

...
```

Use a configuration for Keepalived that allows any of the trusted storage peers (`gluster1`, `gluster2`, `gluster3`, or `gluster4`) to take over the cluster's virtual IP address whenever the current peer serving the virtual IP address fails.

```
pi@gluster1 ~ $ sudo bash

root@gluster1:/home/pi# cat <<EOD >/etc/keepalived/keepalived.conf

vrrp_script chk_glusterd
{
        script "killall -0 glusterd"
        interval 2
        weight 2
}

vrrp_instance VI_1
{
        interface eth0
        state MASTER
        virtual_router_id 13

        priority 100
```

```
        virtual_ipaddress
        {
            192.168.2.100
        }

        track_script
        {
            chk_glusterd
        }
    }

EOD

root@gluster1:/home/pi# exit

exit

pi@gluster1 ~ $
```

Finally, restart the Keepalived service.

```
pi@gluster1 ~ $ sudo systemctl restart keepalived.service

pi@gluster1 ~ $
```

Now, the virtual endpoint can be mounted instead of a trusted peer.

```
pi@gluster4 ~ $ sudo mount -t glusterfs 192.168.2.100:/vol0 /mnt

pi@gluster4 ~ $ ls -l /mnt
total 7900
-rwxr-xr-x 1 root root 4032544 Nov  1 00:47 kernel7.img
-rwxr-xr-x 1 root root 4056224 Oct 31 23:37 kernel.img

pi@gluster4 ~ $
```

See also

- **GlusterFS** (http://www.glusterfs.org/): GlusterFS is a scalable network filesystem. Using common off-the-shelf hardware, you can create large, distributed storage solutions for media streaming, data analysis, and other data and bandwidth-intensive tasks. GlusterFS is free and open source software.

- **GlusterFS** (https://en.wikipedia.org/wiki/GlusterFS): This Wikipedia article describes the GlusterFS design.

Creating a supercomputer

This recipe turns four Raspberry Pis into a super computer using Apache Spark.

Apache Spark is a fast and general engine for large-scale data processing. In this recipe, Apache Spark is installed on four Raspberry Pis that have been networked into a small computer cluster. The cluster is then used to demonstrate the speed of super computing by calculating the value of pi using a Monte Carlo algorithm.

After completing this recipe, you will have a Raspberry Pi super computer.

Getting ready

The following ingredients are required to create a supercomputer:

- ▸ Four basic networking setups for the Raspberry Pi
- ▸ A high-speed network switch

This recipe does not require the desktop GUI and could either be run from the text-based console or from within LXTerminal.

With the Secure Shell server running on each Raspberry Pi, this recipe can be completed remotely using a Secure Shell client. Typically, a website is managed remotely.

All the Raspberry Pis should be connected directly to the same network switch.

How to do it...

Perform the following steps to build a Raspberry Pi supercomputer:

1. Log in to each Raspberry Pi and set its hostname. One Raspberry Pi will be the Spark master server, and the other three will be Spark slaves. Name the four Raspberry Pis `spark-master`, `spark-slave-a`, `spark-slave-b`, and `spark-slave-c`.

2. Now, let's set up secure communication between master and slaves. Use the `ssh-keygen` command on `spark-master` to generate a pair of SSH keys. Press `<enter>` to accept the default file location (`/home/pi/.ssh/id_rsa`). Then, press `<enter>` twice to use an empty passphrase (the Spark automation requires an empty passphrase).

   ```
   pi@spark-master ~ $ ssh-keygen

   Generating public/private rsa key pair.
   ```

```
Enter file in which to save the key (/home/pi/.ssh/id_rsa):

Enter passphrase (empty for no passphrase):

Enter same passphrase again:

Your identification has been saved in /home/pi/.ssh/id_rsa.
Your public key has been saved in /home/pi/.ssh/id_rsa.pub.
The key fingerprint is:
29:0e:95:61:a6:e6:30:8f:23:66:cd:68:d3:c4:0c:8e pi@spark-master

The key's randomart image is:
+---[RSA 2048]----+
| .    +          |
|o +  + o         |
|E.o+o o          |
|  *B .  .        |
|.*o++ . S        |
|+... o .         |
|      .          |
|                 |
|                 |
+-----------------+

pi@spark-master ~ $
```

3. Use the `ssh-copy-id` command to copy the newly created public key from `spark-master` to each of the Spark slaves (`spark-slave-a`, `spark-slave-b`, and `spark-slave-c`).

    pi@spark-master ~ $ **ssh-copy-id pi@spark-slave-a.local**

    ```
    The authenticity of host 'spark-slave-a.local (192.168.2.6)' can't be
    established.
    ECDSA key fingerprint is e9:55:ff:6c:69:be:5d:8f:80:de:b2:d9:85:eb:1b:90.

    Are you sure you want to continue connecting (yes/no)? yes

    /usr/bin/ssh-copy-id: INFO: attempting to log in with the new key(s), to
    filter out any that are already installed
    /usr/bin/ssh-copy-id: INFO: 1 key(s) remain to be installed -- if you are
    prompted now it is to install the new keys

    pi@spark-slave-a.local's password:

    Number of key(s) added: 1
    ```

> Repeat step *3* for each of the slaves: `spark-slave-a`, `spark-slave-b`, and `spark-slave-c`.

4. Note that a secure shell login (`ssh`) from `spark-master` to the slaves no longer requires a password for authentication:

```
pi@spark-master ~ $ ssh spark-slave-a.local

The programs included with the Debian GNU/Linux system are free software;
the exact distribution terms for each program are described in the
individual files in /usr/share/doc/*/copyright.

Debian GNU/Linux comes with ABSOLUTELY NO WARRANTY, to the extent
permitted by applicable law.
Last login: Mon Nov  2 21:29:28 2015 from 192.168.2.1

pi@spark-slave-a ~ $
```

5. Now, it's about downloading the Apache Spark software distribution. Use a web browser to locate the correct Apache Spark software distribution package on the Apache Spark website's download page (`http://spark.apache.org/downloads.html`), which is shown in the following screenshot:

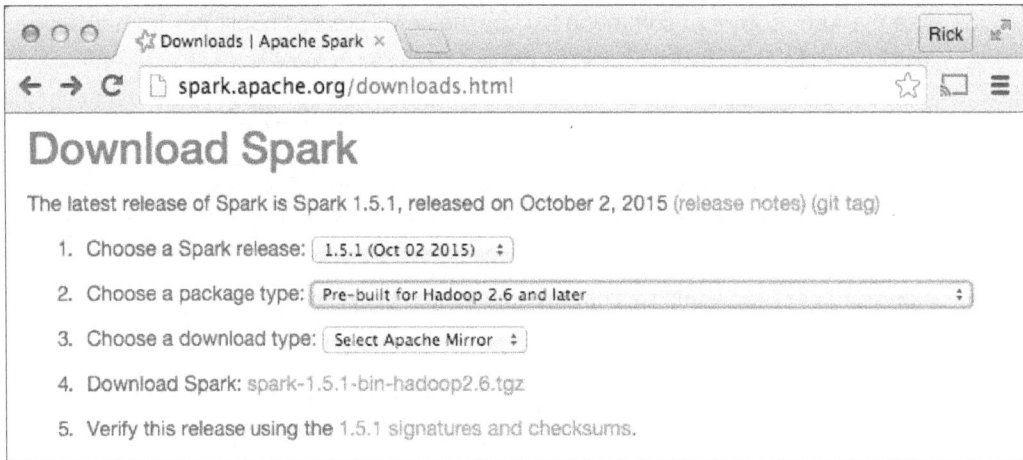

6. On the download page, use the following drop-down options:

    1. **Choose a Spark release: 1.5.1 (Oct 02 2015)**

    2. **Choose a package type:** Pre-built for Hadoop 2.6 and later

    3. **Choose a download type**: Select Apache Mirror

Once the correct choices have been made for **1**, **2**, and **3**, click on the link (`spark-1.5.1-bin-haddop2.6.tgz`) that appears at **4**. Download Spark.

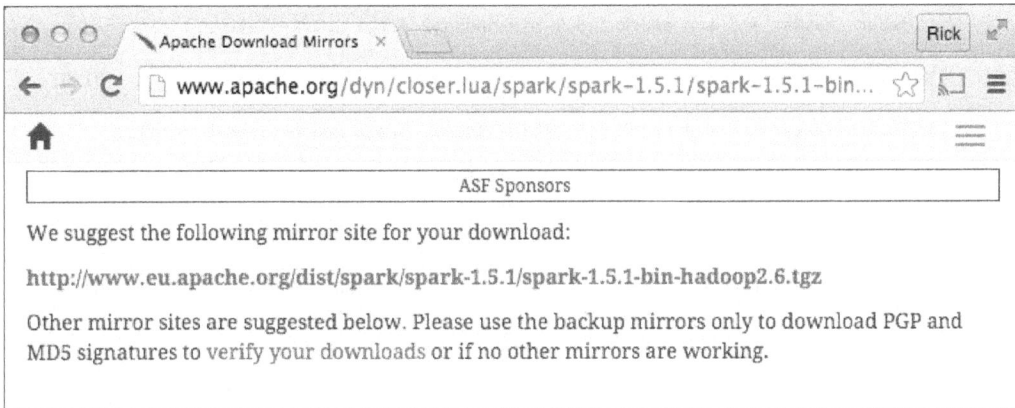

7. Note that the next web page displays the actual download link for the correct Apache Spark software distribution package (`http://www.eu.apache.org/dist/spark/spark-1.5.1/spark-1.5.1-bin-hadoop2.6.tgz`).

8. Use the `wget` command on `spark-master` to download the Apache Spark software distribution page, as follows:

```
pi@spark-master ~ $ wget http://www.eu.apache.org/dist/spark/spark-1.5.1/
spark-1.5.1-bin-hadoop2.6.tgz

--2015-11-05 17:41:01--  http://www.eu.apache.org/dist/spark/spark-1.5.1/
spark-1.5.1-bin-hadoop2.6.tgz
Resolving www.eu.apache.org (www.eu.apache.org)... 88.198.26.2,
2a01:4f8:130:2192::2
Connecting to www.eu.apache.org (www.eu.apache.org)|88.198.26.2|:80...
connected.
HTTP request sent, awaiting response... 200 OK
Length: 280901736 (268M) [application/x-gzip]
Saving to: 'spark-1.5.1-bin-hadoop2.6.tgz'

spark-1.5.1-bin-hadoop2.6.tgz   100%[=============>] 267.89M   726KB/s   in
4m 38s

2015-11-05 17:45:39 (987 KB/s) - 'spark-1.5.1-bin-hadoop2.6.tgz' saved
[280901736/280901736]

pi@spark-master ~ $
```

9. Use the `tar` command to unpack the Apache Spark software distribution on each Raspberry Pi (spark-master, spark-slave-a, spark-slave-b, and spark-slave-c), as follows:

```
pi@spark-master ~ $ scp spark-1.5.1-bin-hadoop2.6.tgz spark-slave-a.local:.

spark-1.5.1-bin-hadoop2.6.tgz                    100%  268MB   4.4MB/s   01:01

pi@spark-master ~ $ scp spark-1.5.1-bin-hadoop2.6.tgz spark-slave-b.local:.

spark-1.5.1-bin-hadoop2.6.tgz                    100%  268MB   4.0MB/s   01:07

pi@spark-master ~ $ scp spark-1.5.1-bin-hadoop2.6.tgz spark-slave-c.local:.

spark-1.5.1-bin-hadoop2.6.tgz                    100%  268MB   5.2MB/s   00:47

pi@spark-master ~ $
```

10. Use the `tar` command to unpack the Apache Spark software distribution on each Raspberry Pi (spark-master, spark-slave-a, spark-slave-b, and spark-slave-c), as follows:

```
pi@spark-master ~ $ tar xvfz spark-1.5.1-bin-hadoop2.6.tgz

spark-1.5.1-bin-hadoop2.6/
spark-1.5.1-bin-hadoop2.6/NOTICE
spark-1.5.1-bin-hadoop2.6/CHANGES.txt
spark-1.5.1-bin-hadoop2.6/python/
spark-1.5.1-bin-hadoop2.6/python/run-tests.py
spark-1.5.1-bin-hadoop2.6/python/test_support/
spark-1.5.1-bin-hadoop2.6/python/test_support/userlibrary.py
spark-1.5.1-bin-hadoop2.6/python/test_support/userlib-0.1.zip
spark-1.5.1-bin-hadoop2.6/python/test_support/sql/
spark-1.5.1-bin-hadoop2.6/python/test_support/sql/people.json
spark-1.5.1-bin-hadoop2.6/python/test_support/sql/orc_partitioned/
spark-1.5.1-bin-hadoop2.6/python/test_support/sql/orc_partitioned/b=1/
spark-1.5.1-bin-hadoop2.6/python/test_support/sql/orc_partitioned/b=1/c=1/

...
```

> Repeat step *10* on each Raspberry Pi, namely spark-master, spark-slave-a, spark-slave-b, and spark-slave-c.

11. Use the `mv` command to move the Apache Spark installation directory (`spark-1.5.1-bin-hadoop2.6`) to a more convenient location on each Raspberry Pi (`/opt/spark`), as follows:

```
pi@spark-master ~ $ sudo mv spark-1.5.1-bin-hadoop2.6 /opt/spark

pi@spark-master ~ $
```

12. Now, configure the Spark master. Use the `cat` command on `spark-master` to create a list of slaves, as follows:

```
pi@spark-master ~/ $ cat <<EOD >/opt/spark/conf/slaves

spark-slave-a.local
spark-slave-b.local
spark-slave-c.local

EOD

pi@spark-master ~/ $
```

13. Use the `scp` command on `spark-master` to copy the Spark execution environment configuration file (`spark-env.sh`) to each Spark slave (`spark-slave-a`, `spark-slave-b`, and `spark-slave-c`), as follows:

```
pi@spark-master ~ $ echo "SPARK_MASTER_IP=`hostname -I`" >/opt/spark/conf/spark-env.sh
```

14. Use the `scp` command on `spark-master` to copy the Spark execution environment configuration file (`spark-env.sh`) to each Spark slave (`spark-slave-a`, `spark-slave-b`, and `spark-slave-c`), as follows:

```
pi@spark-master ~ $ scp /opt/spark/conf/spark-env.sh spark-slave-a:/opt/spark/conf/spark-env.sh

spark-env.sh                                    100%   30     0.0KB/s   00:00

pi@spark-master ~ $ scp /opt/spark/conf/spark-env.sh spark-slave-b.local:/opt/spark/conf/spark-env.sh

spark-env.sh                                    100%   30     0.0KB/s   00:00

pi@spark-master ~ $ scp /opt/spark/conf/spark-env.sh spark-slave-c.local:/opt/spark/conf/spark-env.sh

spark-env.sh                                    100%   30     0.0KB/s   00:00

pi@spark-master ~ $
```

15. Use the `echo` command on `spark-master` to append an additional memory constraint (`SPARK_DRIVER_MEMORY=512m`) to the execution environment (`spark-env.sh`) of the Spark master server (`spark-master`) so that enough memory remains free on the master server to run spark jobs, as follows:

```
pi@spark-master ~ $ echo "SPARK_DRIVER_MEMORY=512m" >>/opt/spark/conf/
spark-env.sh

pi@spark-master ~ $
```

16. Use the `echo` command on `spark-master` to append the local IP address (`SPARK_LOCAL_IP`) to the execution environment (`spark-env.sh`). This reduces the warnings in the output from Spark jobs:

```
pi@spark-master ~ $ echo "SPARK_LOCAL_IP=$(hostname -I)" >>/opt/spark/
conf/spark-env.sh

pi@spark-master ~ $
```

17. Use the `sed` command to change the logging level of Spark jobs from `INFO` (which produces a lot of informational output) to `WARN` (which produces a lot less output).

```
pi@spark-master ~ $ sed 's/rootCategory=INFO/rootCategory=WARN/'
spark/conf/log4j.properties.template >/opt/spark/conf/log4j.properties

pi@spark-master ~ $
```

18. At this point, the Spark cluster is ready to start.

> The next steps calculate pi both with and without the Spark cluster so that the duration of the two calculation methods can be compared.

19. Now, calculate pi without using the Spark cluster. Use the `cat` command on `spark-master` to create a simple Python script to calculate pi without using the Spark cluster, as follows:

```
pi@spark-master ~ $ cat <<EOD >pi.py

from operator import add
```

```
from random     import random
from time       import clock


MSG  = "Python estimated Pi at %f in %f seconds"

n = 1000000


def f(_):
    x = random() * 2 - 1
    y = random() * 2 - 1
    return 1 if x ** 2 + y ** 2 < 1 else 0


def main():
    st = clock()
    tries = map( f, range( 1, n + 1 ) )
    count = reduce( add, tries )
    et = clock()
    print( MSG % ( 4.0 * count / n, et - st ) )


if __name__ == "__main__":
    main()


EOD

pi@spark-master ~ $
```

20. Use the `python` command on `spark-master` to run the script for calculating pi (`pi.py`) without a Spark cluster.

    ```
    pi@spark-master ~ $ python pi.py

    Python esitmated PI at 3.141444 in 13.430613 seconds

    pi@spark-master ~ $
    ```

21. Note that it took one Raspberry Pi (`spark-master`) more than 13 seconds (`13.430613` seconds) to calculate pi without using Spark.

22. Now, calculate pi using the Spark cluster. Use the `cat` command on `spark-master` to create a simple Python script that parallelizes the calculation of pi for use on the Spark cluster, as follows:

```
pi@spark-master ~ $ cat <<EOD >pi-spark.py

from __future__ import print_function

from operator   import add
from random     import random
from sys         import argv
from time        import clock

from pyspark     import SparkConf, SparkContext


APP_NAME = "MonteCarloPi"
MSG      = "Spark estimated Pi at %f in %f seconds using %i partitions"

master     =      argv[ 1 ]   if len( argv ) > 1 else "local"
partitions = int( argv[ 2 ] ) if len( argv ) > 2 else 2

n = 1000000


def f(_):
    x = random() * 2 - 1
    y = random() * 2 - 1
    return 1 if x ** 2 + y ** 2 < 1 else 0


def main(sc):
    st    = clock()
    tries = sc.parallelize( range( 1, n + 1 ), partitions ).map( f )
    count = tries.reduce( add )
    et    = clock()
    print( MSG % ( 4.0 * count / n, et - st, partitions ) )
```

```
if __name__ == "__main__":
    conf = SparkConf()
    conf.setMaster( master )
    conf.setAppName( APP_NAME )
    sc = SparkContext( conf = conf )
    main( sc )
    sc.stop()


EOD

pi@spark-master ~ $
```

23. Use the `start-all.sh` shell script on `spark-master` to start the Apache Spark cluster. Starting the cluster may take 30 seconds.

```
pi@spark-master ~ $ /opt/spark/sbin/start-all.sh

starting org.apache.spark.deploy.master.Master, logging to /home/pi/spark/
sbin/../logs/spark-pi-org.apache.spark.deploy.master.Master-1-spark-
master.out
spark-slave-c.local: starting org.apache.spark.deploy.worker.Worker,
logging to /home/pi/spark/sbin/../logs/spark-pi-org.apache.spark.deploy.
worker.Worker-1-spark-slave-c.out
spark-slave-b.local: starting org.apache.spark.deploy.worker.Worker,
logging to /home/pi/spark/sbin/../logs/spark-pi-org.apache.spark.deploy.
worker.Worker-1-spark-slave-b.out
spark-slave-a.local: starting org.apache.spark.deploy.worker.Worker,
logging to /home/pi/spark/sbin/../logs/spark-pi-org.apache.spark.deploy.
worker.Worker-1-spark-slave-a.out

pi@spark-master ~ $
```

24. Use a web browser to view the status of the cluster by browsing to the cluster status page at `http://spark-master.local:8080/`.

25. Wait until the Spark master server and all three slaves have started. Three worker IDs will be displayed on the status page when the cluster is ready to compute. Refresh the page, if necessary.

26. Submit the Python script (`pi-spark.py`) that is used to calculate pi to the Spark cluster, as follows:

```
pi@spark-master ~ $ export SPARK_MASTER_URL="http://$(hostname -I | tr -d
[:space:]):7077"

pi@spark-master ~ $ export PATH=/opt/spark/bin:$PATH


pi@spark-master ~ $ spark-submit pi-spark.py $SPARK_MASTER_URL 24

15/11/04 21:39:38 WARN NativeCodeLoader: Unable to load native-hadoop
library for your platform... using builtin-java classes where applicable
15/11/04 21:39:51 WARN MetricsSystem: Using default name DAGScheduler for
source because spark.app.id is not set.
```

```
[Stage 0:>                                                    (0 +
0) / 24]15/11/04 21:40:00 WARN SizeEstimator: Failed to check whether
UseCompressedOops is set; assuming yes
15/11/04 21:40:05 WARN TaskSetManager: Stage 0 contains a task of very
large size (122 KB). The maximum recommended task size is 100 KB.

Spark esitmated Pi at 3.143368 in 0.720023 seconds using 24 partitions

pi@spark-master ~ $
```

27. Notice that it took the Spark cluster less than a second (`0.720023 seconds`) to calculate pi. That's more than 185 times faster!!

28. The Raspberry Pi super computer is working!

How it works...

This recipe has the following six parts:

- Setting up secure communication between the master and slaves
- Downloading the Apache Spark software distribution
- Installing Apache Spark on each Raspberry Pi in the cluster
- Configuring the Spark master
- Calculating pi without using the Spark cluster
- Calculating pi using the Spark cluster

The recipe begins by setting the hostnames of the four Raspberry Pi computers. One Raspberry Pi is selected as the Spark master (`spark-master`), the other three Raspberry Pis are the Spark slaves (`spark-slave-a`, `spark-slave-b`, and `spark-slave-c`).

Setting up secure communication between master and slaves

After the hostnames have been set, the `ssh-keygen` and `ssh-copy-id` commands are used to establish a secure communication link between the Spark master (`spark-master`) and each of its slaves (`spark-slave-a`, `spark-slave-b`, and `spark-slave-c`).

The `ssh-keygen` command is used to create a secure key pair (`/home/pi/.ssh/id_rsa` and `/home/pi/.ssh/id_rsa.pub`). The `ssh-copy-id` command is used to copy the public key (`id_rsa.pub`) from `spark-master` to each of the slaves.

After the public key of `spark-master` has been copied to each slave, it is possible to log in from `spark-master` to each slave without using a password. Having a secure login from a master to a slave without a password is a requirement for the automation of the startup of the cluster.

Downloading the Apache Spark software distribution

The Apache Spark download page (`http://spark.apache.org/downloads.html`) presents a number of choices that are used to determine the correct software distribution.

This recipe uses the 1.5.1 (Oct 02 2015) release of Spark that has been pre-built for Hadoop 2.6 and later. Once the correct choices have been made, a link is presented (`spark-1.5.1-bin-hadoop2.6.tgz`), which leads to the actual download page.

The `wget` command is used to download the Spark software distribution from the actual download page to `spark-master` using the link presented on the actual download page (`http://www.us.apache.org/dist/spark/spark-1.5.1/spark-1.5.1-bin-hadoop2.6.tgz`).

The software distribution has a size of 280 MB. It will take a while to download.

Once the Spark software distribution (`spark-1.5.1-bin-hadoop2.6.tgz`) is downloaded to `spark-master`, it is then copied using the `scp` command to the three slaves (`spark-slave-a`, `spark-slave-b`, and `spark-slave-c`).

Installing Apache Spark on each Raspberry Pi in the cluster

The `tar` command is use to unpack the Apache Spark software distribution (`spark-1.5.1-bin-hadoop2.6.tgz`) on each Raspberry Pi in the cluster (`spark-master`, `spark-slave-a`, `spark-slave-b`, and `spark-slave-c`).

After the software distribution has been unpacked in the home directory of the user, `pi`, it is moved by using the `mv` command to a more central location (`/opt/spark`).

Configuring the Spark master

The `cat` command is used to create a list of slaves (`/opt/spark/conf/slaves`). This list is used during the cluster startup to automatically start the slaves when `spark-master` is started. All the lines after the `cat` command up to the **end-of-data** (**EOD**) mark are copied to the list of slaves.

The `echo` command is used to create the Spark runtime environment file (`spark-env.sh` under `/opt/spark/conf/`) with one environment variable (`SPARK_MASTER_IP`) that is set to the IP address of `spark-master` (`hostname -I`).

The Spark runtime environment configuration file, `spark-env.sh`, is then copied from the `spark-master` to each slave (`spark-slave-a`, `spark-slave-b`, and `spark-slave-c`).

After the configuration file (`spark-env.sh`) has been copied to the slaves, two additional configuration parameters specific to `spark-master` are added to the file.

The echo command is used to append (>>) the SPARK_DRIVER_MEMORY parameter to the bottom of the configuration file. This parameter is used to limit the amount of memory used by the spark-master to 512m (512 MB). This leaves room in the spark-master memory pool to run the Spark jobs.

The echo command is also used to append the SPARK_LOCAL_IP parameter to the bottom of the configuration file (spark-env.sh). This parameter is set to the IP address of the spark-master (hostname -I). Setting this parameter eliminates some of the warning messages that occur when running the Spark jobs.

The sed command is used to modify the logging parameters of spark-master. The log4j.properties file is changed so that INFO messages are no longer displayed. Only warning messages (WARN) and error messages are displayed. This greatly reduces the output of the Spark jobs.

At this point, the Spark cluster is fully configured and ready to start.

Calculating pi without using the Spark cluster

Before the Spark cluster is started, a simple Python script (pi.py) is created using the cat command to calculate pi without using the Spark cluster.

This script (pi.py) uses the Monte Carlo method to estimate the value of pi by randomly generating 1 million data points and testing each data point for inclusion in a circle. The ratio of points inside the circle to the total number of points will be approximately equal to *Pi/4*.

More information on calculating the value of Pi, including how to use the Monte Carlo method, can be found on Wikipedia (https://en.wikipedia.org/wiki/Pi).

The Python script that is used to estimate the value of pi takes more than 13 seconds to run on a single standalone Raspberry Pi.

Calculating pi using the Spark cluster

Another Python script (pi-spark.py) is created using the cat command.

This new script (pi-spark.py) uses the same Monte Carlo method to estimate the value of pi using 1 million random data points. However, this script uses the SparkContext (sc) to create a **resilient distributed dataset** (**RDD**) that parallelizes the million data points (range(1, n + 1)) so that they can be distributed among the slaves for the actual calculation (f).

After the script is created, the Spark cluster is started (/opt/spark/sbin/start-all.sh). The startup script (start-all.sh) uses the contents of the /opt/conf/slaves file to locate and start the Spark slaves (spark-slave-a, spark-slave-b, and spark-slave-c).

A web browser is used to validate that all the slaves have started properly. The `spark-master` produces a small website (`http://spark-master.local:8080/`) that displays the status of the cluster. The Spark cluster's status page is not refreshed automatically, so you will need to continually refresh the page until all the workers have started.

Each Spark slave is given a Worker ID when it connects to `spark-master`. You will need to wait until there are three workers before you can submit the Spark jobs, with one worker for each slave (`spark-slave-a`, `spark-slave-b`, and `spark-slave-c`).

Once all the slaves (workers) have started, the `pi-spark.py` Python script can be submitted to the cluster using the `spark-submit` command.

The `spark-submit` command passes two parameters, namely `$SPARK_MASTER_URL` and `24`, to the `pi-spark.py` script.

The value of the `SPARK_MASTER_URL` is used to configure (`SparkConf conf`) the location of the Spark master (`conf.setMaster( master )`).

The second parameter of the `pi-spark.py` script (`24`) determines the number of compute partitions that are used to parallelize the calculations. Partitions divide the total number of calculations into compute groups (24 distinct groups).

The number of partitions should be a factor of the number of available computer cores. Here, we are using 2 partitions for each available computer core (24 = 2 x 12). There are twelve cores available—four cores in each of three Raspberry Pi slaves.

The `SPARK_MASTER_URL` and `PATH` environment variables are updated to simplify the `spark-submit` command line.

The `SPARK_MASTER_URL` is set to the IP address of the `spark-master` using the `hostname -I` command. The `tr` command is used to strip (`-d`) the trailing space (`[:space:]`) from the output of the `hostname -I` command.

The location of the Spark command directory (`/opt/spark/bin`) is prepended to the front of the `PATH` environment variable so that the Spark commands can be used without requiring their complete path.

Submitting the `pi-spark.py` script to the cluster for calculation takes a few seconds. However, once the calculation is distributed among the workers (slaves), it takes less than a second (`0.720023` seconds) to estimate the value of pi. The Spark cluster is more than 185 times faster than a standalone Raspberry Pi.

The Raspberry Pi supercomputer is running!

There's more...

This recipe only begins to explore the possibility of creating a supercomputer from low-cost Raspberry Pi computers. For Spark (and Hadoop, on which Spark is built), there are numerous packages for statistical calculation and data visualization. More information on supercomputing using Spark (and Hadoop) can be found on the Apache Software Foundation website (`http://www.apache.org`).

See Also

- **Apache Spark** (`http://spark.apache.org/`): Apache Spark™ is a fast and general engine for large-scale data processing.

- **Apache Hadoop** (`http://hadoop.apache.org/`): The Apache™ Hadoop® project develops open-source software for reliable, scalable, and distributed computing.

- **ssh-copy-id** (`http://manpages.debian.org/cgi-bin/man.cgi?query=ssh-copy-id`): Uses locally available keys to authorize logins on a remote machine. The Debian man page for `ssh-copy-id` describes the command and its options.

- **tr** (`http://manpages.debian.org/cgi-bin/man.cgi?query=tr`): This is used to translate or delete characters. The Debian man page for tr describes the command and its options.

- **Monte Carlo methods for estimating pi** (`https://en.wikipedia.org/wiki/Pi#Monte_Carlo_methods`): This Wikipedia article on pi describes a number of ways to calculate pi, including the Monte Carlo method.

Index

login password
changing, passwd used 55-57

M

Mac OS X disk utilities
dd 12-15
diskutil 12-14
MagPi
about 8
URL 8
man command
URL 91
used, for reading built-in
documentation 88-90
Man-in-the-middle attack
URL 55
media centers 3
MediaWiki
URL 180
memory usage
configuring, with raspi-config
command 36-38
Monte Carlo method
URL 321
mount
URL 120
move (rename) files
URL 191
MTR
URL 207
MTR (My traceroute)
URL 207
Multicast DNS
URL 24
mythic beasts
URL 207

N

Networked Attached Storage (NAS)
about 128
URL 133
network hubs 4

network protocol analyzer
capture filters 213, 214
installing 208-212
promiscuous mode 212
terminal-based user interface 212, 213
network trace utility
installing 205-207
New Out of Box Software. *See* NOOBS
Nginx
URL 176
nmbd
URL 139
Node-RED
URL 259
NOOBS
about 9
booting with 10-12
copying, to SD card 11
URL 12
NOOBS ZIP file
URL, for downloading 10

O

on-board components, Raspberry Pi
LAN9512 6
SoC 6
OpenSSH
URL 43
operating system
updating, apt-get command used 64-68

P

package
installing, apt-get command used 77-81
passwd
URL 57
used, for changing login password 55-57
Pi
calculating, without Spark cluster 319
calculating, with Spark cluster 319-321
URL 319
pianobar
URL 88

W

web.py website
URL 248
web server
about 204
Apache2, installing on 282
configuration files 173
dynamic pages 173
installing 167-172
lighttpd web server 174, 177
Nginx 175
other servers, defining 173
scaling 287
setting up 281
static content 173
testing 282
unique test web pages, creating for 282
web server failure
load balancer failure, testing 286, 287
normal operation, restoring 287
testing 285, 286
wget command
reference 318
wiki
installing 177-190
Win32DiskImager.exe
about 15
URL, for downloading precompiled binary 16

Windows 10IoT
about 10
URL 10
wireless access point
creating, with hostapd 191-199
starting 203
wireless firewall 204
wireless USB adapter
checking 200
Wireshark
about 214
URL 214
wireshark-filter
URL 214

X

x11vnc
URL 167
Xively
URL 269
xrdp
URL 162

Z

Zero-configuration networking
URL 269

Thank you for buying
Raspberry Pi Networking Cookbook
Second Edition

About Packt Publishing

Packt, pronounced 'packed', published its first book, *Mastering phpMyAdmin for Effective MySQL Management*, in April 2004, and subsequently continued to specialize in publishing highly focused books on specific technologies and solutions.

Our books and publications share the experiences of your fellow IT professionals in adapting and customizing today's systems, applications, and frameworks. Our solution-based books give you the knowledge and power to customize the software and technologies you're using to get the job done. Packt books are more specific and less general than the IT books you have seen in the past. Our unique business model allows us to bring you more focused information, giving you more of what you need to know, and less of what you don't.

Packt is a modern yet unique publishing company that focuses on producing quality, cutting-edge books for communities of developers, administrators, and newbies alike. For more information, please visit our website at www.packtpub.com.

About Packt Open Source

In 2010, Packt launched two new brands, Packt Open Source and Packt Enterprise, in order to continue its focus on specialization. This book is part of the Packt open source brand, home to books published on software built around open source licenses, and offering information to anybody from advanced developers to budding web designers. The Open Source brand also runs Packt's open source Royalty Scheme, by which Packt gives a royalty to each open source project about whose software a book is sold.

Writing for Packt

We welcome all inquiries from people who are interested in authoring. Book proposals should be sent to author@packtpub.com. If your book idea is still at an early stage and you would like to discuss it first before writing a formal book proposal, then please contact us; one of our commissioning editors will get in touch with you.

We're not just looking for published authors; if you have strong technical skills but no writing experience, our experienced editors can help you develop a writing career, or simply get some additional reward for your expertise.

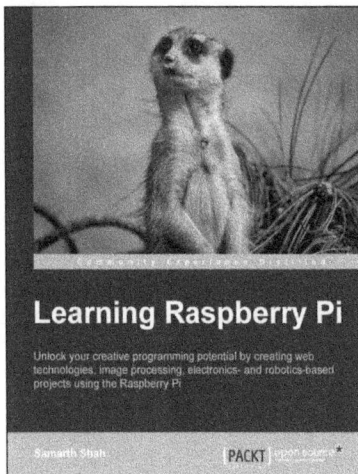

Learning Raspberry Pi

ISBN: 978-1-78398-282-0   Paperback: 258 pages

Unlock your creative programming potential by creating web technologies, image processing, electronics- and robotics-based projects using the Raspberry Pi

1. Learn how to create games, web, and desktop applications using the best features of the Raspberry Pi.

2. Discover the powerful development tools that allow you to cross-compile your software and build your own Linux distribution for maximum performance.

3. Step-by-step tutorials show you how to quickly develop real-world applications using the Raspberry Pi.

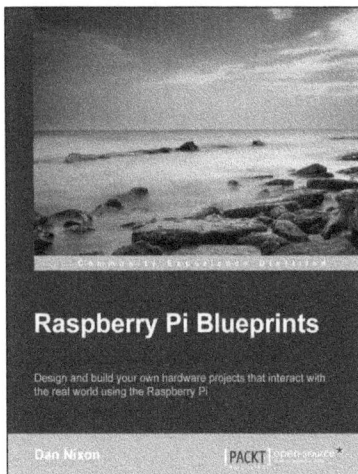

Raspberry Pi Blueprints

ISBN: 9978-1-78439-290-1   Paperback: 284 pages

Design and build your own hardware projects that interact with the real world using the Raspberry Pi

1. Interact with a wide range of additional sensors and devices via Raspberry Pi.

2. Create exciting, low-cost products ranging from radios to home security and weather systems.

3. Full of simple, easy-to-understand instructions to create projects that even have professional-quality enclosures.

Please check **www.PacktPub.com** for information on our titles

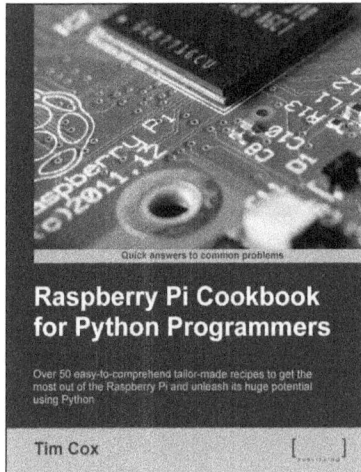

Raspberry Pi Cookbook for Python Programmers

ISBN: 978-1-84969-662-3   Paperback: 402 pages

Over 50 easy-to-comprehend tailor-made recipes to get the most out of the Raspberry Pi and unleash its huge potential using Python

1. Install your first operating system, share files over the network, and run programs remotely.

2. Unleash the hidden potential of the Raspberry Pi's powerful Video Core IV graphics processor with your own hardware accelerated 3D graphics.

3. Discover how to create your own electronic circuits to interact with the Raspberry Pi.

4. Interface with purpose-built add-ons and adapt off-the-shelf household devices.

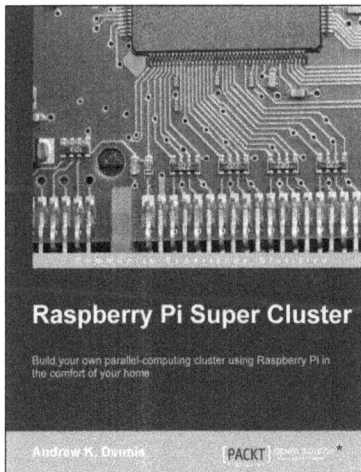

Raspberry Pi Super Cluster

ISBN: 978-1-78328-619-5   Paperback: 126 pages

Build your own parallel-computing cluster using Raspberry Pi in the comfort of your home

1. Learn about parallel computing by building your own system using Raspberry Pi.

2. Build a two-node parallel computing cluster.

3. Integrate Raspberry Pi with Hadoop to build your own super cluster.

Please check **www.PacktPub.com** for information on our titles

www.ingramcontent.com/pod-product-compliance
Lightning Source LLC
Chambersburg PA
CBHW080910220326
41598CB00034B/5537